Liberal Loyalty

Liberal Loyalty

Freedom, Obligation, and the State

Anna Stilz

PRINCETON UNIVERSITY PRESS
PRINCETON AND OXFORD

Published by Princeton University Press, 41 William Street,
Princeton, New Jersey 08540
In the United Kingdom: Princeton University Press, 6 Oxford Street,
Woodstock, Oxfordshire OX20 1TW

Stilz, Anna, 1976–
Liberal loyalty : freedom, obligation, and the state / Anna Stilz.
p. cm.
Includes bibliographical references and index.
ISBN 978-0-691-13914-2 (hadcover : alk. paper) 1. Citizenship. 2. Justice. 3. Liberalism. I. Title
JF801.S74 2009
323.6—dc22 2008040053

British Library Cataloging-in-Publication Data is available

This book has been composed in Sabon

Printed on acid-free paper. ∞

press.princeton.edu

Printed in the United States of America

10 9 8 7 6 5 4 3 2 1

Contents

Preface

This book is called *Liberal* Loyalty because it offers a defense of loyal or committed citizenship. It is not an argument in favor of supererogatory displays of patriotism—dying for one's country—nor for political loyalty at all costs—"my country right or wrong."[1] Instead, it defends loyal citizenship in a more restrained, everyday sense: obeying the law, paying one's taxes, voting and participating politically, and showing a special concern for the equality and well-being of one's compatriots. It argues that we have important political obligations, and that we should take them seriously.

The book is called Liberal *Loyalty*, on the other hand, because it claims that the reason we should be loyal citizens—the reason we should take our political obligations seriously—is simply that we care about liberal justice, and not that we share a national identity, are especially patriotic, or cherish a sentimental attachment to our state. An appeal to rationalist and universal principles, I argue, is sufficient to establish the importance of committed citizenship, and it provides a more normatively attractive basis for defending citizenship than do other views. Many people, of course, already believe that committed citizenship is important. I fear, though, that those who are already loyal citizens may not be so for the right reasons—that is, for liberal reasons, and not patriotic or nationalist ones. And I also fear that liberals are increasingly drawn to question the value of loyal citizenship in favor of a more cosmopolitan vision. On both fronts, then, there is something to be said.

This book has been several years in the making, and in the process, I have accumulated debts to friends and colleagues that I cannot hope to properly repay. The book developed out of a dissertation that was written in Harvard University's Department of Government under the supervision of Richard Tuck. For his restrained guidance and penetrating criticisms—and even more for providing me the model of a truly gracious intellectual life—I am very grateful. Both Nancy Rosenblum and Sharon Krause read the whole manuscript carefully and provided comments and

[1] This remark has been attributed to a US naval commander—Stephen Decatur—in an 1816 toast and was revived by Senator Carl Schurz from Illinois in an 1872 Senate speech.

support at many crucial points. Several of the early chapter drafts were written in the year I spent as a graduate fellow at the Center for Ethics at Harvard University under the guidance of Michael Blake. His criticisms and his philosophical acumen have improved my work immeasurably.

Special thanks must also go to the many friends and colleagues who read versions of the manuscript. First, I must thank Verity Smith, Noah Dauber, and Bruno Macaes—my writing partners in the final summer of graduate school—for comments on the first full draft and for making the process of finishing the dissertation actually an enjoyable one! Joshua Dienstag also read an early version of the manuscript and gave very helpful comments, and has provided encouragement since my early days as an undergraduate at the University of Virginia. Special thanks as well to Melissa Schwartzberg, Bryan Garsten, and Karuna Mantena—members of a writing group formed in my first year as an assistant professor—who read a much revised version in the summer of 2007, and who have provided just the right combination of sympathetic support and critical questions as the final version of the project took shape. Last, I must express my gratitude to Daniel Viehoff and Martin Sandbu, both of whom read large parts of the manuscript at a late date and helped me to clarify crucial parts of the argument.

I was fortunate to be able to produce the final version of the manuscript in the welcoming environment of the Department of Political Science at Columbia University, where my colleagues provided both intellectual stimulation and warm friendship. I also enjoyed the benefit of a postdoctoral fellowship year at the Berlin Program for Advanced German and European Studies, as well as the support of the Center for European Studies at Harvard University. Finally, portions of the project have been presented at various points along the way to audiences at the political science departments of Columbia University, Dartmouth College, Harvard University, Georgetown University, and Princeton University; to New York University's Monday Group; to the Berlin Program's Fellows Colloquium; to the graduate fellows seminar at Harvard's Center for Ethics; and at meetings of the New England Political Science Association and the American Political Science Association. I learned much from the comments and questions offered by audience members at each of these presentations.

In addition, I must thank all those people who read parts of the manuscript over the last few years, or who engaged in important conversations and exchanges with me about these issues: Bob Amdur, Charles Beitz, Michael Bratman, Jean Cohen, Jon Elster, John Ferejohn, Eviana Hartman, Istvan Hont, David Johnston, Ira Katznelson, Dimitri Landa, Helene Landemore, Reidar Maliks, Patchen Markell, Jan-Werner Mueller, Isaac Nakhimovsky, Amalia Navarro, Japa Palikkathayil, John Parrish,

Pasquale Pasquino, Alan Patten, Philip Pettit, Thomas Pogge, Simon Rippon, Andrew Sabl, Andrea Sangiovanni, Nadia Urbinati, and Tim Waligore. Their criticisms and thoughts all affected the evolution of the manuscript at crucial stages.

My first tentative thoughts about this project were born among an inimitable group of friends in Cambridge, Massachusetts, none of whom are responsible in any way for what is said here—and who usually did the best they could to help me forget about it—but whose companionship and support have contributed immeasurably to it nonetheless. I must thank the original inhabitants of 6 Marie Avenue—Casey Klofstad, Will Phelan, and Ros Rickaby—for memories and companionship I shall cherish for many years to come. I owe thanks to countless other friends I have met along the way, but these three deserve pride of place.

Finally, I must end by expressing my debts of gratitude to those people who are most special to me: my family. To my mom, my dad, Pam, Coley and John Paul, I owe the strength and the support to complete a project like this one, and I am grateful for the love that they never fail to express. Without them, I would have given up long ago. To Hillel Soifer I owe more than I can fully say. He has been with me every step of the way.

PART ONE

Equal Freedom and the State

1

Introduction

Of the many facts about the contemporary world that we tend to take for granted, one of the most pervasive is that it is a world of separate states. We may have much else to say about the character of these states—that they ought to protect human rights, or that they ought to be democratic—but, at least until recently, the fact that organized political life will take the form of a plurality of sovereign states was not often drawn into question.[1] Moreover, we not only tend to assume that the state will *exist* as a background fact about our political life, but we also think that its existence can make a moral difference. We usually hold, that is, that the citizen or resident stands in a special relationship to the institutions of her own state, and to the compatriots with whom she shares them—at least when these institutions are reasonably just, democratic, and legitimate. On this view, the fact of being a member of a particular state can matter morally: it makes a difference to one's practical reasoning about what to do. When deliberating about what is required of her, we think a citizen or resident ought to take her membership to have a kind of *moral salience*, one that marks this particular relationship as a source of special duties.

Imagine for a moment the case of a representative democratic citizen: let's call her Sally from Toronto. The fact that Sally is a citizen of Canada who resides in its territory, and is not a citizen or resident of Germany, or the United States, or Japan, will make some difference to what we (as a matter of everyday common sense) think that Sally is required to do. For example we may think that Sally, when going about her daily business, ought to obey Canadian laws rather than the laws of some other, equally just, state: the United States, say, or Argentina. And obeying Canadian law rather than some other law will make a difference to her behavior. If she is a novelist, then because Canada prohibits certain kinds of speech with racist or defamatory intent, she ought not depict this kind of speech

[1] In the last fifteen years, a spate of works reflecting on our assumptions having to do with sovereignty and the state have appeared, some of which I will treat in more detail below. The most common proposed alternative to the state is a system of dispersed sovereignty, which has been proposed in different form by Onora O'Neill, Thomas Pogge, David Held, and Simon Caney. See O'Neill, *Bounds of Justice*, 168–202; Pogge, "Cosmopolitanism and Sovereignty"; Held, *Democracy and Global Order*; Caney, *Justice beyond Borders*, 148–88.

in her work, even though in a neighboring liberal state (the United States), that sort of speech would be constitutionally protected.[2] And if Ontario requires biannual car inspections, while Argentina does not, then according to our assumptions Sally has a reason to get her car inspected, simply because Ontario requires it. She may have other reasons to believe that such car inspections ought not to be required at all—perhaps, after careful study, she has decided that the environmental benefits do not outweigh the costs. But despite this, on most liberal-democratic theories, she would still not be justified in simply electing to follow Argentina's policy on this matter, because it better corresponds with her own (perhaps even carefully considered) views. The duty to obey the law, if there is one, is an obligation that binds only those persons who stand in some special institutional relationship—those who fall within the territorial domain of a given state. This duty extends to residents and even tourists in Canada, as well as those, like Sally, who hold full citizenship.

In addition, many of us think that as a citizen of Canada, Sally not only has a duty to obey Canada's laws, she also has a duty to participate in formulating them. By debating political issues, voting for representatives, staying informed, working for a campaign or advocacy group, and participating in social movements or even committing acts of civil disobedience, citizens like Sally contribute their voices and votes to the legislative process. If Sally never votes or reads the newspaper, and shows no concern when Canada's laws or policies turn out to be unjust or inefficient, we may criticize her for neglecting her civic obligations. Since Sally and her fellow-citizens have a voice in electing the government that puts this legislation in place, she should do what she can to ensure that the laws of her country are just and its policies effective. But we generally assume that citizens have a responsibility to involve themselves in the legislative process only in their own state, and not in legislative processes in other states. If Sally omits to involve herself in the political affairs of Argentina—if she does not read Argentine newspapers, or get involved in any Argentine social movements or political campaigns—we would hardly say that she was neglecting a political obligation in the same way. To take an interest in Argentine politics might be a charitable thing for Sally to do, but we would not criticize her for failing to do so.

Beyond her relationship to Canada's laws, we also take it for granted that Sally ought to pay her taxes to the revenue authorities in the state where she lives and works, and not to the revenue authorities of some other equally just and legitimate state. We assume, therefore, that Canadian citizens like Sally, as well as those who reside and work on Canadian territory, ought to positively contribute to the state institutions that formulate and coercively impose laws on herself and others within their juris-

[2] *Criminal Code of Canada*, sec. 318–19.

diction.[3] The tax rates in Michigan might be lower, but Sally cannot simply elect to pay her taxes there. Perhaps Sally's tax money would do more good and make a more appreciable difference to other people's lives if she sent the check to the government of Argentina. But despite this, we generally assume that Sally should pay her tax money to her *particular* authorities, and not to the authorities in a just and legitimate state of her own choosing.

Finally, Sally is also expected to contribute to redistributive policies and to the provision of public goods that benefit fellow citizens in Canada, instead of contributing to redistribution that takes place in other, perhaps much poorer, countries. Her contribution will most likely take the form of tax money, but it may also come as a demand for compliance with affirmative action initiatives that benefit the less advantaged. Her taxes may go to provide public schooling for children of Canadian families, to contribute to the pension plans of the Canadian elderly, or to provide health insurance for fellow Canadians. Sally is expected to contribute to redistribution in Canada despite the fact that there are many people in the world whose needs are much more urgent and basic than any of the "comrades of fate" who benefit from her tax dollars. Redistributive social-welfare and public goods programs of this sort are underpinned by the idea that citizens and residents owe special obligations to their compatriots. If they exist, such special obligations extend beyond those obligations that are thought to be owed to all other human beings, like basic nonharm and the provision of minimal subsistence. In all of these ways, then, the aid of an average member of an industrialized democracy benefits those who fall within her state substantially more than it benefits those who fall outside it. And most traditional theories of social democracy take this to be morally warranted by the existence of special rights and duties between members of the same state.

The Particularity Assumption

We could find yet further examples of particular obligations that depend on an individual's standing in a special relationship to his own state—think, for example, of the duty to do military or civil service, to defend

[3] In chapter 7, I offer an account of the sources of our political obligations that emphasizes the significance of a state's territory in defining membership. On the view I endorse, the differences between the obligations of a visitor to a state's territory and obligations of residence or citizenship are less thoroughgoing than it might seem. The distinction between them is only a matter of degree, not of kind. Citizens are simply those persons who have the most permanent and enduring connection to a particular territorial state. Tourists have only a fleeting connection to it, and temporary residents are somewhere in between. I thank Martin Sandbu for pressing me to be clearer about these matters.

one's country in a just war, or to contribute to reparations, each of which is also thought to bind only members of one particular political community. Of course, there are important differences among these duties. Some of the obligations we have mentioned are territorial obligations: obligations to obey the law bind everyone within a state's jurisdiction, even mere tourists or short-term visitors. Some are obligations of residence: all long-term residents have an obligation to pay taxes and to contribute to redistribution. And finally some are obligations of citizenship: only full citizens are bound by duties to vote and participate politically, to defend their country in war, to do civil or military service.[4] But what is common to all of these civic duties is that they are grounded on the belief that the existence of separate states makes some moral difference to what we ought to do. Such duties all invoke the existence of political obligations, special "moral requirement[s] to support and comply with the political institutions of one's country of residence."[5] "Political obligation," as A. John Simmons puts it, "is something like the obligation to be a good citizen in a fairly minimal sense."[6]

Our commonsense view, then, presupposes that there is a special bond or obligation that ties the citizen or resident to her state, and to her compatriots, and not to others, and requires her to support *these* people and *these* institutions and not others. Following Simmons's work on political obligation, I will call this the *particularity assumption*.[7] If the particularity assumption is correct, I am not constrained to obey or to support every just state, or to support, as a matter of preference, the *most* just state in the world. Instead, I am bound to obey and support *my own* state, at least as long as it is sufficiently just. If someone like Sally has civic obligations, then they must depend on the special relationship that she stands in with her state: it is this relationship that ties her to her political community and its institutions. As we have seen, the particularity assumption—and the idea of a special relationship to the state that it implies—is deeply embedded in our everyday moral judgments as well as in traditional accounts (liberal and otherwise) of political obligations.

[4] As I state in footnote 3, later in the book I will give an account of these obligations that shows why the differences between them are less significant than it might seem. This territorial view of membership also has implications for granting citizenship rights: on the view I endorse, anyone who can prove a permanent connection to the state should be eligible for full civic rights. Dual citizenship may be acceptable, but only if the citizen can prove a connection to both territories and can discharge both sets of civic obligations.

[5] Simmons, *Moral Principles and Political Obligations*, 29.

[6] Simmons, *Moral Principles and Political Obligations*, 155.

[7] Simmons calls it the "particularity requirement" in *Moral Principles and Political Obligations*, 31.

The fact that the particularity assumption is embedded in our commonsense views does not make it a justified assumption, however. And some contemporary liberal theorists have denied that the particularity assumption is actually justified at all. One can see why they might be uneasy about it. For the particularity assumption (at least at first blush) seems to hold that the fact of simply *finding oneself* to be a member of a state is an important part of the argument for one's having obligations to that particular state. Sally was most likely born into the role of citizen, and it seems that certain obligations to her state and to her compatriots are simply predicated of her because of that fact. But liberals have traditionally been uneasy about appealing to the brute fact of our membership in institutional schemes, or of our being born into certain relationships, as a moral justification for our having obligations to those relationships or schemes.[8] The mere fact that I find myself to be subject to a tyrannical despot, and that he expects me to comply with his orders, gives me no obligation to obey him. Nor does the fact that I happen to be a member of a Mafia family give me an obligation to support and further its activities, even though that might be what the Mafia conventionally expects of its members. By parity of reasoning, we might suppose that Sally's happening to have been born in Canada gives her no obligation to do what Canada conventionally expects of its members. The bare existence of a particular state, like the bare existence of any other relationship, institution, or practice, cannot constitute an adequate ground for our having special obligations to it on a liberal view. If these obligations are to be justified, we must appeal to some further line of reasoning.

But if the mere existence of separate states is not sufficient to justify our having civic obligations, then what could justify those obligations? Liberals have traditionally looked to extra-institutional principles to ground our obligations. If institutional schemes can be justified with respect to such principles—principles such as respect for the freedom and equality of persons—then perhaps we can be shown to have a moral obligation to support and uphold them. On this view, the mere fact that an institution or practice requires something of me, taken by itself, never gives me a moral reason to do it. If conventional obligations cannot be justified on the basis of an appeal to extra-institutional principles, then despite the fact of our membership, and despite the tug of our commonsense moral views, perhaps we should accept the conclusion that we actually have no real duties to support and uphold the institution in question.

[8] In some cases, liberal discomfort about unchosen obligations even extends to denying the most paradigmatic of these unchosen obligations: obligations to family. Simmons, for example, denies that children have any moral obligations to support and aid their parents, since they did not choose to be born. *Justification and Legitimacy*, 38.

This would be the liberal conclusion about our responsibilities to a tyrant or to our fellow members of the Mafia, for example. Whatever attachments we may feel to these relationships, they impose no justified obligations on us: instead we should revise our attachments, since they are unjustifiable and misguided. This intuition, of course, partly depends on the fact that the tyrant and the Mafia both establish schemes or practices that are morally wrong. But interestingly, a liberal would come to the same conclusion about my unchosen membership of a morally beneficial practice: if I simply happen to be born into it, it does not bind me.

Imagine I am born into a commune that my parents joined before my birth. Suppose I come of age and I no longer wish to serve in the commune's work-rotation—planting vegetables and washing dishes for the other members—but instead decide to pursue my fortunes in the wider world. No liberal would argue that I am bound to continue in the work-rotation forever, simply because of my birth membership in the commune. This is so even if this commune is a benevolent enterprise (set up, let us say, to care for the poor). The liberal is unwilling to say that I have an obligation to stay because to claim that I am bound by unchosen obligations to the commune would negate my personal freedom to choose the shape of my own life. On the liberal view, then, it is generally not acceptable to force obligations on people to participate in institutions and practices—even morally justified or beneficial practices—against their will. Following this line of thought, it may seem that even if Canada is a just and morally worthy state—like the beneficial commune—Sally has no unchosen obligations to support and comply with it simply because she happened to be born there. Perhaps, as a free human being, she ought instead to obey Michigan's free speech laws or start an advocacy project to influence Argentina's next election, if that is what she decides is the most morally and rationally justified thing for her to do. If that is the case, then we would need to revise our moral intuitions about the state.

But while revising our moral intuitions about Sally's case would be one possible outcome of extended reflection about them, I do not think it is likely to be the correct result. Instead, in this book I hope to vindicate Sally's (and our) intuitions about her obligations to her state and to her compatriots. I will claim that Sally really does have the obligations to obey the law, to participate politically, to pay taxes to her own state, to contribute to civic redistribution, to perform civil or military service, to contribute to war reparations and the like, that we usually ascribe to her and other citizens. The sort of vindication I hope to offer is not a commonsense but rather a philosophical one, and it proceeds on broadly liberal grounds. In what follows, I will argue that we can show Sally's obligations to be justified if we think deeply enough about what the extra-institutional principles of freedom and equality—to which liberals are already committed—really require. A successful defense of political obligations to particular states, on my view, therefore need not appeal to any "brute" moral force found in the existence of states, to Sally's commonsense intuitions, or to her felt attachments to her fellow members or her state institutions. Instead, I think it can be discovered purely in sustained reflection about what is truly involved in guaranteeing the freedom and equality of persons. That a purely liberal vindication of the particularity assumption of the sort I will attempt could be successful is not obvious, however. Indeed, the general trend of contemporary political theory has been to deny that it is possible.

The Cosmopolitan Challenge

Although it plays an important role in many traditional liberal theories of political obligation and distributive justice, the particularity assumption highlighted above has been exposed in recent years to much criticism on liberal grounds, especially by cosmopolitan theorists. Cosmopolitans have argued that, on reflection, we ought to hold that special obligations of citizenship are fundamentally incompatible with a liberal theory of justice. On the cosmopolitan view, then, the particularity assumption *cannot* be justified on the basis of any appeal to extra-institutional principles, and as a result it ought to be abandoned, and our commonsense intuitions revised accordingly.

The problem, in their eyes, stems from the fact that the principles of freedom and equality, on which a liberal theory of justice is based, are meant to be universally applicable. As Thomas Pogge puts it, "Every human being has global stature as the ultimate unit of moral concern."[9] Individual persons, and not states, nations, associations, or other groups, are the fundamental bearers of liberal rights, and individual persons hold this status solely in virtue of features that seem to be universally shared: features like rational agency, the power of free choice, or the possession of a set of common human interests. It is therefore all persons everywhere, and not just the members of particular states or associations, that are owed respect on the most foundational liberal principles. Some cosmopolitans extend this point to argue that it is very difficult to see how an individualistic, universalist, right-based political theory could *ever* justify any sort of particularized and differentiated political obligations, like those the particularity assumption invokes. On their view, state boundaries do not impose any restrictions on justice, which is always universal in scope.[10]

[9] Pogge, *World Poverty*, 169.
[10] Tan, *Justice without Borders*, 11.

The seeming contradiction between liberal moral premises and the particularity assumption arises because bounded political obligations presuppose that we owe more *as a matter of justice* to persons who have certain particular, and nonuniversal features (e.g.,that they are our compatriots, or that they share our institutions). But such a partial weighting seems inconsistent with a universalist standpoint (like the liberal one) that is *impartial* between persons, and attributes to all persons—no matter where they are, or what relation they have to ourselves—the same degree of moral worth. For cosmopolitans, then, an appeal to this sort of partial weighting seems to sneak in a whole set of nonliberal considerations at the foundation of a liberal political theory. Indeed, the particularity assumption seems to appeal to just the sort of considerations that liberal ideals have traditionally been mobilized to overcome and fight against: morally arbitrary facts about our birth. "Citizenship," claims Joseph Carens in a memorable phrase, "is the modern equivalent of feudal privilege."[11] Martha Nussbaum adds:

> Why should we think of people from China as our fellows the minute they dwell in a certain place, namely the United States, but not when they dwell in a certain other place, namely China? What is it about the national boundary that magically converts people toward whom we are incurious and indifferent into people to whom we have duties of mutual respect?[12]

Cosmopolitans therefore reject any attribution of special moral significance either to a citizen's membership in a particular state or to her institutional relationship to her compatriots, since, on their view, the scope of justice is always universal.

Simon Caney, for example, points out that all the available liberal rationales for granting civil, political, and economic rights appeal to features of the person that are universally shared.[13] He claims on this basis it must follow that all civil, political, and economic rights, including rights to distributive shares of goods, must be "general rights," in H.L.A. Hart's terminology: all human beings possess them equally. A general right, in Hart's typology, is a right whose origin is not due to any social institutions or interaction, but rather belongs to each human being qua human. The scope of general rights is universal: they are rights held against everybody. For Caney, then, the full panoply of rights to freedom of action, speech, association, belief, the right to vote, to a fair trial, to equal pay, to equal opportunity, and to economic redistribution should apply to all persons,

[11] Carens, "Aliens and Citizens," 252.

[12] Nussbaum, "Patriotism and Cosmopolitanism," 4.

[13] Caney, *Justice beyond Borders*, 72.

no matter in what state they are situated.[14] No civil, political, or economic rights are "special rights," applying to persons solely in virtue of some particular social or institutional relationship, such as that person's country of residence or citizenship.

Of course, cosmopolitans do recognize and accept that because of the nature of our current political circumstances, each human being is born a member of a particular state, but this fact, on their view, should be treated as a brute reality that carries no moral significance. Persons' rights are the true carriers of significance, and for cosmopolitans the existence of separate states makes no difference to what rights persons actually possess.[15] Some cosmopolitans, including Caney, concede that there are cases where institutions or associations can create special rights and duties between their members: as when joint stockholders form a corporation, for example. But states, for Caney, are not associations that fall into this category. Caney argues that, to really create such special obligations, an institution must be voluntarily brought into being by its participants, binding them in virtue of their acts of consent or promising. Since we do not contract into the state, but are born into it, states create no special obligations of this sort between their citizens:

> Individuals who hold the right to freedom of speech, action, association, and so on can make contracts with each other, in which case the contracting parties, but not others, have certain special rights. The key point, though, is that these special rights arise in a background in which persons have universal civil and political rights.[16]

The only justification for the existence of special, nonuniversal rights and duties on Caney's cosmopolitan line, then, is that individuals have voluntarily brought such duties into being, by contracting into a particular association.

Caney, Nussbaum, Kok-Chor Tan, and others are what Thomas Pogge has termed *interactional* cosmopolitans: that is, they take the view that duties to respect other persons' civil, political, and economic rights are "general" or "natural" duties binding on human beings as such and hold independently of any institutional scheme. To assert the existence of a human right, for someone like Caney, is thus to assert that "some or all individual and collective human agents have a moral duty not to deny X to others or to deprive them of X."[17] If I have a right to an egalitarian

[14] For a similar argument, see Barry, "Humanity and Justice," 235.

[15] Arneson, "Patriotic Ties," 128. On this subject, see also Pogge, "The Bounds of Nationalism"; Miller, "Cosmopolitan Respect"; Goodin, "What Is So Special"; Scheffler, "Relationships and Responsibilities"; Tan, "Patriotic Obligations."

[16] Caney, *Justice beyond Borders*, 78.

[17] Pogge, *World Poverty*, 65.

distributive share of world resources, then all other persons have a positive duty to provide it to me.[18]

Cosmopolitans have extended their critique of obligations of citizenship to our existing state-centric schemes of distributive justice. They claim that giving priority to fellow citizens in matters of wealth redistribution and the provision of public goods, as we do in most industrialized welfare states, reflects an indefensible "patriotic bias" that draws an irrelevant distinction between persons based on arbitrary facts of geography and birthright membership. Placing moral weight on shared citizenship or territorial residence, these theorists argue, is equivalent to placing moral weight on any other purely cosmetic feature of a person: it is a form of discrimination, equivalent in seriousness to discrimination based on race, gender, or religion. On their view, distributive principles (of justice) should not "be constrained or limited by state or national boundaries."[19]

When we put our tax money toward the needs of the poor in our own country, on this view, surely we are just neglecting the economic rights of a much larger and more deserving population, with whom we simply

[18] Pogge argues against this interactional view, claiming that duties to respect human rights are not duties that concern our personal moral conduct toward others, including distant strangers. Pogge instead takes the position that human rights are best conceived of as claims on the proper organization of *institutions*. For Pogge, "The postulate of a human right to X is tantamount to the demand that, insofar as reasonably possible, any coercive social institutions be so designed that all human beings affected by them have secure access to X" (*World Poverty*, 46). The corresponding duty to protect human rights, argues Pogge, is held by all participants in a social system, who are obliged to organize themselves in such a way as to ensure that the institutions in which they participate secure the human rights of others.

This might seem to make room for the sorts of special duties of citizenship invoked in the particularity assumption: if human rights are claims on institutions and the members of those institutions, then it would seem that they have an important *associative component*: that is, they bind only participants in the institutional scheme in question, not humanity at large. Indeed, one possible reading of Pogge's view (which would bring him quite close to the position I advocate in this book) would be that institutions on which claims of human rights could be made are coercive legal institutions. But Pogge expressly denies that this is the right reading of what he means by an institution: he suggests, to the contrary, that human rights can be guaranteed by various kinds of nonlegal institutions: "A society may be so situated and organized that its members enjoy secure access to X, even without a legal right thereto. . . . One's human right to adequate nutrition, say, should count as fulfilled when one has secure access to adequate nutrition, even when such access is not legally guaranteed" (*World Poverty*, 46). For Pogge, then, perhaps a human right can also be a claim on *nonlegal* institutions, such as associations, families, universities, churches, or firms, a view I shall contest in chapter 2. In general, though, Pogge argues that demands of justice do stem from membership in particular contexts of institutional interdependence and not from natural duties all humans owe to one another, but he claims that in our current world, these contexts of interdependence are global. In such a situation, then, the demands of an interactional and an institutional conception of rights are much the same in practice.

[19] Tan, *Justice without Borders*, 19.

happen, for contingent reasons, not to share a state. And how can this be anything more than a form of prejudice or arbitrary favoritism? Surely our compatriots are no more morally deserving than others; so why do we consider ourselves bound to aid them to a greater degree? Indeed, some authors have claimed that these supposed "obligations to compatriots" enshrine arbitrary prejudices, thinly veiling forms of discrimination among equal persons that are equivalent to racism:

> Large percentages of the populations of many countries, particularly in the southern parts of the world, fail to get enough calories to lead a normal, active life, making for short life expectancy. Moral universalism must regard this as very bad. If, as seems plausible, favoritism by nationals of more prosperous countries for hungry compatriots over others would contribute to this situation, then such favoritism is, from a universalist standpoint, no better than racism.[20]

The basic moral challenge of the cosmopolitan argument is that defending special obligations to fellow citizens or residents requires us to draw an arbitrary distinction between persons based on a morally irrelevant property: the brute fact of their happening to share a state. As Pogge puts it, "Nationality is just one further deep contingency (like genetic endowment, race, gender, and social class), one more potential basis of institutional inequalities that are inescapable and present from birth."[21]

As we can see, the cosmopolitan challenge to traditional liberal assumptions is a forceful one. Cosmopolitans have pressed traditional liberals with ever-increasing urgency to explain how the special obligations of membership invoked by the particularity assumption could possibly be defended on the basis of fundamentally universalist moral principles of freedom and equality, which purport to be impartial between persons. Wouldn't it be more consistent with the moral basis of liberalism, they ask, to ground our political obligations not on facts about our membership in particular states, but on the universal duties of justice owed by each of us to all other human beings?

In order to vindicate their point of view, along with the particularity assumption upon which it relies, those liberals who believe in the moral importance of citizenship would have to show that this cosmopolitan challenge was misguided in a fundamental way. And to demonstrate *this*, they would have to prove that the basic analogy at the center of the cosmopolitan case—the analogy between placing moral weight on state membership and placing moral weight on purely arbitrary features of the

[20] Gomberg, "Patriotism Is Like Racism," 109; see also McCabe, "Patriotic Gore, Again."

[21] Pogge, *Realizing Rawls*, 247.

person, like race or gender—is actually a false one. This would show that civic membership was not a morally irrelevant property, like the other cosmetic features of the person to which the cosmopolitan analogy appeals. Moreover, traditional liberals would have to demonstrate this without appealing to any irrelevant assumptions—such as the alleged moral "force" of simply being born into a particular relationship—that are prima facie inconsistent with liberal theory. What traditional liberals require, then, is an argument that shows why the particular facts about our relations to our own states and to our compatriots are of some lasting moral significance. And to really do the job, this would have to be an argument that was based solely on the "universal" and "impartial" grounds of a regard for equal freedom.

But while it seems clear that such an argument would be what is necessary to lay the cosmopolitan challenge to rest, a look at the contemporary literature shows that producing that argument has proved to be very difficult.[22] Instead, contemporary liberals have largely been content to work within the parameters marked out by the particularity assumption without trying to defend it, and this, as we shall see, has opened them to the charge that they simply take the boundaries of the nation-state for granted as an unquestioned background to their political theory. Moreover, because traditional liberals have been largely unable or unwilling to offer an argument about why the principles of freedom and equality can justify bounded political obligations to particular states and groups of citizens, cosmopolitans have continued to mount ever-bolder attacks on their point of view.

The Liberal-Nationalist Counterargument

This lacuna in contemporary liberal theory's ability to justify the assumption that citizens do stand in a special relationship to the institutions of

[22] The best contemporary efforts to develop such an argument are found in Blake, "Distributive Justice"; and Nagel, "Problem of Global Justice." The argument I will lay out in the first section of this book is sympathetic to some of their views, but adopts a different approach. In particular, while these thinkers emphasize, in a Rawlsian way, the repercussions of state coercion for citizens' autonomy, I derive my defense of the moral importance of citizenship primarily from a reading of Kant and Rousseau. Going back to these early modern thinkers, I think, allows us to get clearer on *how* exactly the relationship of common citizenship is morally important in terms of equal freedom. As I will try to show over the following chapters, citizenship is morally important because we need state authority in order to enjoy certain categories of rights, particularly rights of property, and because the definition of these rights must be one we produce together, through democratic legislation. Since I emphasize the connection between rights and democratic authority, my account is rather different from those of the above authors.

their own state and to their compatriots has led theorists from other camps to step in and offer an account of a member's special bond to her state that does appeal to the "moral force" found in the "brute" existence of relational ties or the fact of group belonging. One such answer to the cosmopolitan challenge has recently been put forward by a group of theorists who call themselves *liberal nationalists*, a group that includes David Miller, Yael Tamir, Will Kymlicka, and Margaret Canovan, among others. Liberal nationalists argue that "patriotic biases" of the sort attacked by cosmopolitans are not just arbitrary prejudices, but are actually essential features of democratic politics. They claim that "only within nation-states [is there] any realistic hope for implementing liberal-democratic principles."[23]

To defend their view, nationalists charge that the practice of existing liberal democracies, along with many theories of liberalism, in fact already "tacitly presupposes" the prior existence of the cultural nation.[24] The thesis that liberalism presupposes the nation has two parts. First, liberal nationalists argue that the theory of liberal democracy incorporates claims about boundaries, membership, and political obligation—summed up in the particularity assumption—that require ultimate reference to the cultural nation in order to be morally justified. And second, liberal nationalists further claim that, as an empirical matter, democratic institutions can only function effectively if citizens share a sense of solidarity and trust, which can only be provided by a national culture. We will have a chance to investigate the nationalist position in greater detail in chapter 6; but for now it is worth sketching the view in outline, to show why the nationalist argument for bounded political obligations—one of the few that is currently on the table—cannot be understood as a truly liberal argument, precisely because it claims that certain ascriptive facts have overwhelming normative significance in determining our obligations. For this reason, although it has received significant attention in recent years, the liberal-nationalist position cannot provide a universalist and extra-institutional justification for the particularity assumption of the sort we are seeking.

Liberal nationalists begin their argument for the nation's indispensability by observing that there seem to be important background difficulties in liberal-democratic theories of a broadly Rawlsian stripe. Rawls, for example, begins his *Theory of Justice* from the assumption that principles

[23] Kymlicka and Straehle, "Cosmopolitanism."

[24] Samuel Scheffler has offered a similar account of the "particularist dimension" of liberalism in his recent work: "Many liberal theories that explicitly reject associative duties seem tacitly to rely upon them, or at least to incorporate elements that serve to mimic such duties in important respects." See *Boundaries and Allegiances*, 69.

of justice apply to the basic structure of a "closed society," whose members "enter it only by birth and leave it only by death,"[25] and he resists the attempts of cosmopolitans (such as Thomas Pogge or Charles Beitz) to apply his ideal of justice as fairness globally.[26] But Rawls does not offer an argument about why the closed nation-state is the correct unit to which to apply such principles. For this reason, liberal nationalists have maintained that Rawls—and other liberals who make background assumptions that are similar to his—must be invoking a national community as an unquestioned background circumstance that underpins his theory. Rawls and other liberals, they claim, simply take nation-states for granted. And with good reason, according to liberal nationalists, since national community is actually a prerequisite to democracy, justice, and fairness:

> There is a longstanding though much denied alliance between liberal and national ideas that might explain the inconsistencies pervading modern liberal theory: why is citizenship in a liberal state more commonly a matter of birthright and kinship rather than choice? Why do liberals believe that individuals owe political loyalty to their own government—as long as it acts in reasonably just ways—rather than to the government that is demonstrably the most just of all? Why does the liberal welfare state distribute goods among its own citizens, while it largely ignores the needs of nonmembers? The answers to these questions direct us to the national values hidden in the liberal agenda.[27]

Tamir and other liberal nationalists assert that the pervasive acceptance among liberals of the background assumptions with which we began—that a citizen or resident stands in a special relationship with the institutions of her own state and with her compatriots, a relationship that grounds her particular political and redistributive obligations—ultimately shows that liberals must be tacitly relying upon or invoking the cultural nation as the backdrop to their politics. Only the cultural nation, it is argued, could explain why political obligations and redistributive duties are bounded in the way that we usually assume them to be.

But why might the nation serve to explain why political obligations are bounded? According to the nationalists, our political obligations are bounded because they in fact coincide with certain special associative obligations that we *already* owe to fellow members of our cultural nation. To defend this idea, they point out that we commonly think of other important personal relationships as giving rise to "special obligations," obli-

[25] Rawls, "Political Liberalism," 12.
[26] See Beitz, *Political Theory*; and Pogge, *Realizing Rawls*.
[27] Tamir, *Liberal Nationalism*, 69.

gations that are not derivable from, or reducible to, universal moral duties owed to all human beings, but which instead depend on the intrinsically valuable nature of a particular relationship to us. Examples of such duty-generating relationships are friendships, or the relationship between parents and children, or between husbands and wives. We do not believe that the obligations we owe to our children, for example, are derived from their status as unaffiliated and morally free human beings, but rather from their status as *our* children, from the fact that they stand in a special relationship to ourselves. Certain valuable relationships are already held by commonsense morality to generate self-standing special obligations, and according to liberal nationalists like Tamir or Miller, the special relationship of cultural nationhood ought to be added to this list.

Liberal nationalists hold that the relationship of cultural nationhood is a duty-generating one, like the special relationships of family or friendship, because like these other relationships, it creates certain valuable goods for the persons involved. Cultural nationhood, they argue, plays a central role in constituting individual identity, and it shapes the exercise of our personal freedom. A national context makes certain cultural options meaningful to us, and provides us with a context in which we can make choices, since "familiarity with a culture determines the boundaries of the imaginable."[28] Growing up in a certain national culture, on this view, is a fact that has special moral force for an individual, because it shapes his identity and gives him a context for choice. And because his identity and freedom are very great personal goods—perhaps among the most significant personal goods—the member of a nation owes an obligation of support to the relationship that produces these goods. That relationship is one of cultural nationhood; therefore the member owes a special obligation of support to his cultural nation.

Thus, by reconceiving of our relationship to the cultural nation as the source of important special obligations, liberal nationalists claim that we can vindicate our sense—expressed in the particularity assumption—that citizens owe special duties to their own institutions and to their fellow compatriots, at least as long as the boundaries of the nation coincide with those of the state.[29] Conationals owe each other more, suggest Tamir

[28] Margalit and Raz, "National Self-Determination," 449.

[29] This assumption is problematic, as some nationalists have realized. For the boundaries of relatively few states actually coincide with the boundaries of cultural nations. For this reason, the cultural nationalist thesis can be used at least as easily to advocate *dismantling the state*—because our special obligations to the nation do not in fact coincide with the boundaries of the existing polity—as to support our political obligations to any actually existing state unit. Will Kymlicka and Yael Tamir, for instance, have both recognized this, and argued on this basis for devolving more political rights to small national groups, while maintaining supranational political institutions at either the federal (Canadian) or European

and Miller, because they identify with the national community that shares a particular state, and they identify with this community because its national culture is constitutive of who they are. On the basis of their central thesis, then, liberal nationalists have forcefully argued that the only consistent way for more traditional liberals to vindicate their background assumptions (and to avoid being pressed into a cosmopolitan stance) is to adopt some form of liberal nationalism, by conceding that the cultural nation is an important prerequisite for justice, since nationhood explains how bounded political obligations might be generated, and therefore helps us to vindicate the particularity assumption that is so deeply embedded in many of our beliefs about the state. "Liberal theorists," notes Will Kymlicka, "invariably limit citizenship to the members of a particular group, rather than all persons who desire it. The most plausible reason for this . . . [is] to recognize and protect our membership in distinct cultures."[30]

As we can see, then, the nationalists too have put forward an influential defense of the particularity assumption. But despite the force of many of the liberal nationalists' claims, I believe we ought to be dissatisfied with their account. The problem with the liberal-nationalist view is that it minimizes or neglects the importantly *universalist* moral justification for liberal politics, in favor of a form of ethical partiality that is based on exclusivist cultural ties. In holding that an individual's identity and obligations depend upon his membership in the cultural nation, nationalists neglect, or at least substantially revise, traditional liberal ideals of autonomy and individualism.

If a fact about a person's upbringing and identity can impose unchosen obligations on him, then liberal nationalists are implicitly committed to conceding that every national culture's members have unchosen obligations to it, no matter what that culture's character or values, simply by the fact of their having been educated to membership. This is like saying that someone who is born a member of the Mafia has unchosen obligations to his fellow members, simply because he has grown up in the group and it has come to play a significant role in his own conception of himself. Yael Tamir, for instance, accepts just such a conclusion:

---

level. But if their argument about the sources of political obligations is correct—that these obligations ultimately derive from associative obligations to national groups—one wonders what could underpin citizens' obligations to these higher-level political institutions. Canada or Europe, by all rights, ought to cease to be able to expect its citizens to contribute to federal redistribution or to obey unpopular laws, if Kymlicka and Tamir are correct. That leaves one wondering what rump-Canada or rump-Europe *could actually do* once their redistributive and legislative authority has been so drastically curtailed, and why Kymlicka and Tamir bring such higher-level institutions into their theories at all.

[30] Kymlicka, *Multicultural Citizenship*, 125.

> One last feature characterizes associative obligations. Since they grow from relatedness and identity, they are independent of the normative nature of the association. There is no reason to assume . . . that only membership in morally worthy associations can generate associative obligations. For example, members of the Mafia are bound by associative obligations to their fellow members.[31]

But surely any liberal would want to say that the mafioso has no such obligations, and to the extent that his identity or conception of himself leads him to think that he does, that conception is misguided, and his identity should be revised. Liberals wish, in other words, to find a source of external evaluation for our identities and practices, one that appeals beyond the self-conception of members to some further set of moral criteria. In the end, by refusing external evaluation, nationalists import into their political theory a set of ascriptive considerations that are not in any sense derived from the liberal values of freedom and equality and that are often in grave tension with these principles.

Despite this, however, the liberal-nationalist project does have the advantage of offering a clear answer to the cosmopolitan challenge on the possible *moral sources* of the differentiated and bounded political obligations invoked by the particularity assumption, albeit it one that more traditional liberals have been reluctant to adopt. Because of their uneasiness with the nationalist response to the cosmopolitan challenge, though, traditional liberals find themselves in a rather uncomfortable position. We might describe their situation by saying they face a war that must be fought on two fronts.

Traditional liberals are up against challenges from nationalists and cosmopolitans alike, and this poses them a painful dilemma. On the one hand, they could concede (with the cosmopolitans) that the moral principles on which liberalism is based should apply globally to all individuals, without reference to their geographical location, and therefore that special obligations to our own states and compatriots are in fact morally unjustifiable. This would save the liberal claim to moral universalism, but at the expense of adopting the cosmopolitan position. On the other hand, traditional liberals could admit that democratic institutions tacitly presuppose a cultural nation, which provides the real demarcating criterion for who may and who may not belong, and defines the group of persons to whom we have political obligations. This would save the particularity assumption, but at the expense of betraying liberal universalist background principles. If these are the only two options for traditional liberals,

[31] Tamir, *Liberal Nationalism*, 101. Tamir does go on to say that these obligations can be (and in the case of a mafioso, would be) overridden by other moral reasons. But they still exist and retain moral force, even when overridden.

however, they face the usual fate of those who fight wars on two fronts: they will find themselves annexed from both sides. If the traditional liberal position is not to be undermined, a third and better option must be found.

How to Vindicate the Particularity Assumption: A Sketch of the Argument

To vindicate the particularity assumption without falling on either horn of the dilemma put to them, liberals have to formulate a response that shows why the citizen's relationship with her particular state and with her fellow citizens is in fact morally important, and they would have to formulate this response purely in terms of freedom and equality, without invoking any moral "force" that might be based on ascriptive claims about culture, language, or ethnicity, or the brute fact of finding oneself subject to an institutional scheme. Such a response would show why the salience of *particular* relations of civic membership could be morally relevant on impartial, universal, and extra-institutional grounds. This may seem like a very difficult task. Fortunately, though, I believe that such a response already exists—it is in fact one of the key arguments of early modern political theory—and the aim of this book is to reconstruct, update, and defend it. In my view, the main outlines of just such a view can be found in two of the most important philosophical antecedents of the idea that any legitimate state must guarantee the equal freedom of its citizens: the writings of Kant and Rousseau.

But if the answer already exists, then why have contemporary liberal political philosophers found it so difficult to defend the particularity assumption? I believe it is because contemporary philosophers tend to hold the false view that all our obligations to other persons must spring from one of two possible sources: either they are clear and determinate "natural moral duties" that are owed to human beings as such, like obligations not to murder or assault, rape, or lie; or they are duties that antecedently autonomous individuals have specifically contracted to undertake, by acts of promising or explicit commitment. Political obligations and special redistributive duties to compatriots, however, are not easily assimilable to either of these two models. Political obligations, if they exist, are "particularized" to one bounded political community, and so do not apply to the entirety of humanity in the manner of "natural duties" of interpersonal morality. And most citizens of modern democracies cannot be meaningfully said to have consented to stand in any "special" relationship to their compatriots—since most of them were born, and not naturalized, into the state—so these duties cannot be understood as obligations that are based on some prior contract. Since these obligations cannot be readily explained by reference to natural duty or to consent, many liberal theorists fall into skepticism, conceding that it is hard to see how any obligations of citizenship or "special" redistributive duties could be justified, as the particularity assumption holds them to be.

Nevertheless, I believe that particular political obligations can be defended if we step outside this two-part moral structure, and that there is good reason to think that the nature of equal freedom as a political value may actually require us to step outside it. There may, in other words, be a third variety of liberal value with reference to which our obligations to particular states and compatriots might be justified, and this third variety would consist in those duties that are mediated, and thus "filled out" or fully defined, only by the establishment of public authorities. When we reflect on our commonsense views about Sally's situation, we notice right away that all the obligations we attribute to her rest on her relationship to a public institution—the *state*—and through that state, to her compatriots. Whatever might ground these obligations, then, is going to have to address the existence of that state in some fashion. What is striking about contemporary political theory, though, is that there is relatively little work that addresses our obligations to the state. Instead, cosmopolitans speak of our duties to humanity; consent theorists speak about our duties to keep our promises to other people; and nationalists invoke a set of moral duties to the cultural nation, but not to the state. My purpose in the first part of this book, then, is to attempt to recover from early modern political theory a language in which we might speak intelligibly about the moral importance of legitimate state authority.

Invoking a set of moral values that are mediated by just states does not violate the liberal constraint on justifications with which I began: that they must appeal to some extra-institutional principle to ground obligations of citizenship. For the fact that institutional structures must be brought into being to make the exercise of freedom possible does not mean that equal freedom itself has no extra-institutional basis. In a similar way, we can think that there are other things of preinstitutional value to human beings—say, the need to secure basic health—that require the construction of institutional schemes to be realized: the creation of a health care *system*. On this sort of argument, the existence of the state as an institution can be justified by the fact that it helps us realize some preinstitutional value that could not possibly be realized without it.

In the next two chapters, I will argue that Kant and Rousseau thought that the value of equal freedom could only be realized through the state. The reason they thought equal freedom required this kind of mediation was that prior to the establishment of the state, the value of equal freedom is *indeterminate* with respect to certain key questions. That moral ideal, on their view, does not yet carry with it a complete set of clear and definite "natural duties," which are publicly knowable to all individuals upon reflection, and which can answer certain fundamental questions, especially questions about the legitimate extent of our property and the limits of our "acquired" rights. Rousseau and Kant held, then, that in order to implement the value of equal freedom, we require reference to an authority that can provide some public definition to resolve these questions, and that this authority can only be the legitimately constituted state. For this reason, these two thinkers argue that it is only with reference to the laws of a legitimate state that the bounds of each citizen's personal sphere of freedom can be fully defined and guaranteed.

In part 1 of this book, then, I will be defending the view that the cosmopolitans go wrong because they overlook equal freedom's mediation by state authority. Instead, cosmopolitans mistakenly believe our duties of equal freedom to be equivalent to a set of natural duties that are clearly knowable to all individuals upon reflection, and apply to personal moral relationships, rather than to states. If freedom is instead a value that takes an institutionally mediated form, as Kant and Rousseau thought it did, then it follows that the existence of the state is not morally irrelevant to establishing a condition of equal freedom. Instead, on the view I put forward, *only a state can create the conditions in which equal freedom between individuals is realized.* By drawing a set of reciprocal bounds to individuals' choices, the legitimate state guarantees each of its subjects a private sphere of liberty exempt from the interference of other persons. And in so doing, it renders them free for the very first time, able to exercise autonomous control over their own affairs.

In part 1, I will also defend Rousseau's view that the only kind of state that could possibly define a set of adequately equal and impersonal restrictions on our sphere of freedom must be a *democratic* state that guarantees certain basic rights. We do not want to obey any and all states, including tyrannical or morally objectionable ones, if we are interested in equal freedom. If freedom can give us a moral reason to obey states, then surely it gives a reason to obey *only those states that guarantee at least a minimal threshold of freedom to each citizen.* I believe that this further restriction is warranted because it gives us some important moral criteria for judging the institutions to which we delegate political authority. If a state is not a democracy, or is not likely to meet these minimal guarantees, then, on a Rousseauian account like the one I endorse, we have no obligation to obey it.

Democratic Solidarity and Civic Allegiance

Despite all this, my argument in part 1—the central claim of which is that equal freedom must be mediated by state authority—does not lay the liberal-nationalist case to rest. We may well agree that Kant and Rousseau give us good reasons for thinking that democratic states are necessary in order to realize a condition of equal freedom between individuals. Democratic states, on this sort of argument, are objectively necessary in order to guarantee justice in the world. But still, agreeing with their argument does not fully show why a citizen's general duty to promote justice gives her a greater reason to support her own state rather than to support all just states, or perhaps to support the most just state. It doesn't yet say anything about what a citizen's subjective relationship to her own state should be. Should she conceive of herself as a committed member of a particular state, with important obligations to her compatriots, and to her political institutions? Or should she conceive of herself as a detached individual, fortunate perhaps to live in a world where there are freedom-guaranteeing states, but under no particular obligation to support one of them? Or, finally, should she conceive of herself as a promoter of just institutions everywhere, doing what she can to support all just states? So although part 1 tries to show that there are general reasons of justice to construct states, it does not (yet) show that citizens have a special reason for solidarity with their own compatriots and for allegiance to their particular institutions rather than to persons and just institutions anywhere. In part 2 of the book, therefore, I examine these further problems. Do liberal values, by themselves, provide any justification for a citizen's allegiance to her own particular state, and for solidarity with her compatriots?

Rousseau offers us one kind of controversial answer to these problems: he claims that in order to legislate generally and impartially on one another's behalf, the citizens of a democratic state must share a special bond of identity, one that motivates them to show concern for the freedom and welfare of their compatriots. On Rousseau's view, in order to legislate impersonal laws—laws that will truly protect each citizen's freedom equally—each citizen must be capable of taking up the viewpoint of the general interest or common good, a perspective that requires solidarity with her fellow citizens. Therefore he claims that well-ordered states should foster bonds of solidarity among their citizenries. In some of his writings, Rousseau argues that this is best accomplished by promoting shared cultural practices and a common national identity. If national identity shapes citizens' ethical obligations, then inculcating it is one way of generating a special reason for citizens to show greater concern for their compatriots' freedom and interests and to develop a particular allegiance to their state.

Liberal nationalists agree with Rousseau that a common identity is an indispensable precondition for the success of liberal institutions, and they argue that only a national culture can provide it. Sharing a national culture, on their view, gives us an essential reason why citizens belong together, because they have preexisting bonds and ethical obligations to their conationals, and these bonds give them a special reason for allegiance to their national state. When asked why citizens are loyal to their own state, then, at least in the ideal case, nationalists have a ready answer: they are loyal to it because it preserves and reflects their national culture, which is an important part of their identity, and ought to be morally respected.

Thus, despite the fact that part 1 of the book argues that a condition of equal freedom requires state authority to be brought into being, it has not laid to rest the nationalist concerns about whether principles of justice, taken by themselves, can provide an adequate justification for democratic solidarity and civic allegiance to particular states, and not simply a recognition of the moral importance of state structures in general. My argument in part 2 therefore seeks to prove that we do not need to invoke a common national culture if we are to show why citizens should be committed to their own state.

In my view, citizens' endorsement of justice as an important value gives them perfectly sufficient reasons for allegiance to their state and for solidarity with their compatriots. Other thinkers have also endorsed justice-based accounts of allegiance like mine: Jürgen Habermas, for example, has put forward an account of civic allegiance he calls "constitutional patriotism," and which he claims can reappropriate the radical democratic potential inherent in Rousseau's theory without any appeal to a nation defined in cultural terms. A key feature of Habermas's alternative is his belief that shared citizenship can be as effective a source of political unity as the cultural nation. Habermas is often vague, though, on whether his view can do without any invocation of national culture, and liberal nationalists remain unconvinced: they have criticized Habermas's account as "too abstract" and even "bloodless."[32]

In part 2 I offer my own theory about why Habermas's central thesis—the thesis that shared citizenship can serve as effectively as the nation in particularizing our obligations—is actually correct. Drawing on recent developments in the analytic philosophy of collective intention and action, I argue that the unity of the democratic state can be understood as created solely by the shared intentions of its members. It is her possession of such a shared intention that allows a democratic citizen to regard herself as a member of a political group engaged in a collective endeavor to which her compatriots also contribute. Mutual recognition of these shared intentions among a group of citizens is all that is required to generate a collective agent, or democratic "we," that can act together politically.

[32] For these claims, see Canovan, *Nationhood and Political Theory*, 87–97.

Before moving on, I will say one final word of explanation about the book's two-part structure. As I have indicated, the first part of the book lays out an argument to prove that states are morally significant institutions. But showing this is not sufficient to provide a full defense of the particularity assumption, which—in invoking our intuitions about Sally's situation—is what we set out to do. To defend the particularity assumption, we need to show not only that states are morally important in general, but also that citizens and residents have special moral reasons to uphold the institutions of their own state, at least when those institutions are reasonably just. Therefore, in part 2, I additionally make the case that a commitment to the value of democratic justice provides sufficient grounds for a member to take up a subjective attitude of democratic solidarity with her compatriots and to show allegiance to her particular institutions. My central argument is that justice is a value that requires collective cooperation together with others to be attained. Once we understand that, we can explain why justice—despite being a universal value—can give us reasons for supporting our particular state institutions and for solidarity with our fellow members.

In this book, then, I make two essential and overarching claims. The first is that we have impartial and universal reasons, grounded in freedom and equality, for placing moral weight on relations of shared civic membership. This is because the democratic state helps to give our innate right to freedom a set of determinate public contours, by legislating general and reciprocal restrictions that define each citizen's civil rights. Equal freedom is not the kind of value that could ever be realized without the construction of political authorities, without bringing into being an institution that can legislate public laws to define what it requires. My second claim is that we have reason for showing democratic solidarity and civic allegiance simply because of the fact of citizenship *itself*, and without appeal to any extraneous supplements of the sort provided by background commonalities of language, ethnicity, or culture. This, I believe, is because the kind of freedom that we attain as democratic citizens—specifying and guaranteeing equal civil rights through public law—is a very great good to us, and one that we have reason to value. Like other goods that are of great significance and value, it gives us sufficient reason to act by itself, without any appeal to extraneous desires or commonalities.

If my two overarching claims are correct, then this book provides a defense of the particularity assumption of the sort that liberals require in order to escape from the dilemma that is put to them by cosmopolitans and nationalists. This defense is couched solely in terms of a universal value—the value of equal freedom—that applies impartially to all persons and that explains why it nonetheless warrants our placing moral weight on relations of membership within particular states. If the argument presented here is right, then it shows why the dilemma of liberal particularism is not a real dilemma: it is one that can and should be dissolved.

2

Authority

As we saw in the introduction, there is a tendency within cosmopolitan political philosophy—illustrated in its critique of the particularity assumption—to view the citizen's relationship to the state as a matter of moral irrelevance, a mere artifact of geography. For interactional cosmopolitans, a citizen like Sally owes no special political obligations to her state or her compatriots; instead, she only has moral duties of justice to her fellow human beings. As I indicated, one way of defending the political obligations that we intuitively attribute to Sally is to argue that the state is a morally important association because it helps to "mediate" or "fill out" the terms of its members' equal freedom. But claiming that states mediate equal freedom in turn requires we show that states can be legitimate authorities, that is, that they can have the moral power to require action on the part of their subjects, by defining their rights and duties to one another.

The idea that states can possess legitimate authority has been the subject of a vehement critique by the "philosophical anarchist" school that has gained currency in contemporary political philosophy in recent years. Theorists like A. John Simmons, Leslie Green, and M.B.E. Smith have forcefully challenged the view that *any* state, even a just one, can legitimately claim political authority over its members.[1] To have political authority, for these thinkers, means to have a right to rule, "a general right to make binding law and policy" for a set of subjects, with which those subjects have an obligation to comply.[2] If a just state rightfully held authority over its subjects, then subjects would be under a correlative political obligation to obey its laws and directives. But philosophical anarchists deny that any state, no matter what its moral character, could ever have

[1] As Allen Buchanan sums it up, "The single most compelling conclusion to be drawn from the recent normative literature on political authority is that virtually no government possesses it, not because no government is morally justified in exercising political power nor because we have no sufficient reason to comply with the rules governments impose, but because the conditions for citizens having an obligation to their government to comply with the laws are not satisfied and not likely to be satisfied." See Buchanan, *Justice, Legitimacy, and Self-Determination*, 240.

[2] I take this phrasing from Simmons, *Justification and Legitimacy*, 110. See also Smith, "Prima Facie Obligation"; Green, *Authority of the State*.

the right to direct anyone's actions. Instead, like cosmopolitans, these critics of authority hold that human beings have moral duties of justice to one another qua individuals, and insofar as the state directs them to do what promotes these duties, they should comply with its laws. This is not because they are obligated to obey the law, but rather because they have independent reasons for performing morally required actions. Critics of political authority therefore conclude that even in a legitimate and just political system, the fact of the state's requiring an action does not provide one with a reason to do it.

In this chapter, I challenge the views of political authority and allegiance that are put forward by philosophical anarchists, by showing that their views involve a misrepresentation of what liberal and universal principles of freedom and equality ought to commit us to. Indeed, I think that a fundamental error shared by both the cosmopolitan and anarchist positions is the belief that our rights and duties of justice can be defined and guaranteed without political authority, but simply through individuals' fulfillment of clear and obvious interpersonal moral duties. On their view, the state is at most necessary to provide a sanctioning mechanism for morality. Against this, I argue in this chapter that equal freedom *cannot be defined or made determinate without state authority*, and therefore that justice, when rightly understood, must commit us to accepting the authority of legitimate states.

Throughout the discussion, I will use *equal freedom* synonymously with *justice*: I assume that what justice most fundamentally requires is that individuals possess a set of rights that guarantees their standing as free and equal persons. In chapters 3 and 4, I will say more about what kinds of states actually are legitimate, and when we are genuinely under political obligations to them. And in the book's second half, I show that equal freedom not only gives us reason to establish states in general, it also gives us a special reason to show allegiance to our own state, and to view shared citizenship as a morally significant relation.

The claim argued for in this chapter, then, is that justice can only be brought into being by constructing a state: there is no other way to do it. In defending this view, I will draw partly from Kant's work, but also from a Kantian reading of Rousseau. Both these theorists claimed that equal freedom between human beings could not be realized outside the state, because any condition of equal freedom will always require the existence of public laws, which only a state can bring into being. For this reason, their views about political authority are distinct from those offered by many contemporary theorists, even those who claim Kantian origins for their ideas. In order to highlight the distinctiveness of these two approaches, I will begin by saying something more about the contemporary view, and then, in this chapter and the next, examine the reasons why Kant and Rousseau may have disagreed with it.

Skepticism about Political Authority

As we noted, contemporary political philosophy is marked by a general skepticism about the claims that have traditionally been made on behalf of state authority. "Philosophical anarchists"—among them M.B.E. Smith, A. John Simmons, and Leslie Green—argue that we actually have no political obligations, and therefore that the state cannot possess legitimate authority over us.

Perhaps the most prominent current defender of philosophical anarchism is Simmons, and so we can usefully examine the general approach by considering his work. Simmons begins his reflections on state authority by suggesting that in any condition where political institutions did not exist—in a state of nature, for example—we would still have certain interpersonal "natural" rights and duties to all other human beings. These are "general" rights and duties that bind us prior to any voluntary transactions we might undertake. Broadly following H.L.A. Hart,[3] Simmons distinguishes between two types of obligation: natural or "general" duties (which are correlative to the natural rights of other persons) and special duties, which arise from our deliberately and voluntarily contracting into an association or special relationship. Persons' natural rights, according to Simmons, "centrally include, and perhaps add up to no more than," a right to free self-government or independence.[4] Among our natural duties are negative duties "to refrain from directly harming others," in their "lives, liberty, and property"—duties of respect for their natural right to free self-government—and positive duties to "do [our] share in supporting the helpless needy"—duties of charity.[5] A good example of an interpersonal natural duty of this kind is the obligation not to assault others physically.[6]

Simmons believes that we could comply with these natural duties to other persons without the state, simply by acting morally on our own, or perhaps by establishing informal cooperative systems, but certainly without establishing political institutions. For this reason, he thinks that we ought to conceive of a possible state of nature as a condition in which individuals would each enjoy an equal right to pursue their goals and projects independent of others' interference:

[3] See Hart, "Are There Any Natural Rights?" 67–68.

[4] Simmons, *Justification and Legitimacy*, vii.

[5] Simmons, *Justification and Legitimacy*, 138.

[6] Simmons, *Justification and Legitimacy*, 45.

> Persons' natural condition is "a state of perfect freedom to order their actions, and dispose of their possessions, and persons as they think fit.". . . Our "uncontrollable liberty to dispose of . . . our persons or possessions" (as always, within the bounds of natural law) is in part a moral freedom to pursue our own life plan.[7]

The idea of such a preinstitutional condition of equal freedom and independence, for Simmons, establishes a moral "baseline" with reference to which all institutional departures must be specially justified. We should note here too that Simmons's moral baseline includes not only the inviolability of our bodies, but also the inviolability of a share of the external world: for Simmons, our natural right of independent self-government extends to rights of property, to control over objects.

Because he thinks that human beings would be equally free without the state, simply by acting on their duties of interpersonal morality, Simmons believes there is only one morally acceptable way in which such states might come to have the rights to direct and coerce them characteristic of political authority: namely, through the voluntary consent of these individuals. To hold otherwise, argues Simmons, would negate the liberal commitment that a person's life-plan should be determined by his own actions and decisions. In many everyday situations, we ascribe to ourselves such a moral power to restrict our freedom by our own consent: by undertaking a promise, say, to sell you my bookshelf for your cash, I thereby create in you a new "special" right to restrict my freedom—by demanding the bookshelf—that you would not otherwise have had. But this restriction of my freedom does not infringe my right to self-government in any way, since I have personally willed it. Appealing to consent seems to be an especially attractive liberal method for reconciling the existence of special obligations to institutions and practices with the more fundamental principles of freedom and autonomy. Simmons simply extends this appeal to the power of consent from personal contractual relationships to all institutional relationships.

Like other liberals, Simmons rejects any appeal to the brute fact of our membership in certain institutional schemes as a justification for our having obligations to those schemes. "Since being born into a political community is neither an act we perform, nor the result of a decision we have made," argues Simmons, "we feel that this should not limit our freedom by automatically binding us to the government of that community."[8] And if special obligations need to be made consistent with our personal freedom in order to bind us, we may think that there is one surefire way

[7] Simmons, *Lockean Theory of Rights*, 77, quoting Locke, *Second Treatise of Government*, 8.

[8] Simmons, *Moral Principles and Political Obligations*, 68.

of knowing when they are really consistent with our freedom: that is, if we have explicitly agreed to undertake them. For Simmons, then, we have special obligations to those relationships, *and only to those relationships*, to which we have voluntarily consented at some point in time.

Consent to obligations of citizenship in particular is morally important because states purport to impose a number of coercive measures upon us. To establish the right to impose these, Simmons suggests, our interactions with a political authority would have to be of a very clear and obligation-producing sort, like the act of "signing up" to a voluntary association. Were we to consent in this explicit way to membership, Simmons argues, then the state would acquire legitimate authority over us, simply because we would have altered the natural moral baseline, by ceding the state new rights. So consent is one possible "liberal" grounding for obligations of citizenship: were we to consent, we would bring a special obligation to our own particular state into being, and according to Simmons, we would do so on a basis that is fully consistent with the "preinstitutional" principles of equal freedom.

The obvious problem with this justification of political authority, though, is that only a very few members (such as naturalized citizens or those who have taken loyalty oaths) are bound under Simmons's consent criterion. Rather than legitimating any existing state's right to direct and coerce its citizens, then, the standard of consent actually debunks all such claims. Indeed, Simmons concludes that citizens generally "have no special bonds which require that they obey and support the governments of their countries of residence."[9] He acknowledges, of course, that the members of a political community may feel that they are tied to their own state by a special moral bond, and therefore that they owe support to its institutions and obedience to its laws, support they do not owe to the institutions of other countries. But Simmons argues that this belief is mistaken, unless we have consented to the authority of our government via some meaningful historical act. Such nonconsenting citizens, on Simmons's view, remain in a state of nature with respect to their political institutions.

For Simmons, then, the just state is like a just insurance company: an instrument that some of us may choose to explicitly hire or contract with in order to better attain our aims:

> The mere fact that a business is on balance morally acceptable and a good thing to have around seems to give me no moral reason to do anything for it, unless my failure to act will in some way affect the performance of my duties to others. (Must I support, let alone buy a

[9] Simmons, *Moral Principles and Political Obligations*, 192.

> policy from, some insurance company that is efficient and charitable and offers good bargains on its policies, say?) . . . As long as I mind my moral business, good insurance companies and just states can be created at will by those who want them; but the virtues of these arrangements give them no moral claim on my allegiance.[10]

Think of CIGNA, for example, as a just insurance company: it provides health coverage for many people, and so it is a beneficial and morally justified operation. As a person who is unaffiliated with it, I may still have good moral reasons to promote (and certainly not to hinder) its attainment of its goals, since they benefit other people, to whom I have certain duties. And someday my own health interests might lead me to take out a policy. But imagine how alarmed I would be if CIGNA, a company with which I have no prior history, showed up at my door one day demanding large sums of money from me—in return for some package of benefits for which I had never contracted—and threatened me with violence if I did not pay up. CIGNA's otherwise generally just and beneficial features just do not seem to give it any right to do these things to me: I never consented to be a part of its scheme, no matter how justified, desirable, or beneficial to others that scheme is. Simmons's main claim is that in the absence of our explicit historical consent, we should view the state's authoritative and coercive demands (for our tax money, military service, vote, and obedience to its laws) as an analogously unwarranted imposition. No matter how justified or desirable the state is, if we have not voluntarily consented to undertake obligations to it, we owe it nothing: "Even if a man is born into a *perfect* state, he remains free not to assume those bonds of obedience and support which would make him a member of the political community."[11]

It is important to see, however, that Simmons's rejection of a special obligation to obey the state still allows him to recognize that there are many circumstances in which we have good reasons not to frustrate or even to promote the state's activities. Beyond the moral reasons we have to comply with the state whenever doing so fulfills some preexisting natural duty, Simmons notes that the state, like CIGNA, can often help to promote other people's interests, or it may threaten us with punishment, which can create a prudential reason for us to comply. But none of these reasons, Simmons insists, are of the kind that is constitutive of political authority: I never have reason to do something *just because the state requires it*. Instead, I have reasons to help other people, to perform my natural duties, or not to get myself punished. Unless we have contracted

[10] Simmons, *Justification and Legitimacy*, 138.
[11] Simmons, *Moral Principles and Political Obligations*, 69.

with the state, then, our reasons for complying with the law are always just the normal reasons that would apply to our practical decision making anyway: "We often have reasons, or even duties, to do what the law requires, quite apart from its being commanded by law."[12] Indeed, in cases where I think I have no preexisting moral or prudential reasons for obeying, I should not do so.

While Simmons's denial of political authority is thus not tantamount to claiming that citizens are free to disobey the law whenever they like—since they remain bound by the moral baseline—his philosophical anarchist view is still revisionist in significant respects. On his account, I have no particular reason to support the just state in which I live, rather than just states somewhere else, in much the same way that, even if I care about others' health, I have no special reason to support CIGNA rather than Blue Cross as long as I have not taken out a policy with one of them. Thus, Simmons takes an essentially cosmopolitan view of how we ought to act on our "baseline" interpersonal duties. No general duty to respect others' natural rights or to promote their well-being could ever ground particular obligations of residence or citizenship, since such duties will always require me to respect people's rights and promote their well-being everywhere, and not simply in my own community. And since I can fulfill my natural duties as an unaffiliated human being rather than as a citizen of any particular state, I am perfectly justified in acting morally on my own or in electing to support whatever institutions can best further these duties.

> Even if you had perfectly general duties to promote justice or happiness, say, and consequently duties to support just or happiness-producing states, these duties would require of you that you support all such states, providing you with no necessary reason to show any special favoritism or unique allegiance to your own just state, and proving none of those with any special right to impose on you additional duties.[13]

Simmons's theory is elegantly presented and often impressively argued. But I believe there are reasons for thinking that his views about freedom, consent, and political obligation are deeply inadequate. His view gains most of its traction by noting that there are certain existing practices—like a just insurance company—that may be perfectly well justified or acceptable, but they have nothing to do with my own aims, interests, or prior acts. I have not "signed up" to CIGNA, and so surely Simmons is right to hold that I am under no obligation to it if it can get along without

[12] Simmons, *Moral Principles and Political Obligations*, 194.
[13] Simmons, *Justification and Legitimacy*, 137.

me and no one else's freedom is harmed by my not participating in it. To insist that I actually do have some obligation to an insurance company I never joined would mean granting that my own autonomy and control over my life means nothing at all. Simmons notes this, and proceeds to argue that the state is just like the insurance company. But I believe that Simmons is importantly wrong about the parallelism between the state and CIGNA. If in fact the two organizations are not analogous, we may have obligations to the state that we could not possibly have to a voluntary association, like the just insurance company or a club, team, or other secondary association.

Unlike Simmons, I will claim that we must distinguish between those practices and institutions without which a background condition of equal freedom between individuals would be impossible, and practices and institutions that can be voluntarily brought into being once such a background condition of equal freedom has been securely established. Let us suppose for a moment that the state was the sort of institution without which a condition of justice and equal freedom among individuals would not be possible. In this case, then, it would be consistent with Simmons's own premises to hold that my preexisting duty to respect others' freedom would give me an obligation, independent of my own consent, to contribute to the state, since state institutions are necessary to make others' freedom possible. If it could be shown that there is no way to establish a condition of equal freedom without the state, then Simmons would have to concede that we were obligated to the state on grounds of natural duty alone.[14] By establishing a framework of uniform public laws, in other words, it may actually be that a legitimate state brings a condition of equal freedom into being for the very first time.

In what follows, I will argue that the value of equal freedom does require the establishment of legitimate states. If this line of thought can be shown to be correct, then we must accept that there is an important difference between the state and voluntary associations like the just insurance company. An insurance company is not required to bring about background conditions of equal freedom and independence between individuals, so I have no natural duty to contribute to it. And once I have done my natural duty, by contributing to those institutions that *are* necessary to establish background conditions of freedom, I ought to be able to contribute to other practices (or not) as I so choose, simply because no one's freedom is radically jeopardized by my abstention from them. Practices that take place within a basic freedom-guaranteeing framework are rightly conceived of as "voluntary associations," like a club, a team, or an insurance company. Consent is the proper criterion of special obliga-

[14] Jeremy Waldron makes a similar point in "Special Ties," 28.

tion in these cases. Where Simmons goes wrong, however, is to take voluntary association as the model for all social organization.

Simmons recognizes this possible objection to his approach explicitly, and it is one reason why he takes a Lockean rather than a Kantian approach to the problem of political legitimacy:

> If we can act morally without accepting membership in a political community, the Kantian cannot successfully argue that the state is for each of us "morally necessary" or that the unwillingness to cooperate to produce political solutions is "unreasonable" or morally objectionable.[15]

As Simmons implies, a very powerful argument for the view that equal freedom depends on the state can be found in Kant's political writings, and I think it is high time we revive it.

The Problem of Acquired Rights: The Example of Property

Why might we think that establishing background conditions of equal freedom requires the state? I suggest there are two reasons: first, a state is required to *define* certain sorts of acquired rights—rights that we do not possess solely as a matter of natural interpersonal morality, and paradigmatically rights to property; and second, a state is required to *enforce* all our rights—both rights to bodily inviolability and rights to property—in a way that does not subject some persons to domination by others. In arguing that the state is necessary to define rights to property, my Kantian view denies Simmons's contention that these rights could be made fully determinate in a state of nature. As we noted above, Simmons holds that the interpersonal moral baseline of natural rights and duties that applies even in a state of nature includes not only a right to bodily inviolability—with correlative duties on others not to assault or murder us—but also a right to the inviolability of a share of the external world, our property.

For Simmons, a human being's rightful sphere of freedom consists in a zone or area of control over the external world that can be defined without reference to any political institutions, but simply through good-faith moral reflection. Since our sphere of freedom preexists the state, Simmons therefore claims that we always need some special explanation for why the state can place restrictions upon it. And if we are interested in safeguarding freedom, then it looks like the best answer is simply to say that the state can place as few restrictions on it as possible, namely, only those that naturally free individuals have explicitly consented to. This argument

[15] Simmons, *Justification and Legitimacy*, 153.

leads him to embrace a certain view of the state: it is an organization set over and against free individuals who could get along more or less successfully (and perhaps more freely) in its absence.

A key reason why Simmons is led to the view that our sphere of freedom can be defined without any reference to the state, though, is that he takes a broadly Lockean line (perhaps based on a heterodox reading of Locke) when it comes to explaining property rights. He argues that the natural right to property is grounded in the more general right to independence or self-government:

> Locke's mixing argument begins with a broader right of self-government (control over one's body and labor), which is, of course, in part just a right of noninterference with respect to other persons. This emphasis on self-government, including control over one's plans and projects, is explicit in Locke's texts. And property is an indispensable condition of self-government. Property does not, then, just insure survival; it is also the security for our freedom, protecting us against dependence on the will of others and the subservience to them that this creates.[16]

To actualize one's natural right of self-government, Simmons holds, one may legitimately appropriate, through one's own labor, up to a "fair share" of the earth's resources as one's natural property. A fair share, for Simmons, is "a portion of the earth's resources as large and as good as the best share that could simultaneously be privately held by everyone with a right to appropriate," that is, roughly an equal share.[17] Taking up to this amount of world resources does not injure anyone else, because it leaves them free to appropriate a similar share within which to actualize their own right of self-government. And since their natural rights are in no way infringed by our appropriation, others' consent to our property is not required. Our fair share of resources, then, importantly defines the *spatiotemporal* bounds of our natural right to independent self-government. It is within our fair share, for Simmons, that we have a right not be interfered with by other people as long as we do not interfere with them.

For Simmons, then, the need to recognize property rights by specifying fair shares gives us no special reason to enter the state. Of course, if we choose to consent to the state's authority over us, then we will submit our fair share of resources to the jurisdiction of its government, which will acquire the right to adjudicate the bounds and limits of our property vis-à-vis others'. But nothing about the need for us to establish a system of private property requires us to enter the state. If we do not choose to

[16] Simmons, *The Lockean Theory of Rights*, 274.
[17] Simmons, *The Lockean Theory of Rights*, 281.

consent to the state's authority, then jurisdiction over the bounds and limits of our share remains with our own moral judgment, and the enforcement of these bounds will depend on our own arms.

One key reason Kant does not accept the skeptical view of political authority, as put forward by Simmons, is that, when it comes to rights over external resources, he does not see the value of freedom as having the moral structure that Simmons attributes to it. Kant and Simmons, however, (along with Rousseau, whom we will examine in the next chapter) do share the same conception of freedom at the most basic level, a conception we can call *freedom as independence.* Since this notion of freedom as independence is one I will use throughout this book, it is worth a few words of clarification here. To be free-as-independent, as all these thinkers conceive it, is not to be forced to obey the will of another person; it is to enjoy a sphere of independent self-government within which others cannot interfere. This notion of freedom is thus particularly concerned with the relationships between *persons.* It is not concerned in the same way with whatever restrictions may be placed on our choices by natural obstacles or constraints. Being unable to hike up a mountain because a tree blocks the path does not make me less free, on the freedom-as-independence view. But being unable to hike up a mountain because you have tied me up, or because I have to seek your permission to engage in any leisure activities, does make me unfree. Freedom as independence, therefore, always refers to a relation between one person's will and another's: to be unfree is to be forced to obey someone else's will rather than one's own.

For both Kant and Simmons, attaining this sort of freedom as independence requires people possess rights of property in external things. This is because the only way one person can be free from subjection to another person's will is to have exclusive control over a sphere of the physical world within which those others are not allowed to interfere with his actions. And to have that sort of control is to have property. This exclusive sphere of property includes (*a*) rights of control over one's own body and (*b*) rights of control over specific objects. While Kant agrees with Simmons that freedom requires property, he also claims that property is only possible through the state. As a result, he concludes that freedom as independence is only possible through the state. Since Kant believes that there is a basis in natural right for claiming private property, and he believes that private property requires the state, he concludes that the state is not an optional or voluntary association. Indeed, he goes so far as to suggest that we may be forced into the state against our will.[18]

[18] Kant, *The Metaphysics of Morals*, 90. I cite Kant's writings by the standard German edition of Kant's works, *Kant's Gesammelte Schriften*, edited by the German Academy of

Kant: External Freedom as Independence

How does Kant reach these conclusions? Kant begins his *Metaphysics of Morals* with the argument that every human being possesses an innate right to *external freedom*, which as we have seen, is a right to *independence* from being coerced or constrained by another person's will in carrying out our choices. This, he says, is the "only original right belonging to man by virtue of his humanity."

> *Freedom* (independence from being constrained by another's choice [*Willkür*]), insofar as it can coexist with the freedom of every other in accordance with a universal law, is the only original right belonging to every man by virtue of humanity. This principle of innate freedom already involves the following authorizations, which are not really distinct from it (as if they were members of the division of some higher concept of a right): innate *equality*, that is, independence from being bound by others to more than one can in turn bind them; hence a human being's quality of being *his own master* (*sui iuris*), as well as being a human being *beyond reproach* (iusti), since before he performs any act affecting rights he has done no wrong to anyone; and finally, his being authorized to do to others anything that does not in itself diminish what is theirs, so long as they do not want to accept it—such things as merely communicating his thoughts to them, telling or promising them something, whether what he says is true and sincere or untrue and insincere (*veriloquium aut falsiloquium*); for it is entirely up to them whether they want to believe him or not. (*MM*, 6:238)

As the sole human right, for Kant, the right to freedom as independence gives us several kinds of prerogatives. First, it gives us the title to do anything to other people that we may do to them without actually diminishing *their* freedom as independence, like simply communicating our thoughts to them: it thus grounds rights to freedom of speech and thought. Second, it gives us title to insist that we not be bound by any restrictions to freedom that are not reciprocal restrictions, that do not bind other people in the same way: it justifies a right to equal treatment. In addition, Kant holds that the innate right includes a minimum of bodily inviolability: someone who physically interferes with my body without my consent "affects and diminishes what is internally mine (my freedom), so that his maxim is in direct contradiction with the axiom of right" (*MM*,

---

Sciences (Berlin: Walter de Gruyter, 1900–). These numbers are widely noted in the margins of English translations. *MM* stands for Kant's *Metaphysics of Morals*, and *TP* for Kant's essay "On the Common Saying: That May Be Correct in Theory, But It Is of No Use in Practice."

6:250). Since my faculty of self-determination can only be exercised through my body, anyone who uses direct physical force on my body interferes with all possible expressions of my freedom.[19] These titles—to freedom of thought and communication, to equal treatment, and to a minimum of bodily inviolability—together comprise our *original* claims to freedom.

Unlike internal or metaphysical freedom, though, on Kant's theory, external freedom is defined by the individual's capacity to set and pursue ends in the outside world, by acting. So in order to be *externally* free, I must be able to take up and use physical means—at the very least, spaces and also potentially objects—in order to carry out my choices. I am not externally free merely by thinking or wishing or setting myself a goal, without taking any concrete actions; I cannot be externally free in chains. I am externally free only when I can do something to further my projects. And this means that I must be able to actually take up some means to my ends without fear of your interference with my acts. External freedom thus involves the use of pieces of the physical world, where this use is potentially subject to interference by other persons.[20]

While all rights involve some sort of claim to external freedom, Kant draws a important distinction between rights that belong to us innately (like all those described above) and those we must acquire. Here, Kant differentiates between what he calls the internal and external "mine" (*meum*). Some rights—like the innate titles—are *internally mine*: I am born with them; they are my inalienable property; I do not have to do anything to acquire them. Other rights are acquired, and so belong to what Kant calls the *external mine*: these rights do not belong to us by birth, but require a particular act to be established (*MM*, 6:237). Kant refers to three broad kinds of acquired rights: rights to "(1) a (corporeal) *thing* external to me; (2) another's *choice* to perform a specific deed (*praestatio*); (3) another's *status* in relation to me" (*MM*, 6:248). These three kinds of acquired rights specify (1) my claims of ownership or property; (2) my contractual claims against others; and (3) my status as an occupant of a role, as a spouse, parent, or head of household.[21] And shortly after introducing the innate right, interestingly, Kant suggests that it can more or less be laid aside in his political theory, in favor of a discussion of *acquired rights*: "It can be put in the prolegomena and the division

[19] Kant should not be understood as a partisan of unlimited self-ownership in the Lockean sense. We only have rights to those uses of our body that are compatible with the freedom of others. But still, we have some claim to freedom of bodily movement because that is the only way our freedom can manifest itself in the external world.

[20] For a useful discussion of this distinction, see Mulholland, *Kant's System of Rights*, 176.

[21] See Hruschka, "Permissive Law," 62.

of the doctrine of right can refer only to what is externally mine or yours" (*MM*, 6:238). Most of Kant's political theory, then, is concerned not with the innate right, but instead with acquired rights, which define the precise bounds of our sphere of control over the external world. The fundamental task of a science of right, as Kant sees it, is to show how these rights to an "external mine" should be defined and guaranteed: "The doctrine of right wants to be sure that *what belongs to each* has been determined (with mathematical exactitude)" (*MM*, 6:233). As we shall see, Kant concludes that we cannot acquire these sorts of rights without a state.

One reason for this is that unlike our titles to freedom of thought and communication or to minimal bodily inviolability, our rights to specific external objects are not naturally determinate. Freedom as independence requires that I have rights of control over a particular body (my own), but not that I have rights of control over a particular object. In order to be free-as-independent, I must have a right to some sphere of property, but it does not matter which specific objects I have a right to.[22] Kant's position can perhaps be made more intuitive if we reflect that any system of property will require the existence of a set of rules that is complex and to some extent conventional: rules about what sorts of things are eligible to be held as private property, what precisely are the conditions defining voluntary exchange, what constitutes an exploitative agreement, what are the conditions of publicly recognized spousal or parental rights, and how to distribute opportunities, education, and income. The conditions specifying these sorts of rights would be imprecise and difficult to judge in a state of nature.

The basic thought here is that while a principle of equal freedom provides us some information about what just property distributions should look like, the principle's content is underspecified, and therefore cannot be directly applied. The equal freedom principle suggests that whatever system of property we implement, it ought to be consistent with everyone's possession of a zone of freedom that is guaranteed against others' coercive interference. Nevertheless, many possible systems of property—collective allocation, market socialism, unfettered private ownership—are potentially consistent with that sense of equal freedom. And under each one of these many possible systems, there will again be many possible particular rules consistent with everyone's freedom—rules about the precise bundle of claims conferred by ownership, about how exchange is to be regulated, about which objects belong to which particular persons. And finally, any system of property will also have to include some aspects that are wholly conventional: rules about what precise formalities are required to conclude a contract, exactly how long a statute of limitations to institute, down, indeed, to what side of the road to drive on.

[22] I am grateful to Martin Sandbu for this formulation.

Still, we might imagine that private actors could somehow come to coordinate their expectations about all these matters, perhaps by hitting on that option—among a menu of options that were consistent with everyone's freedom—which was "salient" or "focal," given these actors' situation and the details of their history. David Hume puts forward a theory of property that relies on private actors establishing conventions in this sort of way.[23] But Kant denies that any private method of establishing the bounds to our property could be rightful and just. Instead, property, for him, can be conclusively acquired only in the state, and it is a natural duty for any set of individuals that wishes to acquire property to institute such a state to define and enforce their rights.

Acquiring Property in a State of Nature

But why exactly does Kant believe that it would be impossible to have acquired rights without the state, and that our attempts to define them—while admittedly difficult—would necessarily fail? Kant begins by asking what would happen if humans tried to acquire rights to property by their own efforts, by unilaterally appropriating objects in a state of nature. To illustrate how this process might play out, Kant conducts a thought experiment, which is contained in the section of *The Metaphysics of Morals* called "Private Right." There he connects a right with an authorization for an individual in the state of nature to use coercion to protect his own sphere of property: indeed Kant says that "right and the authorization to use coercion mean one and the same thing" (*MM*, 6:233).

Because a right is connected with the authorization to use coercion, on Kant's view, any private efforts to define and secure acquired rights will necessarily involve us in the private coercion of other people. To the extent that other persons interfere with those objects to which I have a right, they infringe my external freedom and I have the right to coerce them: "If a certain use of freedom is itself a hindrance to freedom in accordance with universal law, coercion that is opposed to this hindrance is consistent with freedom in accordance with universal laws, that is, it is right" (*MM*, 6:232). According to Kant, then, we begin as self-enforcers of our own rights.[24] And Kant's strategy is to show that that we can justify political authority as necessary for freedom if we see that it is the only rational solution to difficulties that *would be inherent in any system of private*

[23] For a useful discussion of convention, see Lewis, *Convention*; for Hume's views on property, see *A Treatise of Human Nature*.

[24] Throughout this section, I have drawn heavily on Arthur Ripstein's excellent interpretation of Kant's theory of public law in "Authority and Coercion."

definition and enforcement of our acquired rights to property, like the one he imagines in his "state of nature" thought experiment.

For Kant, our innate right to freedom initially gives us title to use the common resources of the world unmolested by others. Kant calls this sort of innate right a title to *empirical possession*: it is a right not to be prevented by others from using external objects. In this vein, Kant suggests that someone who tried to wrest an apple from my hand, for example, or to drag me away from my resting place, would wrong me with regard to my innate freedom, which gives me a title to minimal bodily inviolability (*MM*, 6:250). But Kant argues that this title to empirical possession is not sufficient to fully realize and guarantee our more basic right to independence; instead, securing our independence requires us to acquire new rights of private property over the external world.

In order to freely pursue any minimally sophisticated project, we need more than simply the right to use objects while we are physically holding them. Imagine, for example, that I want to paint a landscape. It is clearly insufficient for me to achieve this goal that I possess the use-right to dispose of paint, brushes, and canvas without fear of assault by others while I am holding them. For it is consistent with such a right that as soon as I put down the materials, someone else could come in and undo what I have done. To pursue any sophisticated goal, then, we have to be capable of making objects ours, by annexing them to our own rightful private sphere in the external world. Property rights are in this way essential conditions of agents' autonomy. Kant therefore claims that freedom requires *intelligible* possession of objects, a form of possession that does not require us to physically hold a thing in order for us to wronged by someone else's use of it without our consent. Rights of intelligible possession "maintain things in a state of being possible objects of choice even when they are not in one's physical possession."[25]

But what sort of act could allow me to add a right of intelligible possession to my innate or human rights, and thereby impose a new obligation on all others to respect my new acquisition? Moreover, how could I do this without their consent, simply by depriving them of their claim to make use of it? Kant suggests that it is a "postulate of pure practical reason" that rightful appropriation of property has to be possible even in a state of nature, since no system of freedom as independence could be realized otherwise:

> If the use of [an object] could not coexist with the freedom of everyone in accordance with a universal law (would be wrong), then freedom would be depriving itself of the use of its choice with regard to an object

[25] Weinrib, "Propter Honoris Respectum," 7.

> of choice, by putting *usable* objects beyond any possibility of being *used*; in other words, it would annihilate them in a practical respect and make them into *res nullius*, even though in the use of things choice [*Willkür*] was formally consistent with everyone's outer freedom in accordance with universal laws. (*MM*, 6:251)

Since almost all potential uses of our freedom require the exclusive use of objects, to postulate that it was contrary to right to acquire the objects necessary to our pursuits would seem to hinder the very establishment of freedom in the world and thus paradoxically force justice to prohibit its own realization.

On this basis, Kant concludes that, at least under certain conditions, it would be permissible for me to acquire objects and resources in a state of nature, and to exclude others from their use, since otherwise my autonomy would be radically jeopardized. Kant suggests that acquiring a right to a thing requires "*everyone* to accept an obligation not to interfere in property that some individual person has acquired and declared to be his own."[26] For this reason, rights to property in land can only be acquired if my unilateral will to appropriate

> is included in a will that is united *a priori* (i.e., only through the union of the choice of all who can come into practical relations with one another) and that commands absolutely. For a unilateral will (and a bilateral but still *particular* will is also unilateral) cannot put everyone under an obligation that is in itself contingent: this requires a will that is *omnilateral*, that is united not contingently but *a priori* and therefore necessarily, and because of this is the only will that is lawgiving. For only in accordance with this principle of the will is it possible for the free choice of each to accord with the freedom of all, and therefore possible for there to be any right, and so too possible for any external object to be mine or yours. (*MM*, 6:263)

For my possession of this particular object or piece of land to genuinely impose an obligation on others to recognize and respect it, it has to be something that they could agree to, viewed as free and independent individuals who also have a similar interest in holding property. And in order for them to be able to agree, my holdings cannot infringe their human right to independence: for if a regime of external property jeopardized this right, then their hypothetical consent would be impossible to obtain. This means two things: first, that my property rightfully extends only to a "fair share," one that is consistent with others' exercising a similar right. And second, I am reciprocally bound to recognize others' property once

[26] For this formulation, see Byrd and Hruschka, "Natural Law Duty," 260.

I have appropriated my own, for otherwise I would dominate them by forcing them to recognize a right in me that I am not prepared to grant others.[27] My property rights, in sum, must be justifiable to others as free and independent persons if they are to impose valid obligations.[28]

Kant therefore thinks it would be permissible for me to acquire objects as (intelligibly) mine in a state of nature, and to forcibly exclude others from their use even when I am not holding them, since otherwise my freedom would be jeopardized, and my external freedom is what I innately have a coercive right to protect. Kant calls this postulate of practical reason a permissive law (*Erlaubnisgesetz*): a permissive law provides us with an authorization to do something that would not normally be morally allowed.[29] In this case, it permits me to unilaterally limit your original common right to the use of external objects by coercing you to respect my private possession (*Besitz*) of certain things, even when I am not holding them. The permissive law

> gives us an authorization that could not be got from mere concepts of right as such, namely to put all others under an obligation, which they would not otherwise have, to refrain from using certain objects of our choice because we have been the first to take them into our possession. (*MM*, 6:247)

A permissive law tells me when I am authorized to regard a given external object as rightfully mine—in a preinstitutional condition, and without the agreement of other individuals—and to forcibly exclude others from its use. I am authorized to do so, suggests Kant, whenever I am the first person in possession of the object (when I would not have to force some prior occupant off it), when I give a sign of my possession, and when I regard my possession as springing from an a priori general will that would confirm that my property in this object was actually justifiable to others (*MM*, 6:258).

Why Freedom Cannot Exist outside the State

It might seem, then, that Kant, like Simmons, would hold that although our acquired rights are initially indefinite, our private acts of appropriation in a state of nature can function to more clearly delimit their contours. Once I appropriate an external object—for example, my piece of land in the state of nature—the boundaries of my right to external

[27] On this issue, see Weinrib, "Propter Honoris Respectum," 7–8.
[28] Forst, "Basic Right to Justification."
[29] For more on the permissive law, see Brandt, "Das Erlaubnisgesetz."

freedom might simply be equivalent to those of the things and spaces that I have appropriated. If this were so, then individuals could succeed in more precisely defining property *without the help of the state*, and simply by coordinating expectations based on their private acts. In order to respect and acknowledge my external freedom, on this view, you would just have to cede me the spot I have rightfully occupied and to refrain from infringing on my choices within that sphere. Yet Kant does not take this position: he argues that the rights made possible by the postulate of practical reason are problematic. Whatever rights our private acts of appropriation outside the state confer upon us can only be understood as provisional rights, that is, they are not conclusive and settled (*peremptorische*): indeed, for him, "It is possible to have something external as one's own only in a rightful condition, giving laws publicly, that is, a civil condition" (*MM*, 6:255).

What is the problem with these private methods of defining our rights to property? Why are they so unsatisfactory, from Kant's perspective? The essential problem with acquiring property rights in a state of nature, for Kant, seems to be that we cannot unilaterally—through private will—impose a new obligation on other persons to respect our property that they would not otherwise have had.[30] "By my unilateral choice I cannot bind another to refrain from using a thing, an obligation he would not otherwise have; hence I can do this only through the united choice of all who possess it in common" (*MM*, 6:261).[31] Even claiming to interpret the a priori general will on another person's behalf, says Kant, is attempting to impose a law on them on my own private authority, since every act of appropriation is "the giving of a law that holds for everyone" (*MM*, 6:253).[32] And he worries that this claim to private authority over others is a potential source of injustice: "Now when someone makes arrangements about *another*, it is always possible for him to do the other wrong; but he can never do wrong in what he decides upon with regard to himself (for *volenti non fit inuria*)" (*MM*, 6:314). My will to appropriate, in the belief that my appropriation is justifiable to others, cannot yet serve as a (coercive) law for everyone else, because it cannot put them under an obligation.

[30] See Waldron, "Kant's Legal Positivism," 1557: "Acquisition involves one person's creating obligations for others, obligations that are wholly for the benefit of the appropriator. . . . Thousands of other people, including people he has never met and people who have never even heard of him, suddenly find themselves laboring under obligations that they did not have before. Moreover, the duties that they acquire in this way are potentially onerous ones."

[31] For a useful discussion of this, see Kersting, *Wohlgeordnete Freiheit*, 226.

[32] A similar point is made by Weinrib, "Propter Honoris Respectum," 5.

Kant suggests, in other words, that figuring out how to carve up shares of the external world consistently with everyone's freedom does not exhaust the entire problem of justice involved in acquiring rights to property. We might appeal to criteria of salience or convention to help coordinate our expectations on which of the many possible property distributions to choose. But we face an additional difficulty: how do we impose one of these distributions without at the same time arrogating to ourselves the private authority *to lay down the law for an equally free being*, one who has an innate right not to be constrained by our private will? In coercing someone to respect our view of our property rights, we are also necessarily claiming the right to impose our private will upon that person. If it is to really respect everyone's freedom, Kant thinks, a property distribution cannot be unilaterally imposed in this way.

This additional dimension of the problem of justly acquiring rights—the problem of unilateral imposition—is rooted in each person's basic "right to do *what seems right and good to him* and not to be dependent upon another's opinion about this" (*MM*, 6:312). This right to do what seems right and good to him derives from the moral equality of persons: no one has an innate right to decide in another person's behalf. And because each person is an equally authoritative judge, it is therefore impossible—in a state of nature—to put him under an obligation of justice that he himself does not recognize.

> The will of all others except for himself, which proposes to put him under obligation to give up a certain possession, is merely *unilateral*, and hence has as little lawful force in denying him possession as he has in asserting it (since this can be found only in a general will). (*MM*, 6:257)

In conditions of equal authority—such as those that exist in any state of nature—one is obligated only by what one recognizes, by one's own lights, as an objectively valid requirement of justice. For that reason, no other person's merely unilateral will can bind one in the face of one's own disagreement.

Kant concludes from this that "no particular will can be legislative for the commonwealth" (*TP*, 8:295), since no private person's will can effectively claim to impose an obligation on others. Instead, Kant says that "all right," that is to say all claims that impose binding duties on others, "depends on laws" (*TP*, 8:294). Law overcomes the problem of unilateralism inherent in imposing new obligations on others on one's own authority, by substituting an *omnilateral* will in place of a unilateral one: "Only the concurring and united will of all, insofar as each decides the same thing for all, and all for each, and so only the general united will of the people, can be legislative" (*MM*, 6:314). But why is law—imposed from a public perspective—consistent with everyone's freedom in a way that particular wills—based on our private judgments—are not?

Fundamentally, Kant argues that defining and enforcing both our rights over our bodies and our rights to external objects through public and nonarbitrary laws is the only way to secure ourselves against the coercive interference of other private persons in our affairs. For Kant, then, the only sort of property distribution to which we could all hypothetically consent must necessarily be one that is defined and enforced by the state, since all privately enforced distributions have the inevitable side-effect of subjecting us to the wills of others. To show this in more detail, Kant points out two different ways that unilateral private enforcement undermines our right to independence: first, through unilateral interpretation—a particularly pervasive problem in the enforcement of property rights, since these rights are fully conventional in a way our rights over our bodies are not; and second, through unilateral coercion, which threatens interference by others in all our rights, both our rights over our bodies and our rights over external things.

The Problem of Unilateral Interpretation

Kant centrally appeals to the idea that to conclusively possess a right, it must be an objective right, rather than a subjective right based on one individual's private interpretation of what justice requires. A subjective right is an individual's good-faith belief about his rights: this belief gives him title to coerce others to keep off his property or to allow him bodily inviolability. But it does not yet place other people under a correlative duty. That would be so only if all individuals shared his interpretation of justice. But since individuals are equally authoritative judges in the state of nature, whenever they do not share another person's belief about justice, his belief imposes no duty on them at all. Instead, they are obliged only by the duties imposed by their own good-faith interpretation of justice, which may not be concordant with his. It might be said, by someone of a more Lockean persuasion, that one of these competing interpretations is the one that simply *is* valid as a matter of moral fact. That may be so. But as long as we remain in a state of nature, even this true view of right must remain unrealized, since each person, being an equally authoritative judge, has a right to enforce his or her own interpretation of justice, which means the true view of right places the person under no duties when it does not correspond with the person's own. So as long as we remain our own judges and self-enforcers, there is no means by which we might establish which interpretation of right is morally valid without claiming the authority to serve as judge in another person's behalf and forcibly subject the person to our will. And to claim that authority over someone else, Kant thinks, is refuse to recognize a person's independence as an equally free being.

For this reason, Kant thinks a procedure for the determination of *objective rights* is a constitutive feature of justice, since a common process of adjudication is logically necessary if anyone's rights are to impose any objective duties on other people.[33] Objective rights are rights that are determined through such a process of adjudication, and that impose recognizable duties on us even when we disagree about what justice requires. If each person is threatened with violence every time another person's private interpretation of justice disagrees with her own, she cannot *possibly* enjoy a secure sphere of freedom, since this other person is able to interfere with it whenever he sees fit. Instead, it is a constitutive part of justice that there be one *univocal* interpretation of the rights and duties to which everyone is subject, because only then can people securely enjoy *independence* from each other. Part of what justice demands, then, is a mechanism by which people can have their rights guaranteed in the external world without depending on the concordance of other people's beliefs. Justice cannot be attained in the absence of such a procedure: only once it is in place are we fully independent of interference by other people, as we have an innate claim to be.

To see how the unilateralism of interpretation undermines independence, imagine for a moment that you and I are state-of-nature neighbors. Say we have managed to resolve the indeterminacy of our property rights somewhat, perhaps by appropriating only in accordance with our interpretation of Kant's a priori general will, or by coordinating our expectations based on the most salient just system. So we have hit on some rightful boundary that sets off your property from mine, such that if I desire to live side by side with you in peace, simply by respecting your basic rights, I ought to be able to do so. Let's call our initial "property-owning" equilibrium *E1*.

Now suppose some dispute arises between us over whether your property right has in fact been infringed. Perhaps I have built a huge garage in my area, which blocks the sunlight to your property and makes your garden unusable. Any number of examples are possible; what unites them all is that they represent new contingencies, the disposition of which is going to be indefinite enough according to whatever original criterion of appropriation we are working with to make it likely parties acting in good faith might disagree. In our state-of-nature system, however, the interpretation of what right actually requires in this contingency is left up to you, along

[33] I am indebted to Martin Sandbu for conversation about these distinctions.

with the choice of whether or not to exercise your coercive rights to redress any (perceived) violation.

So let's say that you decide my garage is a violation of your acquired rights, since it makes your entire garden unusable, and so you cross our boundary in order to prevent me from blocking the light and to exact compensation from me. If I do not agree with your interpretation of your rights, I am under no obligation to submit to you: I am an equally authoritative interpreter of justice. I may object to the rightfulness of your boundary-crossing in this case, or, even if I concede that you had a right to exact punishment, I may (in all good faith) think that you have exceeded the bounds of the compensation you are entitled to. So I may struggle against you, and regard myself as doing so rightfully. In this situation we both regard ourselves as having a claim of justice, and since we both act in good faith, we act with full *subjective* right. But in our state of nature, the only thing that can decide the matter between us is a contest of strength, since both sides are equally right from their point of view. As Jeremy Waldron puts it:

> there is an affront to the idea of justice when force is used by opposing sides, confrontationally and contradictorily, in justice's name. The point of using force in the name of justice is to *assure* people of that to which they are entitled. But if force is being used to further contradictory ends, then its connection with assurance is ruptured.[34]

Let's say that in this case you are the stronger, and that you succeed in demolishing my garage and in exacting what you regard as rightful compensation for my supposed infringement—say, one-quarter of my property. Now we have a new property-owning equilibrium, *E2*, in which you possess 125 percent of our combined share and I possess only 75 percent. And keeping with our initial assumption that both parties were acting in good faith, with full subjective right, this new equilibrium would not have come about unrightfully.

Yet there is a real sense in which I retain a claim here, since the only reason you now possess more of the total is that you were stronger, not that I was convinced by your interpretation of justice. But the bounds of our sphere of control in the external world ought not to depend on the contingencies of who is stronger, and our innate independence ought not to be subject to continual interference by others who may coerce us at any moment in accordance with their private views. For this reason, Kant thinks it is a constitutive feature of justice that it be administered by an authoritative legal system, which can impose one set of objective rules about what constitutes an infringement of property—rules we must re-

[34] Waldron, "Kant's Legal Positivism," 1540.

spect even when we disagree about what justice requires—and adjudicate our conflicting claims in a way that is consistent with our continued independence from each other. The idea is that if we want to possess claims that, as objective rights, are actually respected by others in the external world, we will need to recognize *one and only one* common set of rules about rights, not a variety of competing private interpretations that coercively struggle for the upper hand.

Because the state of nature contains no mechanism to determine rights when people disagree, Kant argues that it will always be a condition of unfreedom and dependence, even if we happen to be persons of goodwill who are merely concerned to enforce justice fairly:

> Even if we imagine men to be as benevolent and law-abiding as we please, the *a priori* rational idea of a non-lawful state will still tell us that before a public and lawful state is established, individual men, peoples, and states can never be secure against acts of violence from one another, since each will have his own right to do what seems good and right to him, independently of the opinion of others. (*MM*, 6:312)[35]

The necessity of coercive political authority, then, is not simply due to the presence of malevolent or immoral persons among us. Instead, it lies in the very idea of a condition in which each person is allowed to impose her own private interpretation of the nature and limits of her rights on her moral equals. Even if I make this decision in a good-faith way, *it is still my private decision*, and therefore it is based on an interpretation of our situation that you might not share, and against which you might raise a complaint. As long as we remain in the state of nature, though, the only thing that can decide between our respective points of view is the outcome of our efforts to apply force. Coercion thus necessarily enters into the very definition of our rights as long as we remain in a state of nature.

Recall, though, Kant's definition of our one innate right: it is the right to independence from being constrained by another person's private will or faculty of choice (*Willkür*). Kant's essential insight is that no condition

[35] Not all those contemporary theorists who advocate "Kantian" theories of justice appear to have grasped the extent to which Kant supposes the state to be a necessary condition for freedom, conceived as independence from others' *Willkür.* Even Onora O'Neill, a subtle interpreter of Kant's ethical theory, appears to misinterpret his political theory in this way: "Because human beings are not always well disposed towards one another, justice requires enforcing institutions which unavoidably curtail external freedom. In Kant's view, the first task in developing a more specific account of justice is to recognize this reality, and to accept that justice requires institutions that coerce to limit coercion" (*Bounds of Justice*, 138). But Kant does not think institutions are necessary merely because we are morally ill-disposed. Instead, Kant believes that it is conceptually impossible to think that we could free ourselves from others' *Willkür* in any condition of private enforcement, even if these others were benevolent and well disposed toward us. Even a benevolent master, on Kant's view, is still

of private enforcement of claims to possession could ever produce a situation in which this innate right is adequately guaranteed. In any state of nature, we will necessarily be constrained by the private wills of others all the time, since it is other people's private wills that determine and enforce the limits of my sphere of control. Since the boundaries of others' freedoms are coextensive with the boundaries of my own, in any condition of private enforcement, the extent of my *actual* freedom always depends on their choices about precisely how to interpret and enforce their rights against me. And the more extensive their interpretation of their own rights and the more powerful they are at enforcing it, the more limited my sphere of actual freedom will be. For this reason, our duty to respect others' freedom as independence gives us a moral duty to leave the state of nature, since no one's independence can be secured there. To really establish a situation where we are no longer constrained by others' private wills, we must have reference to one set of objective and publicly ascertainable rules of right.

Unilateral Coercion and Assurance

Indeed, Kant thinks that a condition of private interpretation and enforcement undermines independence even if my state-of-nature neighbors and I happen to agree on the boundaries to our property rights "all the way down," that is, even if there are no problems of interpretation between us. That is because even when you agree on the limits of my rights, I am still dependent on your private will to sustain this agreement at every moment, and Kant argues that this dependence is in itself a form of insecurity and unfreedom. You might respect my rights now, but your will could change at any time, and so you retain the *power* of arbitrary interference with me and my rights, even if you do not in fact exercise it.[36] Kant argues that I should not have to depend on your private will as the only source of security for my rightful claims; instead, if I am to be a free equal, I must have a mechanism to assure me that my rights will be guaranteed, no matter what the status of your will. Inside the state, that mechanism is the public use of coercion. Outside the state, though, I can have recourse to my own arms whenever I am insecure about the reliability of your will and disposition. I do not have to wait until you actually violate my rights;

---

a master, and no situation that accepts such private subjection to others can be called a condition of freedom.

[36] The conception of freedom as independence I am attributing to Kant has affinities to Philip Pettit's view of freedom as nondomination, particularly in the notion that being exposed to someone else's power of arbitrary interference is a form of unfreedom, even when that power is not exercised. See Pettit, *A Theory of Freedom*, 138–39.

instead, since I am dependent on your will, any sign you might be intending to violate them gives me moral title to coerce you.

This makes the enforcement of public law necessary to overcome a serious problem of assurance about others' intentions to respect our rights. Our obligation not to interfere with others' property is conditional upon their guaranteeing to us that they will not interfere with the objects to which we claim a right.[37] But the conditionality of this obligation renders a system of private enforcement of acquired rights wholly problematic in the absence of assurance, since one's obligation to respect the rights of others depends on the presence of a conclusive guarantee that they will respect one's own. As soon as this guarantee is absent, one has a rightful title to preemptively attack others' property to protect one's own acquired rights: "I am therefore not under obligation to leave external objects belonging to others untouched unless everyone else provides me assurance that he will behave in accordance with the same principle with regard to what is mine" (*MM*, 6:256). The conditional obligation allows that if I am at all uncertain whether or not you intend to respect my rights, I am not bound to respect yours. Indeed, Kant goes so far as to claim that the very presence of another person in my vicinity with whom I am not subject to a common scheme of public justice gives me such a right to use preemptive force, simply because, for all I know, he might well encroach upon the external sphere of my freedom at some future point:

> No one, therefore, need wait until he has learned by bitter experience of the other's contrary disposition; for what should bind him to wait until he has suffered a loss before he becomes prudent[?] . . . it is not necessary to wait for actual hostility; one is authorized to use coercion against someone who already, by his nature, threatens him with coercion. (*MM*, 6:307)

In practice, then, in the state of nature I can have a right to attack you—out of mere suspicion of your intentions toward me, since I am dependent on your will—even to the point of infringing on your bodily inviolability and vice versa. So although we have an obligation to refrain from infringing others' rights (both rights to bodily inviolability and rights to property), we also have an equally important obligation to guarantee to others that we will do so, and our initial obligation to refrain from infringing others' sphere of freedom is null and void so long as we have not received such a guarantee from them, and vice versa.[38] This makes the state of nature into a thoroughly coercive condition: not only do individuals have a right to appropriate in accordance with their interpretation of

[37] Here I am following the discussion in Mulholland, *Kant's System of Rights*, 283.

[38] Mulholland, *Kant's System of Rights*, 283.

what would be justifiable to others; not only do they also have the right to interpret all further disputes about the limits of their rights in accordance with their own private judgment and to enforce that judgment to the best of their ability; but they also have a right to judge whether or not someone else might be threatening their acquired rights and to preemptively attack that person.

The Duty to Enter the State

The reason why the state is necessary to conclusively establish justice, then, is that it provides a mechanism for defining and securing rights in the face of disagreement, and for assuring each individual that others will not interfere with his freedom and property, which puts him under a conclusive duty to respect theirs. This frees us from having to rely on others' skill at moral reasoning, their good graces, or our own arms for the security of our freedom. For these reasons, Kant argues that persons have a natural duty of right to enter the state: "When you cannot avoid living side-by-side with all others, you ought to leave the state of nature and proceed with them into a rightful condition" (*MM*, 6:307).

Kant derives the duty to enter the state, then, not from some further postulate, but from "The Universal Principle of Right" itself, which states that an action is right if it can coexist with everyone's external freedom in accordance with a universal law (*MM*, 6:231). Private acquisition and enforcement simply cannot coexist with everyone's freedom; therefore they are wrongful:

> Given the intention to be and to remain in this state of externally lawless freedom, human beings do *one another* no wrong at all when they feud among themselves; for what holds for one also holds in turn for the other, as if by mutual consent. . . . But in general they do wrong in the highest degree by willing to be and to remain in a condition that is not rightful, that is, in which no one is assured of what is his against violence. (*MM*, 6:308)

The duty to enter the state emerged, as we saw, from the thought experiment of the state of nature, which showed that individuals cannot possibly be successful at establishing their external freedom—defined as independence from constraint by others' private wills—through their unilateral acts, even if they act in good faith. In such a condition, no one could securely enjoy a right of noninterference within her own sphere of control, because each other private person retains the prerogative to interfere with her, at every moment, as it seems right and good to him. On Kant's argument, then, if we remain in a state of nature, we have by definition not attained freedom, in that we have not yet achieved a condition in which true independence from others' private wills could ever be secured. Equal freedom itself gives us a moral duty to construct a state, by establishing impersonal and public laws to delineate the boundaries and extent of our respective property claims.

For this reason, unlike Simmons, Kant does not think we have to consent to enter the state in order for it to have legitimate authority over us. Instead, the state is simply a necessary instrument for satisfying precisely the moral background conditions that equal freedom-as-independence already imposes on any system of rights to property. Since our natural duties to others already require us to respect their freedom as independence, and since, because of the problems of unilateral private interpretation and enforcement, the state is necessary for that purpose, we have a natural duty to enter the state. We already will the existence of the state, in other words, as soon as we will the legitimate possession of private property, simply because our duties to respect others' freedom cannot be satisfied in any other way.

As long as the state's system of coercive law really does establish an equal distribution of external freedom between individuals, then, its public use of coercion is just, and it does me no wrong. If the laws create a background condition of justice, then I have no complaint. Indeed, for Kant, I don't even have to specifically agree to these laws or to the establishment of this particular state in order to be obligated by them. For Kant, the state is nothing like a voluntary association; it is not something I have the option to "sign up" for or not, as I so choose:

> In all social contracts, we find a union of many individuals for some common end which they all *share*. But a union as an end in itself which they all *ought to share* and which is thus an absolute and primary duty in all external relationships whatsoever among human beings (who cannot avoid mutually influencing one another) is only found in a society in so far as it constitutes a civil state, i.e. a commonwealth. (*TP*, 8:289)

As a matter of shorthand description, then, we might say that Kant's position differs from Simmons's in that Kant does not see the authoritative and coercive legal order put in place by the state as a kind of second-best remedy for achieving a distribution of freedom that might, were we sufficiently moral or benevolent, have been achieved through our interpersonal behavior. Instead, Kant forcefully argues that the state is a constitutive part of justice, because any system of private interpretation and enforcement of our rights will undermine our freedom altogether:

> Unless it wants to renounce any concepts of right, the first thing [each individual] has to resolve upon is the principle that it must leave the state of nature, in which each follows his own judgment, unite itself with all the others (with which it cannot avoid interacting), subject itself to a public lawful external coercion, and so enter into a condition in which what is to be recognized as belonging to it is determined *by law* and is allotted to it by adequate power (not its own but an external power); that is it ought above all else to enter a civil condition. (*MM*, 6:312)

A Statist Theory of Rights

Had we not seen Kant's argument about the problems of unilateral interpretation and coercion in defining property rights, his claim that we have a natural duty of justice to the *state* might strike us as somewhat odd. This is because, as Simmons exploits, we generally take ourselves to be bound by other natural duties of personal morality, including the duties not to murder, assault, or rape other people, or the duty to rescue. But we don't need institutions to act on these duties. Instead, we are perfectly capable of following through on them all by ourselves, simply by refraining from or performing the acts in question. But, as we have seen, Kant claims that natural duties of justice have a structure that is unique to justice itself, because the precise content of these duties requires further specification in terms of positive law, and this content must be imposed from a public and objective perspective.

Since property cannot be justly acquired outside the state, Kant's state-of-nature idea is purely fictitious: it is not meant to explain how the state arose, but rather to provide the individual inside the state with an explanation of his political obligations. It shows him that his commitment to the state is not a voluntary one, like a commitment to a club or an insurance company, but instead one that is necessarily binding. Nevertheless, thinking through what private rights might have been like in some preinstitutional condition is not a useless exercise, since it allows us to imagine how justice ought to look once we are inside public institutions.

Kant's argument in favor of the state gives us reason to be skeptical whether political authority is really irreconcilable with the principles of freedom and equality, as Simmons and other anarchist critics have claimed. If it is true that (*a*) our rights to property cannot be given determinate and publicly knowable contours without invoking public law, and (*b*) none of our rights—even rights over our bodies—can be enforced outside the state without undermining our independence, then the authority of the state becomes essential to justice. Kant, in the end, offers us what I would like to call a *statist* theory of rights. A statist theory claims that rights to bodily inviolability and to property can only exist in a form that binds other people to recognize and respect them when there is a state to authoritatively define and enforce these rights.

If Kant is correct, then, equal freedom is a necessarily institutional value: it is not one that can ever be secured by our private actions, even if we carry out our moral duties. And because he thinks freedom is an institutional value, Kant rejects the key assumption shared by cosmopolitans and critics of authority: that justice consists in clear and obvious natural duties that apply directly to individuals' personal moral conduct. Instead, Kant holds that justice is a standard that applies to the state—the institution that defines our acquired rights—to ensure that it determines these rights in an equal and reciprocal fashion. And because Kant holds that justice can apply only within a structure of political authority, he suggests that a citizen's relationship to that structure ought not to be viewed as morally irrelevant: instead, citizens have a moral duty of justice to construct and uphold state institutions.

What lessons can we learn from Kant's theory? If we take the statist view seriously, then, like Kant, we will hold that justice is a necessarily *institutional* value. Justice, as we have seen, could not possibly be secured by our private actions, even if we act in good faith and try to carry out our moral duties. This is because no matter how benevolent and well-disposed human beings are, the structure of an extra-institutional situation always gives other persons a form of coercive private control over us that is in contradiction to freedom, since others retain the power to interfere with our choices unilaterally and at will. For these reasons, we should also reject the assumption that justice is an interpersonal moral duty. Indeed, if we take Kant seriously, we ought to believe that one of our most fundamental duties of justice is the duty to belong to a legitimate state.

3

Democracy

In the last chapter, I argued—through a reading of Kant's political theory—that a condition of justice can only be brought into being by means of state authority. As we saw, equally free individuals must possess rights that are not naturally defined—what Kant calls *acquired rights*. Kant's main assertion is that the only way to "fill in" the terms of our acquired rights consistently with each person's innate claim to be treated as a free equal is via a public mediating institution, the state. This is because any private means of settling the bounds of these rights will always leave us exposed to the threat of domination by other people, who retain the power to coerce us in accordance with their own views at every moment. To really attain freedom, we must eliminate this threat of private domination, and that requires we bring into being a public institution—the state—that can authoritatively define, and coercively impose, one objective, impersonal, and binding definition of our rights.

If we take Kant's argument seriously, we will hold that a condition of equal freedom simply cannot be attained in the absence of state authority, and therefore that state institutions are of considerable moral significance. Kant's principal insight is that equal freedom can never be secured when individuals' private wills are allowed to determine the extent of other people's rights. Only impersonal and nonarbitrary laws can determine our rights consistently with everyone's freedom. If we see the matter this way, then we will view the institutions that allow us to regulate our relations by *law*, rather than by private will, as themselves being of moral importance in terms of the value of equal freedom. States are not morally inessential institutions, and they are not potentially dispensable parts of our social fabric. Rather, as soon as we commit to respecting persons as free and equal, we commit to state authority, since there is no other way to define the terms of our respective rights in a nondominating fashion.[1]

What we need, though, if we accept Kant's argument about the moral importance of the state, is a means of ensuring that its laws remain legitimate, that is, that they are sufficiently impersonal and nonarbitrary and that they actually function to secure everyone's equal claim to a sphere of private freedom. If the value of freedom gives us good reason

[1] I am indebted to an anonymous reviewer for part of the phrasing in this sentence.

to establish and obey political authorities, surely it only gives us reason to obey those political authorities that really do guarantee equal freedom. Whatever problems prevent our realizing a condition of equal freedom in the absence of the state, they cannot be so overwhelming as to license our subordinating ourselves to any kind of state whatsoever, even an arbitrary and tyrannical one. Instead, we want some assurance that the laws it enacts will truly reflect the ideal of freedom as independence that Kant defends. Achieving this requires securing independence not just from the choices of other individuals, but also from the private will of the political authority itself.

Unfortunately, Kant's political theory does not provide us sufficient assurance on this score. For Kant, the existence of a civil condition (and therefore of justice itself) is predicated on our surrendering our own title to privately decide when coercion in defense of our rights is warranted. Because political authority is a necessary prerequisite to the establishment of justice, Kant therefore concludes that we have an obligation to obey all existing political authorities, in the hope that justice will eventually be brought about through them. In the end, then, Kant takes every existing government, no matter what the character of its rule, to be a legitimate one. He argues that "the presently existing legislative authority ought to be obeyed, whatever its origin" (*MM*, 6:319).

While Kant concedes that there exists an a priori standard for determining when law is just—whether that law could logically serve as the general will of an entire people, which requires that each member be able to consent to it—for him, this standard is merely a diagnostic tool of which the existing sovereign should make use in order to legislate well. The actual will of the body politic is not given by reference to this a priori standard, but instead through being represented by the particular will of an identifiable agent: a monarch, an aristocracy, or a democratic assembly. Although the sovereign, whoever he is, ought to frame his laws with reference to this standard, Kant suggests that the people have no coercive claim against him if in fact he deviates from it. "The reason for this," Kant claims, "is that the people, under an existing civil constitution, has no longer any right to judge how that constitution should be administered" (*TP*, 8:300). Ultimately, Kant opts for the view that we are obligated to obey whatever state exercises power over us, simply because the establishment of the state—as a public mediating institution—is a necessary precondition for the realization of right. Political authority comes first, and we simply have to hope that justice will follow upon it. Kant's political theory therefore fails to provide us with a useful account of the limits of legitimate state authority.

That is why I turn to Rousseau in this chapter. In what follows, I will argue that Rousseau gives us an account of political authority that is in many ways an attractive alternative to Kant's, and that can go some distance toward establishing a criterion for the legitimacy of the state: this is the criterion of the general will. Rousseau's theory, like Kant's own, has the merit of acknowledging that, because of the threat of private domination in any state of nature, equal freedom can only be realized inside a state. But he also claims that we are not required to obey the will of an unaccountable sovereign in the manner Kant defends. For Rousseau, freedom could never give us a reason to obey the arbitrary will of a particular private person, including the will of a sovereign. Instead, he holds that the only kind of state that we could possibly have a genuine obligation to obey must be one based on a general will—a collective will that protects a set of common interests, and that imposes these protections in the form of an impersonal law. A general will, he claims, is the one authority that can place bounds on our freedom without dominating us in the process.

In this chapter, I will try to uncover what Rousseau might understand by the general will, a fraught and difficult concept. In the next chapter I will argue that the general will, when properly updated in contemporary terms, can still serve as a criterion for assessing the state's legitimacy. Rousseau is a complex thinker, and here I will be offering an expressly Kantian interpretation of his ideas. Although my interpretation is certainly not the only possible one, I do not think it is in any way obfuscating. Kant himself took a number of his central concepts—including the idea of freedom as independence and the idea that the general will is the proper standard of justice—from Rousseau. Moreover, Kant himself read Rousseau as a theorist of freedom inside the rational state, and therefore as a precursor to his own views.[2] But most importantly, the reason why Rousseau ought to be of fundamental interest to us is that he may give us the means of articulating a theory of political legitimacy that avoids the absolutist elements inherent in Kant's own conception. If such a theory can be found, then our use of Rousseau will have been worthwhile, even if a Kantian interpretation of his work is only one among many.

One of the key points that will emerge from our discussion of Rousseau is that he imposes a controversial condition on the formulation of a general will. Rousseau argues that citizens of a democratic state must share a bond of solidarity with one another in order to exercise political authority in a nondominating way. If they are to formulate a general will, citizens must be motivated to take one another's interests into account: the good of each person must matter to all. Therefore a self-interested or a factionalized citizenry, Rousseau argues, will not be able to define a set of civil rights that allows each person to maintain her freedom. Only a patriotic

[2] See Kant's 1786 essay "Conjectures on the Beginning of Human History," 227.

citizenry, strongly identified with one another and with the state, can formulate and obey a general will. In part 2 of the book, we will be investigating this "solidarity requirement" in much greater detail.

Freedom and Legitimacy

Rousseau begins the *Social Contract* by declaring that the purpose of his book is to understand the nature of legitimate political authority: to find "some legitimate and sure rule of administration, taking men as they are, and laws as they can be" (*SC*, 41).[3] The structure of his argument in book 1 is a search for the answer to this question: What form must political authority take in order to place citizens under a genuine obligation to obey?[4] Rousseau's main claim in book 1 of the *Social Contract* is that a legitimate authority must be an authority that preserves our freedom. Rousseau defines freedom as the ability to obey one's own will (*E*, 84; *SC*, 50), or perhaps more perspicuously, as not being subject to someone else's will (*LM*, 260–61). Therefore, he thinks that our freedom is never guaranteed if we are required to submit to the will of some particular agent or group. No condition of one-sided domination could ever create an obligation to obey on the part of those subject to it.

Rousseau's main assertion—that a legitimate authority must necessarily guarantee its subjects' freedom—is actually more difficult to establish than it might at first seem. This is because there existed another powerful and popular argument at the time of his writing that asserted the contrary case. Like Rousseau's own, this argument held that legitimate authority was not based on force, on facts about our birth, or on nature, but instead on artificial conventions made by free human beings. But this theory still asserted that legitimate political authority could be properly understood as a form of domination, and even that it could be directly modeled on a kind of voluntary enslavement. This was a central argument of Grotius and Hobbes, both of whom claimed that a relation of legitimate authority could perfectly well come about through a compact of voluntary slavery. Starting from Rousseau's own first principles, they were able—with the help of a theory of voluntary slavery—to offer a defense of absolute and unaccountable government, which they claimed could be under-

[3] Rousseau, *Social Contract and Other Later Political Writings*. Unless otherwise noted, the translations of Rousseau's writings are taken from this edition or Rousseau, *Discourses and Other Early Political Writings*. Exceptions are *E: Emile*, and *LM: Letters from the Mountain*. The abbreviations are as follows: *SC*: *The Social Contract*; *GM*: *Geneva Manuscript*; *Poland*: *Considerations on the Government of Poland*; *D2*: *The Discourse on Inequality*; *EOL: Essay on the Origin of Languages*.

[4] Melzer, *Natural Goodness of Man*, 126; Dent, *Rousseau*, 187.

stood as the voluntary enslavement of a group of people to the authority of a sovereign power.

Their defense turned on the idea that a fully acceptable use of one's natural freedom is to freely agree to give it up. This is especially relevant, Hobbes and Grotius thought, in situations where one's security or basic subsistence is severely jeopardized. Facing privation or extreme insecurity, an individual might well agree to obey a master's will in perpetuity in return for some desired good, for example, his own subsistence, security, the payment of his debts, or (in the case of a prisoner of war), in exchange for his life.[5] In these types of situations, Grotius and Hobbes suggested, perpetual slavery would be a useful and a rational bargain to make, simply because it guarantees the provision of one's most basic needs. But once a person voluntarily consents to the master's authority, both thinkers argued, a moral and not merely a physically coercive relationship arises between them. By consent, the master acquires a right over the slave, the right to rule or direct his actions, that is, to serve as a legitimate authority for him. In such cases, Grotius and Hobbes argued, relations of domination do involve real normative authority: they are not simply the coercive use of threats and bribes, which the slave would have genuine title to resist, because force confers no right.

Grotius, moreover, thought that conventional slavery provided a useful model for understanding political authority, since in imitation of the voluntary slave, an entire people could alienate its will in perpetuity to a monarch, in the hope of thereby ensuring its preservation or security.[6] Hobbes too described the relation between a master and his slaves as a perfectly good model for the relation between the sovereign and his subjects in the *civitas*.[7] What made it possible for them to equate the relation of sovereign to subject with the relation of master and slave is an essentially shared feature of the two contracts: in both cases, the individual (or people) transfers the right of independent self-government to a master,

[5] On the context of Rousseau's argument against slavery by convention, see Derathé, *Jean-Jacques Rousseau*, 192–207. For another analysis of Rousseau's relationship to the "natural rights" jurists that preceded him, see Tuck, *Rights of War and Peace*, 197—207.

[6] Grotius, *Rights of War and Peace*, 86–87.

[7] Hobbes, *On the Citizen*, 119.

> But first one must refute the view which denies that a commonwealth made up of any number of slaves under one common Master is a commonwealth at all. At V.9. a *commonwealth* was defined as one *person* formed from several men, and his will is to be regarded as the will of all of them, so that he may make use of individuals' strength and resources for the common peace and defence. By the same article of the same chapter, *one Person* exists, when the will of several men are contained in the will of one man. But the will of each slave is contained in the will of his Master, as was shown at VIII.5, so that he may make use of their strength and resources as he pleases. It follows that it is a commonwealth which is formed from a *Master* and a number of slaves.

whose will then serves as an authority for him. And once he has transferred it, the individual cannot repossess his right to choose for himself. By extension, Hobbes held, just as Kant also does, that once a people is subject to a sovereign, it has no right to judge the content of his directives because they have given up their right to judge; they are therefore equivalent to his perpetual (voluntary) slaves.

This account, which equates political authority with a kind of voluntary slavery, is a significant challenge to Rousseau's view. It is challenging because it grants his first principle: that political authority is not a natural fact about the world, rooted in force or birth, but is conventional or artificial, derived from pacts made by free and equal individuals. In order for his alternative view—that a legitimate authority must be one that preserves our freedom—to have purchase, he first has to refute voluntary enslavement as a possible model for legitimate political authority. Rousseau needs to show that our right to freedom is an inalienable right, one that cannot be given up, and therefore that any legitimate authority must always recognize and guarantee this right: it cannot require us to renounce it.

Rousseau refutes voluntary slavery in an interesting way, thereby laying the cornerstone for his own view that a legitimate state must guarantee the ongoing freedom of its subjects. Rousseau argues that the specific kind of convention said to be involved in voluntary slavery has to be invalid. It can be ruled out because it is logically self-refuting: the notion of consent at stake is contradictory, because it undermines the obligation to obey the very contract of slavery that has just been made. Having a right to make, to enforce, and to be obligated by any contract with someone else, for Rousseau, always presupposes that one retains one's status as a person, as a being with legal standing, who can continue to possess rights against others. These rights are the background moral conditions that make contractual obligation and voluntary association with others possible in the first place. To give up one's status as a being with any legal claims and to turn oneself into someone else's property (as the slave does) is necessarily also to give up the ability to make contracts and to be obligated by them.[8] In this way Rousseau hopes to show that a free decision to give up one's freedom must be held to be null and void—it is a decision that no one can be legally obligated to carry out, because in making it, one disavows one's very capacity to be placed under legal obligations: "To renounce one's freedom," Rousseau says, "is to renounce one's quality as man, the rights of humanity, and even its duties" (*SC*,

[8] Kant also interprets the inalienability of freedom this way: "And no one can voluntarily renounce his rights by a contract or legal transaction to the effect that he has no rights but only duties, for such a contract would deprive him of the right to make a contract, and thus would invalidate the one he had already made" (*TP*, 8:292).

45). No one who has given up all his rights can be placed under any duties and obligations; he may be *forced* to obey his master, but he cannot be legally obliged to do so:

> Is it not clear that one is under no obligation toward a person from whom one has the right to demand everything, and does not this condition alone, without equivalent and without exchange, nullify the act? For what right can my slave have against me, since everything he has belongs to me, and his right being mine, this right of mine against myself is an utterly meaningless expression? (*SC*, 46)

In the argumentative strategy of Grotius and Hobbes, recall, the idea of contractual slavery is initially modeled on reciprocal exchange: the master gives the slave his subsistence; the slave in return grants the master his obedience. But once the slave has alienated his freedom, Rousseau argues, the exchange cannot remain reciprocal: the master's obligation to the slave disappears, and vice versa, simply because the slave's personhood, together with his rights and even his will, has been fully subsumed under the master's own: he is his master's property. The slave's right against the master and the master's right against the slave become *one right*: a right of the master against himself. But having a right against oneself is impossible; and therefore Rousseau holds this proves the original agreement to be self-contradictory. Having a contractual obligation to another requires that one remain a legally separate person, with the standing to bring a claim against others; and this means one must preserve at least the essential rights of free personhood. The rights of free personhood are inalienable.[9]

In consequence, Rousseau concludes that if we accept, as Hobbes and Grotius do, that legitimate political authority must be based on a convention between naturally free persons, we must also accept that this authority cannot possibly take the form of one person's domination over others. A convention that requires us to accept *any* act of a master or a sovereign will necessarily be one in which one is not obligated to obey: it is a situation in which one has become a slave, and, by making oneself someone else's property, has renounced all moral titles whatsoever. Since our power to be obligated depends on our retaining moral personhood, the enslaved subject of an unaccountable sovereign no longer has any political obligations at all.

The conclusion that slavery must be ruled out entails far-reaching consequences for Rousseau's investigation into what "legitimate" political authority requires: if it is true that free conventions to give up our freedom are void, then we must always remain just as free inside a well-ordered

[9] For discussions of Rousseau's views on freedom as an inalienable right, see Gildin, *Rousseau's Social Contract*, 26; Parry, "Autonomy and the Citizen," 100–102.

state as we would be in the state of nature outside it.[10] Rousseau therefore cannot hold (as Kant seems to) that a regard to freedom could justify individuals in accepting any and all decisions made by a sovereign's particular and arbitrary will. Citizens cannot accept decisions of a sovereign authority that require them to give up their freedom. To accept that would be to give oneself gratuitously, and that is one contract we do not have the power to make.

So although it is frequently asserted that Rousseau does not believe in any individual moral rights that exist prior to or independent of the state, his views on voluntary slavery clearly show this assertion to be mistaken. Like Kant, Rousseau does believe in one inalienable "natural" right, which cannot be contracted away: this is the innate right to freedom,[11] and it must be recognized if the political association is to be legitimate rather than tyrannical. But Rousseau takes this insight a step beyond Kant: he thinks that preserving our right to freedom cannot possibly license unconditional obligation to any particular person's arbitrary will as a sovereign power. Instead, some way must be found for the individual to recognize an authority over and above his own private will, without this relation of authority taking the form of subjection to the private will of someone else, especially the private will of a sovereign. Rousseau suggests that this can happen if the people construct the standard for their collective life in common according to law. Civil freedom can only exist when nobody rules anyone else at all; when, instead, everyone is ruled by the laws. How this can occur is the subject we must now take up.

The General Will

Recall that Grotius had held that an entire people, in imitation of the voluntary slave, could potentially alienate its collective will to a king.

[10] Rousseau, *LM*, 807: "Il est encore d'une espèce particulière [de convention] en ce qu'il lie les contractants sans les assujétir à personne, et qu'en leur donnant leur seule volonté pour règle, il les laisse aussi libres qu'auparavant." See also *Emile*, 461, where he states that "one is *more* free under the social pact than in the state of nature" (emphasis added).

[11] On this point, see Dent, *Rousseau*, 188–90: Rousseau, as we shall see in more detail later, dissents from the strand in natural rights thinking that holds that the individual reserves certain rights to himself inside the state. But, as Dent properly notes: "It is a mistake to infer that because Rousseau denies this strand in natural rights thinking, he denies natural rights altogether. He does not. Each potential associate brings to the issue of devising legitimate terms for his association with others natural moral titles and claims, which must be fitly accommodated if the conditions of association are not to be tyrannical. But it is a necessary part of the way in which they *can* be appropriately accommodated that no one associate reserves the right of judgment to himself."

If this is true, Rousseau notes, then the body must have constituted a "people"—with a common will—prior to that act. If a people could make legitimate and authoritative decisions for itself on the basis of a common will, then the only possible solution to the problem of authority is not subjection to an unaccountable sovereign. This, he argues, points us toward the proper question about legitimate political authority: what could possibly make a group into "a people" instead of an aggregation of disconnected individuals? "Peoplehood" (as one unified collective) presupposes the existence of relations of obligation, such that the will of the people as an association has authority over the actions of the individual. The real question about political authority, then, is how individuals create a situation where the will of a collectivity comes to have this kind of legitimate claim on their behavior. In order to understand the genesis of these relations of authority, suggests Rousseau, we must refer to an original convention. Moreover, this convention cannot be a convention of the kind that has already been ruled out: it cannot be a convention involving the alienation of freedom. Freedom, as we have seen, for Rousseau means obeying only one's own will, or being subject to no will other than one's own (*SC*, 50).

But how could any convention both subject us to authority and preserve us in the full exercise of our freedom? We can begin to see the outlines of the rather difficult problem formed by the constraints Rousseau has set for himself:

Goal: To understand the constitution of the legitimate authority of the collective.
Premissed Constraints:

a. Authority: the will of the association must have normative significance for my behavior, in a way it does not do automatically in an aggregation or crowd—I must therefore be obligated or bound by it.
b. Legitimacy: a legitimate authority cannot take away my freedom.
c. Freedom: the ability to be subject to no one else's will but my own.

Conclusions:

d. In obeying a legitimate authority, I must obey no one else's will, because only thus do I remain free.
e. Despite (*d*), to move from aggregation to association is to produce a significant change in my behavior.

In order to understand the complex notion of the general will, we must get at what this change might be. The general will is meant to be Rousseau's response or solution to the problem of legitimate authority outlined above, which he glosses in these words: "To find a form of association that will defend and protect the persons and goods of each associate with the full common force, and by means of which, each uniting with all, nevertheless obey only himself and remain as free as before" (*SC*, 49-50). The solution to this problem, he states, comes down to one sole condition: "the total alienation of each associate with all of his rights to the whole community" (*SC*, 50).

In order to constitute a legitimate political authority, then, each participant in the contract must give up the totality of her rights, her possessions, and even the free usage of her own body to society as a whole. As parties to the social contract, we no longer have valid rights against society itself, because the main clause of the social contract is that we agree to treat the will of society as a whole, when formulated in the right way, as definitive of our rights. Were the individual to hold back some rights as nontransferable, according to this way of thinking, no true political authority could exist.

The notion of alienating all one's rights to society sounds rather extreme. But Rousseau emphasizes that we do not alienate our rights to be determined by just *any* decision society might happen to make. Instead, we give up our rights to be determined by society acting under a certain kind of decision constraint, the constraint of defining a set of bounds to our actions that could be willed or consented to by everyone who is subject to them. This decision constraint is what Rousseau calls the general will. Here, it is important to remember that the device of a general will is meant to express the terms to which a political authority would need to conform in order to put us under a genuine obligation to obey it. There is no difficulty in holding that individuals don't possess rights against the general will itself, since the terms of the general will define their rights. The general will delineates the limits of each individual's civil rights to property in land, to other possessions, and to a sphere of free action: the sum total of these rights under the general will is what Rousseau calls *civil freedom*. So we have no rights against society as a whole, as long as the decisions of society as a whole conform to the constraints laid out in the general will. When the decisions of society do not conform to these constraints, however, we are under no obligation to obey them: we retain our natural freedom to decide for ourselves what we wish to do.

Although Rousseau accepts that the total alienation of rights and powers to the community as a whole is logically required in order to constitute the general will, his key move is to reject the thought that such an alienation should place these rights at the disposal and direction of any particular agent or body. That would be to establish the state on the model of master and slaves. Rather, while individuals still alienate their entire selves, under Rousseau's model they alienate themselves to each other, or rather to the collective that they are about to form. We thus alienate ourselves in such a way that there is no superior. Because there is no superior, the condition is equal for all, and each is alienating herself to no one in particular: "Each, by giving himself to all, gives himself to no one, since there is no associate over whom one does not acquire the same right as one grants him over oneself" (*SC*, 50). Rousseau's idea, in sum, is that we can remain free if we obey a will that emanates from no one in particular and applies equally to all. To the extent that we are able to do this, we retain our own freedom, simply because we are not required to obey the will of any particular person, and it is dependence on arbitrary and particular wills that jeopardizes our freedom. Each of us is, of course, dependent on political society as a whole, and the limits to our rights are given by what society as a whole could rationally agree to. But dependence on society's impersonal authority, like dependence on necessary forces, does not violate our autonomy.

Civil and Moral Freedom

In explaining the notion of the general will, Rousseau appeals to the idea that in order to live together socially while at the same time maintaining our freedom, we must place some limits on our actions—we must know where our sphere of freedom ends and that of another person begins. The paradoxical quality of the general will is that it is supposed to impose limits to our actions that are wholly consistent with our remaining free. Rousseau interprets this as meaning that we must replace our "natural freedom," the unlimited right to "everything that tempts us and that we can reach" that we would have enjoyed in a state of nature, with "civil freedom," a right that has "bounds" and grants us "positive title" (*SC*, 54). Like Kant's innate right to independence from constraint by others' *Willkür*, civil freedom requires each citizen to enjoy a personal sphere in which he can pursue his own goals without interference from others.[12] By legislating limits to our actions, we also gain what Rousseau calls "moral freedom," "which alone makes man truly the master of himself; for the impulsion of mere appetite is slavery, and obedience to the law one has prescribed to oneself is freedom" (*SC*, 54).

Understanding why this natural freedom is given up and how the civil and moral freedoms we gain on entering society relate to one another is an important key to comprehending the general will. To see why we can

[12] For a useful discussion of what Rousseau means by civil freedom, see Neuhouser, "Freedom, Dependence," 58.

remain free while having limits placed on our actions by the general will, let us examine the idea of civil freedom more closely. "In the state of nature," Rousseau says, "where everything is common, I owe nothing to those to whom I have promised nothing. I recognize as another's only what is of no use to myself. It is not so in the civil state where all rights are fixed by law" (*SC*, 66). What Rousseau seems to have in mind is that, inside the state, we exchange our natural and unlimited liberty of doing as we like for a limited but secure sphere of action. Within the limits set by law, we are guaranteed against the interference of other private persons in our affairs and their potential domination of us. We all give up the liberty of doing what we like within other people's spheres, and in exchange we receive the secure liberty of doing as we like in our own. These reciprocal limits constitute our civil freedom: they guarantee us a sphere of choice that is truly our own, and within which others cannot interfere. The limits imposed by law also restrain us from interfering with others' spheres of freedom, of course, but it is only by so restraining us that our own sphere can be guaranteed.

Despite the fact that inside the state, our natural freedoms are replaced with a new set of civil freedoms limited by law, Rousseau argues that not just any set of laws can serve as just boundaries or limits. Only those laws that are based on a general will are just boundaries, because only these laws are limits to which everyone could rationally consent. So we do not have a genuine obligation to obey any set of laws the state might enact; we only have an obligation to obey those laws that are based on a general will, which set up a distribution of civil freedom that could be rationally willed by everyone who is subjected to it.

Rousseau, as we saw, also says that in entering the state, we gain another kind of freedom: moral freedom, which entails "obedience to a law we prescribe to ourselves" (*SC*, 54). Rousseau often says that a citizen in a legitimate state "obeys only himself." This statement may seem rather inscrutable, given that a citizen in a legitimate state is subject to laws, some of which he may not have consented to—perhaps he even voted against them—and with which he is coerced to comply. How can a person who is in union with others, under coercive laws, obey only himself alone? At another point Rousseau gives us a little more clarity when he says that "every genuine act of the general will either obligates or favors all Citizens equally. . . . So long as subjects are subjected only to conventions such as these, they obey no one, but only their own will" (*SC*, 63).

By submitting to a set of equal and reciprocal laws that place limits on our sphere of action, Rousseau thinks, we gain back the freedom from others' interference that we would have enjoyed in a totally solitary and independent state of nature, like the one he depicts in the *Discourse on Inequality*. By submitting to law, I make it the case that I do not have to obey another person's will within my own sphere. In that sense, I obey only myself within my sphere of civil freedom, and since law is a precondition for my enjoyment of civil freedom, when I obey the laws, I am helping to secure a sphere within which I can obey only myself. In addition, Rousseau seems to argue that if I am thinking rationally, I will realize that subjecting myself to fair and reciprocal laws is the only way to guarantee me the ability to obey my own will, and so I should subjectively embrace the laws that grant it to me. If I do that, then I am also obeying only myself when I obey the laws in an additional sense: *I will* the laws. Rousseau maintains that the exchange of our unlimited natural liberty for a limited civil freedom combined with security against private interference is one that any rational person should make, since it represents an objective improvement in his condition from the state of nature. That is why, in subjecting himself to such limits, each person is "obeying only himself," since he is doing what it would be rational for him to do, what he would have chosen in the state of nature if he was thinking clearly. He should will or subjectively endorse the laws of the state, if they are just, because these laws secure his freedom.

To be required by law to respect the life and the property of other people on an equal basis with oneself is not to be subject to a constraint, argues Rousseau. It is to be free. If one thinks about it carefully, one will realize that these sorts of constraints are actually necessary and rational, and indeed, that one would choose subjection to them if given the opportunity. Equal and reciprocal constraints free us from the relations of private dependence and domination to which we would otherwise be subject. Once one understands this, one can will and affirm the laws to which one is subject inside the state as rational and desirable limits. It is this kind of affirmation that Rousseau calls *moral freedom* or *obedience to oneself*.

Common Interest and General Will

But what is the content of this general will, which—unlike any private will—cannot possibly dominate us, and which we can obey inside the state while still remaining free? Rousseau claims that in any legitimate society—that is, any society held together by the voluntary recognition of its members, rather than by force—there must always be a unanimous agreement on at least one common interest. Each individual must have been led out of a state of nature and into political society in order to better further her own concerns. Therefore it is logical to think that not only must citizens recognize themselves as standing in a relation of mutual political obligation, but they must also share some general interests.

These, of course, are the very ones that would have brought them together into political society in the first place.

> While the opposition of particular interests made the establishment of societies necessary, it is the agreement of these same interests which made it possible. What these different interests have in common is what forms the social bond, and if there were not *some point* on which all interests agree, no society could exist. (*SC*, 57; emphasis added)

But what is this common interest that constitutes the unity of the body politic? I believe it can only be understood as a *negative* interest, our interest in freedom from dependence on, and from potential domination by, other private persons. Evidence for this view is given by Rousseau's claim that the general will serves to "guarantee citizens against all personal dependence" (*SC*, 53).[13] In order to guarantee the citizen against personal dependence, though, the state will also have to guarantee some of his other fundamental interests, including securing his person and property against interference by others and providing for his basic needs. Having these interests guaranteed by the state prevents him from depending on other individuals to secure these essential claims.

Why do citizens need to be guaranteed against personal dependence in order to be free? Rousseau claims that private dependence is inherently threatening to freedom: "Everyone must see that since ties of servitude are formed solely by men's mutual dependence and the reciprocal needs that unite them, it is impossible to subjugate a man without first having placed him in the position of being unable to do without another" (*D2*, 159). When we are dependent on other people for the satisfaction of our needs or for the guarantee of our rights, there is the ever-present possibility that they will exploit our dependence to force us to obey their will,

[13] Some other commentators have understood Rousseau to be referring to a much "thicker" common good, such as a shared associational end. These commentators argue that the common interest is a *positive* one: some concrete goal, aim, or interest that all individuals have and that all in society share. Some have argued that the common good refers to an ethical or cultural unity—to a common form of life that all citizens recognize themselves as partaking in. See, for example, Scott, "Melodious Language of Freedom," 822–29. Joshua Cohen, for example, interprets this passage as implying that "citizens *share* and it is *common knowledge* that they share, a conception of their common interests (of the "common good") though they may have different beliefs about what might advance those common interests." Cohen, "Reflections on Rousseau," 278. Cohen does not interpret Rousseau as advocating a thickly shared form of life. But he does seem at points to think that citizens share a general interest that is "common knowledge" between them. Hilail Gildin likewise interprets the common good as a public good, the provision of which all individuals separately desire, and recognize that they desire, but which it is not necessarily in their private interest to assure through their voluntary collaboration. See Gildin, *Rousseau's Social Contract*, 33, 55–56.

not our own, by exacting concessions from us in exchange for our compliance. In order to meet our needs, we have to keep them happy, and that means that much of the time we will have to do as they wish, not as we would like. In such a condition, we enjoy our freedom—the ability to obey our own will—only on the sufferance of others, and are exposed to the threat of their interference at all times. By subjecting ourselves to the general will, then, we free ourselves from this condition of dependence on other people's arbitrary and potentially capricious wills.[14]

To understand how the general will secures our freedom by protecting us from personal dependence, however, we must see that our interest in being free from personal dependence is not the same as an interest in independence. In particular, it does not mean independence from the state, since the state is required to set bounds on our freedom of action that prevent other persons from interfering in our pursuit of our own goals, and us from interfering with theirs. Under the general will, Rousseau says, "Every Citizen [must] be perfectly independent of all the others, and excessively dependent on the City" (*SC*, 80). In the state of nature, man was independent because there was no need for his choices to take account of others: he had a natural right to whatever tempted him that he could reach. In the civil state, however, man is necessarily dependent on others for the satisfaction of his material needs and the guarantee of his rights, and therefore his choices must somehow take account of these others. The constitution of a legitimate state enables him to take account of these others in a nonarbitrary way, in a way that limits the potential for capricious interference in others' affairs. Under law, he must respect the bounds of others' sphere of liberty in exchange for their regard to his own. Rousseau argues:

> Many attempts have been made to confuse independence and liberty. These two things are so different that they are even mutually exclusive. When each does what he pleases, he often does what displeases others, and that is not called a free state. Liberty consists less in doing one's will than in not being subject to someone else's; it also consists in not subjecting someone's will to ours. Whoever is master cannot be free, and to rule is to obey. (*LM*, 260–61)

The achievement of equal freedom, argues Rousseau, is only possible in a state of a certain kind, one whose institutions are ordered so as to realize the reciprocal independence of its members. These institutions will impose certain limits on citizens' actions, but such limits—defined by the general will—are rational and necessary in order that all can be equally free of subjection. Realizing our interest in freedom from personal depen-

[14] For the use of the term "capricious will," see Neuhouser, "Freedom," 81.

dence is therefore perfectly consistent with our dependence on the state, and with the obligation to obey its legitimate laws.

Our interest in freedom from personal dependence is a negative interest, since it is purely formal, and presupposes nothing about what our other interests and goals are. No matter what the content of our choices may be, we have an interest in these choices being our own, and not the result of interference or manipulation by some other agent. Insofar as an individual citizen is committed to choosing anything at all, then, she must also necessarily be committed to the end of promoting her own freedom-as-independence, since it is always a precondition for her choosing *this* thing.[15] A unanimous and a priori agreement on freedom as independence is therefore always present among us, no matter what our actual wills, goals, and preferences happen to be. This is because all these wills, goals, and preferences presuppose our ability to choose if they are to truly be ours. This negative interest in freedom from domination and personal dependence, on the interpretation I am putting forward, is the only common interest in a Rousseauian state.

Drawing Boundaries to Freedom

In translating this account of freedom into a positive set of laws, though, we must face an important problem. I am obligated to obey the legitimate state if and only if it promotes my freedom from personal dependence, for this is an interest that I and my fellow citizens share and on the basis of which we could construct a political association. Our collective dependence on the state is therefore meant to guarantee the bounds of a sphere of self-government, a sphere within which each of us can make our own choices free from interference by others. But how am I to know if my free sphere has been adequately guaranteed? Am I sufficiently free only if my choices are not limited in any way at all? If they are somewhat limited? But how much?

A slightly contrived example may clarify the problem here. Imagine that by exercising your power to determine your own ends, you decide that you would like to fish in the local trout stream. But in order to get to the stream, you would have to walk across a yard that I am now using to grow pea plants, thereby pursuing my own freely chosen end of organic gardening. By walking across the yard, you would trample the plants and therefore destroy my ability to pursue my ends in a sphere that is free

[15] The conception of freedom I am attributing to Rousseau is structurally similar to one that has been attributed to Kant and Hegel by some commentators. See, e.g., Korsgaard, "Morality as Freedom," 167–71; Patten, *Hegel's Idea of Freedom*, 91–101.

from the interference of other private wills. Does the protection of my freedom to grow pea plants require the limitation of your freedom to go fishing, or vice versa? In order to share a legitimate state that realizes our interest in freedom, in other words, we must determine some actual limits to freedom—we must know what the civil freedom of another person forbids us. So how are we to decide where the right boundaries lie, and which particular interests are to be protected by the law?

Rousseau thinks no general answer to this question can be given by reference to a theory about which human interests are most basic or fundamentally important. Instead, he opts for a procedural solution to this problem. What matters for civil freedom, he claims, is not where exactly the boundaries on our choices are drawn but instead the manner in which they are determined. To be legitimate, the limits to our actions must be expressed in the form of a law, and a law should always articulate an interest that can be protected equally for all:

> Thus there is no liberty without Laws, nor where someone is above the Laws. . . . A free people obeys, but it does not serve; it has leaders and not masters; it obeys the Laws, but it obeys only the Laws and it is from the force of the Laws that it does not obey men. (*LM*, 261)

Law is special because of its impersonality: in subjecting ourselves to law, rather than to a particular person or group of people, we do not depend on anyone's private will, and therefore we are not dominated by anyone. Depending on an impersonal law to define our rights allows us to retain our freedom.

Concretely specifying what protecting freedom requires in the form of general laws cannot get away without making any reference to particular positive interests, however. To guarantee a condition of equal freedom for everyone, we must come up with a set of general interests that can be protected equally for all citizens in the state. These protected interests will define the concrete bounds of each citizen's sphere of civil freedom.

The way in which Rousseau's theory makes reference to particular protected interests, however, is importantly different from how theories that see the state as guaranteeing some common interest of happiness or well-being do the same. A theory of equal freedom does not base its protection of our interests in any account of human happiness, human nature, or the necessary ends of human beings (apart from freedom). The freedom-protecting state instead simply considers the question of whether not protecting a given interest for all its members might grant some citizens a coercive advantage over others that might jeopardize their freedom from personal dependence. If our not having protected rights to private property, for example, gives you the ability to hold me hostage to your will, then my basic right to free self-government is jeopardized, and the legitimate state should intervene. The key issue for a theory of the state based on freedom from personal dependence, then, is that no citizen be able to obligate another to a sacrifice that is greater than that to which he himself can be obligated.

Rousseau therefore claims that the proper procedural solution to the problem of determining bounds to our respective spheres of freedom is to test which of our particular interests can be willed generally, in the form of a reciprocal law. Interests that cannot be willed generally, whatever their nature, ought not to be legally protected. Indeed, Rousseau suggests that this solution to the problem of equal freedom is entirely original with him:

> Since nothing obligates the subjects except the general will, we shall investigate how this will is manifested, by what signs one is sure of recognizing it, what a law is, and what the true characteristics of law are. This subject is entirely new: the definition of law remains to be made. (*E*, 462)

Because the law is an impersonal and formal institution, in obeying it, we obey no one else's will, and so therefore we remain free.

Constructing the General Will

In any procedure that would define a set of interests that can be protected for all, the opinions of citizens must serve as equal inputs, since no particular person's private will can serve as the rule of right in the state. Rousseau therefore suggests that the general will is best determined through democratic voting. Here, I think we should be careful to read Rousseau as saying that the general will can be expressed through voting under the right conditions, not that every result of a democratic vote is a general will. He is clear that the deliberations of a democratic public will often deviate from a general will: "By itself the people always wills what is right, but by itself it does not always see it. The general will is always upright, but the judgment that guides it is not always enlightened" (*SC*, 68). So it is best to interpret democratic voting as a necessary, but not sufficient, condition for expressing a general will. No will is general when one private person's view is made law. But a will can also fail to be general where many people's views are taken into account, if those views are not properly formulated and expressed.

So what are citizens expressing an opinion about when they vote in such a way as to articulate a general will, a set of interests that should be protected for all? Are they opinions about a citizen's particular interest (when viewed separately from the collective), or are they opinions about the interest of the collectivity as a whole (when viewed from some as-yet-unspecified common perspective)? Each person in the state will have a private will that articulates what he takes to be his interest insofar as he regards himself as a separate person unattached to any others. For example, I may wish to dedicate my life to the cause of art or to become extremely wealthy. A person's private will is the self-referential vision of happiness that she wishes to pursue for herself, perhaps even at the expense of others. A person may also have a corporate will, which represents her interest from the perspective of a member of a partial group within the state. Thus, qua teacher an individual may wish for higher property taxes to subsidize teachers' pay; qua investor she may wish for an exemption on capital gains taxes. Finally, Rousseau suggests that each citizens has a general will that belong to herself when regarded as a citizen. This expresses the most basic interests that are generalizable to all other citizens: at a minimum, perhaps, such interests as security of the person, basic subsistence, and equal respect. Whatever interests can be generalized in this way are the interests that ought to be protected by the state if its citizens' freedom from personal dependence is to be adequately guaranteed.

Rousseau distinguishes in the text between the general will—which citizens can share as an association—and "the will of all," the aggregation of private and particular wills that each person has as an individual:

> There is often a great deal of difference between the will of all and the general will; the latter considers only the common interest, while the former takes private interest into account, and is no more than a sum of particular wills: but take away from these same wills the pluses and minuses that cancel one another, and the general will remains as the sum of the differences. (*SC*, 60)

This is one of the most cryptic passages in Rousseau's *Social Contract.* Here is one interpretation: each individual's particular will is partial to himself, since it considers his needs and interests in a perspective abstracted from any limits placed on them by the needs and interests of others. For example, my will to devote my life to the cause of art may entail a need for the material support necessary to so. I may desire to have this material support provided to me by others. But others will naturally likewise have the desire that I provide them with the material goods necessary to achieve their goals. So these two desires for preference and superiority cancel each other out. Is anything left over? Yes, those interests that we are willing to reciprocally guarantee one another. We each want material well-being; we are each prepared to invest some labor, and there is a minimum level of material well-being that we can agree to guarantee to one another, once our desires for preference and superiority are abandoned.

A general will, then, is a will that all citizens have a reason to obey, since it is one that a person, regarding himself as a citizen in a general respect, could rationally consent to. A citizen could consent to the general will because it provides him with the guarantee of those fundamental interests he needs to be protected if he is to be secured against personal dependence and domination. In obeying such a will, each person can therefore truly be said to obey himself, since this is the will that (rationally regarded in a certain light) he shares, since it secures him the preconditions for his making his own choices. "The will of all," unlike the general will, is simply the additive sum of individuals' conflicting private wills (which look only to private interests), and therefore it cannot serve as the rule of the state. For me to obey an aggregated particular will—the will of a majority of self-regarding individuals—or a corporate will—say, the will of a clique of business owners—would make me, the dissenting citizen, the slave of the majority, since this will is not a will I can share, regarding myself under any description.

Note that in order to voice the general interest that unites them, individuals *must* speak from a certain perspective—the perspective of citizen, rather than that of a private individual or member of a particular faction or corporate group. In taking up the perspective of the common good, then, each relates to the others, not as tools or obstacles to her own designs (or the designs of a sectional group to which she belongs), but as associates whose interests and claims must be incorporated into the proposed terms of cooperation. In articulating the general will, we must try to ignore our particular interests and, with best intentions, vote our judgment about what laws best reflect the common interest. This is a different conception of voting than we commonly use in political science, where it is assumed that, when voting, we are always expressing our particular and private preferences. For Rousseau, in voting we are expressing a judgment or opinion (which can be wrong) about what the common good is, about the interests we can share with others, when we view our situation from a generalized perspective.

While the general will is always the citizen's own will, Rousseau is very clear that one can fail to recognize it as such, and that one may be wrong about its content.[16] This can be the case even though a person may not necessarily refuse obedience to it once what is required is made apparent to him, that is, although he may desire to obey it:

> The Citizen consents to all the laws, even to those passed in spite of him, and even to those that punish him when he dares to violate any

[16] He is also clear that, in order for a will to be general, it does not have to be unanimous: "For a will to be general, it is not always necessary that it be unanimous, but it is necessary that all votes be counted; any formal exclusion destroys generality" (*SC*, 58n).

> one of them. The constant will of all the members of the State is the general will; it is through it that they are citizens and free. When a law is proposed in the People's assembly, what they are being asked is not exactly whether they approve the proposal or reject it, but whether it does or does not conform to the general will, which is theirs; everyone states his opinion about this by casting his ballot, and the tally of the votes yields the declaration of the general will. Therefore when an opinion contrary to mine prevails, it proves nothing more than that I had made a mistake and that what I took to be the general will was not. If my particular opinion had prevailed, I would have done something other than what I had willed, and it is then that I would not have been free. (*SC*, 124)

In such a case, had his own mistaken opinion about it prevailed, the citizen "would have done something other than what [he] had willed." What he always desires to do, then, if he is a loyal citizen, is to obey the general will, or on our interpretation, to ensure that he is guaranteed against personal dependence and domination. This can be the case even when he has mistaken beliefs about what is actually required in this particular instance.

These passages indicate that the general will is not something citizens are unanimous about, and that even in a legitimate and well-constituted polity, citizens may disagree about what the fundamental laws should be. It seems the general will constructs a common interest, rather than merely articulating a shared aim that is already common knowledge. If a vote amid disagreement is actually to express a general will, however, each citizen must make a sincere effort to take the other citizens' interests seriously. He must make an effort to include some opinion about their needs and interests as part of his own determination, since to form an opinion about the *common* good means concerning himself with the freedom and well-being of all other citizens, and not merely his private freedom or the freedom of a partial faction.

As long as the outcome of the procedure truly represents an attempt to construct an opinion that takes everyone into account, and does not merely represent the private or sectional interests of an individual or group, Rousseau suggests, the result of the procedure is suitably general. By depending on this result in the form of law, citizens will not be dominated by the private will of a master or powerful or sectional interests. This is so, Rousseau believes, even if there is disagreement among citizens over what precisely their common interest consists in. As Jeremy Waldron describes it, "Rousseau's settled position appears to have been this: *if* there is disagreement, and *if*, in spite of that disagreement, you can be sure that citizens are nonetheless addressing the general good, then 'the votes of the greatest number always bind the rest' (*SC*, 124)."[17] Provided that a law has truly taken my interests into account, the fact that it disagrees with my opinion does not render it a threat to my freedom: it does not grant other people an unequal share of coercive power over me, because it protects my interests on an equal basis with theirs. A general will has three features, then: first, it defines rights (protected interests) that apply equally to all; second, it defines these rights via a procedure that considers everyone's interests equally; and third, everyone who is coerced to obey the laws has a voice in that procedure. If a will has these three features, then it can be justly imposed upon me even when I disagree with it.

It is a very important corollary that the general will can only be articulated where factions or partial associations are absolutely prevented from arising. By casting a ballot, each citizen is to express her opinion in her capacity as citizen and not in some other private capacity, for when the "general will grows mute," each individual "no more states opinions as a Citizen than if the State had never existed" (*SC*, 122). Factions destroy the common interest that renders the general will equitable and just: they render the will of the state a private will, one that is necessarily dominating. Where partial associations are powerful, one body judges another body that is not part of it, a body whose interests have never entered into its decision calculus. The social body in this case is no longer one body, but is reduced to the partial association and all the rest. At the limit, where the partial association prevails over all the others, the state is ruled by a private will—the will of this faction—and the general will exists no longer. Rousseau seems to believe that individuals have a strong tendency to form such partial associations; this is why he insists that citizens in the rational state must deliberate "with no communication among themselves" (*SC*, 60).

Patriotic Citizens?

In order for Rousseau's model of the general will to work—for it actually to produce nondominating laws—it is essential that each citizen vote an opinion about the general good that is constructed by taking other citizens' interests into account. Where the true interest of the collectivity is not simply obvious but requires construction, it is very important to be clear that citizens are giving a view about the general interest of the collectivity and not about some other interest. Has the citizen in question come up with her opinion solely by considering her own point of view, or the

[17] Waldron, *Liberal Rights*, 412.

point of view of some merely partial group, or has she made an effort to consider the issue from the perspectives of all the others?

If the opinions citizens express in voting have not taken the interests of all individuals in the collective into account, then to form a rule for collective action on the basis of these opinions would be to obey the potentially dominating particular will of an individual or a partial association, not the general will of the collective. A citizen's opinion can therefore only be a genuine opinion about the common interest—one that can serve as a valid input in the construction of a nondominating general will—when his judgment is based on a concern for the freedom and well-being of all other individuals in the state.

As we shall see in more detail in chapter 5, Rousseau argues that since citizens must be concerned with common interests, some form of solidarity between them will be required if they are to formulate an adequately general will. Indeed, Rousseau suggests that where precisely the general will draws bounds on our freedoms—what particular interpretation of our common interests it guarantees—is unimportant, so long as it draws these bounds based on the equal consideration of every citizen. That means that if we are to have confidence in the legitimacy of the laws, we require an even greater confidence in the solidarity and trust that supports our commitment to equal consideration. To be legitimate, the law must attempt to guarantee freedom and equality for all, not the domination of some by others.

Since citizens can only secure their freedom by obeying a general will, Rousseau argues, they will need to be motivationally constituted in such a way that together they can formulate one. As N.J.H. Dent puts it:

> It is only when the promoting of the interests that all have in common becomes the interest of each member that we shall avoid narrow personal or sectional interests usurping the common interest and the general will being replaced by, for instance, a corporate will (perhaps masked, deceptively, as if it were the general will). This is why Rousseau thinks that we are not likely to be able to determine a genuinely general will if we are dealing with a people who do not already feel some sense of common loyalty, purpose, and destiny, such that the good of all, and not just his own, matters highly to each. . . . Not all peoples are equipped to pass laws that will be just and equitable, or to establish a will that is truly general.[18]

As we shall see in chapter 5, Rousseau thinks that this sort of solidarity among citizens is best forged by patriotic education. But we can already see why he might think patriotic motivations are necessary in a well-

[18] Dent, "General Will," 124.

ordered state: for him, they are not simply unreflective habits or prejudices. Rather, Rousseau thinks that patriotic motivations can be justified with reference to the interest in having a nondominating way to define the boundaries to our respective spheres of civil freedom. Without sufficient solidarity, a general will cannot be formulated, and without a general will, we cannot live together in a condition that is free from domination.

Likewise, if we are to construct limits to our actions on the basis of a general will, a sufficient number of citizens must also be willing to voluntarily accept the collective judgment of their fellow citizens as authoritative, without being forced to do so. This in turn requires citizens who are loyal to the state over their own private interests or the interests of a partial group.[19] Rousseau also gives a patriotic explanation of what it means to be loyal, in this way, to the actual general will even when it conflicts with my other private or factional interests. He suggests that to be loyal to the general will is to be a patriotic citizen, to place the good of the state ahead of partial interests. Again, though, Rousseau emphasizes that both we as observers and the citizen himself (upon reflection) can see how this patriotic commitment fosters citizens' freedom. To be loyal to the general will is what it means to be free, and each citizen has a prepolitical interest in being free that he can rationally affirm.

A Rousseauian view suggests, in the end, that each individual's own interest in guaranteeing her freedom from domination and personal dependence gives her an interest in developing the motivations of a citizen, that is, someone who regards her membership in the state, and her relation to her compatriots, as making special claims on her. Citizenship requires a kind of solidarity among compatriots, such that no individual is viewed separately or apart from the whole. Moreover, I think there is plenty of evidence that Rousseau envisioned a motivational transformation in citizens of exactly this kind as a necessary prerequisite for the proper expression of the general will. Indeed, the creation of such solidarity is the key reason for his introduction of the figure of the legislator:

> Anyone who dares to institute a people must feel capable of, so to speak, changing human nature; of transforming each individual who by himself is a perfect and solitary whole into part of a larger whole from which that individual would as it were receive his life and being; of weakening man's constitution in order to strengthen it; of substituting a partial and moral existence for the independent and physical existence we have all received from nature. In a word, he must take from man

[19] The problem cannot simply be solved by appealing to enforcement, because without a sufficient number of individuals who were freely willing to act collectively, enforcement could not be provided. Enforcement simply substitutes a slightly smaller collective action problem for the initial problem.

> his own forces in order to give him forces which are foreign to him and of which he cannot make use without the help of the others. The more these natural forces are dead and destroyed, the greater and more lasting are the acquired ones, and the more solid and lasting also is the institution: So that when each Citizen is nothing and can do nothing except with all the others, and the force acquired by the whole is equal or superior to the sum of the natural forces of all the individuals, the legislation may be said to be at the highest pitch of perfection it can reach. (*SC*, 69)

As Rousseau's invocation of the legislator shows, the individual must be capable of regarding herself as a *member* of the body politic if that body is to be able to produce a general will capable of legitimately defining each citizen's rights. Once this transformation occurs, the interests of each individual—while still privately held—are the interests of a different kind of self, of an individual citizen who is considering herself as a citizen. Indeed, Rousseau sometimes says that an adequately general will requires the prior construction of a people—or *moi commun*—that is, a set of individuals who have the motivation to take one another's needs and interests as making special claims upon them. This solidarity created by the legislator, suggests Rousseau, makes the general will "always upright," because "there is no one who does not appropriate the word *each* to himself, and think of himself as he votes for all" (*SC*, 61).

Forcing Someone to Be Free

Rousseau famously claims that where a citizen's reflection on the conditions necessary to secure his own civil freedom does not lead him to comply voluntarily, he can rightfully be coerced by the state, so long as what he is asked to obey is actually a general will. Coercion is justified insofar as it protects freedom, and a general will—if it exists—specifies the terms of a rightful distribution of civil freedom in the state: it is in this sense that Rousseau can say "the general will is always right" (*SC*, 59):

> Hence for the social compact not to be an empty formula, it tacitly includes the following engagement which alone can give force to the rest, that whoever refuses to obey the general will shall be constrained to do so by the entire body: which means nothing other than that he shall be forced to be free. (*SC*, 53)

Although the recalcitrant citizen is *aware* of what the general will requires, he is lacking a sufficient motive to comply voluntarily, and so must be compelled.

The phrase "forced to be free" that appears in this passage has seemed to some to signal an ominous commitment to totalitarian democracy on Rousseau's part.[20] Proponents of this view argue that Rousseau believes dissenting individuals can be forced into submission by tyrannical majorities, with the justification that such submission is what obedience to their "true" or "rational" selves would require. Yet although Rousseau does hold that democratic voting can, under the proper conditions, express a general will, as we have seen, he never suggests that every decision of a democratic majority is a general will. Indeed, he often claims the contrary: there is good reason to fear that democratic deliberations will diverge from the general will. When the state is close to ruin, Rousseau says, private or factional wills will begin to prevail in the voting process, and majorities will no longer express the general will. But a citizen is only obligated to obey the results of a majority vote, suggests Rousseau, if "all the characteristics of the general will are in the majority. When they cease to be, there is no longer any freedom" (*SC*, 124). What citizens are obligated to obey is always the general will; they are not obliged to obey each and every result of a democratic voting process. Moreover, since Rousseau insists that the purpose of his state is to preserve the individual's liberty rather than to alienate it, and to guarantee his civil freedom—by giving him positive title to all he possesses—it is in my view strange to interpret him as sacrificing the foundational principle of his political theory on the altar of deference to tyrannical majorities.

I believe the phrase "forced to be free" can be given a simpler and less foreboding interpretation. Rousseau begins his theory from the claim that each individual has a rational interest in not being dominated or enslaved by other persons. This is our interest in freedom, in not being subject to someone else's will, or in being the author of our own choices. But to live together socially in dependence upon others while maintaining our own freedom in turn requires us to subject ourselves to a set of reciprocal limits on our actions that are general and apply to each of us in the same manner. These reciprocal limits constitute our civil freedom: they guarantee us a sphere of choice that is truly our own, free from personal dependence and domination, and within which others cannot interfere. These limits also restrain us from interfering with other people's rights, it is true; but without restraining all of us in that way, no one could be free. Since rights to freedom can be legitimately enforced, the state has a right to coerce us to comply with any restrictions that actually do constitute an equal distribution of freedom. To be "forced to be free," then, is simply to be forced to respect the limits that assure each one of us a private sphere

[20] See, for example, Talmon, *Origins of Totalitarian Democracy*, 28–50.

of liberty: it means "hindering a hindrance to freedom," in the vocabulary Kant would later adopt.[21] To refuse to obey these limits—as long as they are properly drawn—is to refuse to recognize their role in constituting our civil freedom.[22]

A corollary of this thesis is that where a democratic deliberation reflects some other will—such as the will of a partial faction—citizens will have no obligation to obey *it*, nor can they be rightfully coerced. As Rousseau puts it, the authority of the democratic sovereign "does not and cannot exceed the limits of general conventions, and . . . everyone may fully dispose of such goods and freedom as are left him by these conventions." As soon as the sovereign begins to "burden one subject more than another . . . it turns into a particular affair, and its power is no longer competent" (*SC*, 63). Thus, on the view of Rousseau I am putting forward, the general will is limited by a set of outcome constraints—a general will must formulate a set of legal rights (based on common interests) that can be protected equally for all, and that burden each subject equally—as well as a set of procedural constraints—everyone subject to the laws must have a say in their formulation, and everyone must vote their view of the common interest.[23]

When one subject is burdened more than another, the bond of obligation that forms the state is simply dissolved, and the state itself—as a moral body—disappears.[24] What is left is simply a relation of force in which some are attempting to become masters by dominating others, and these persons are equally justified in resisting, since they are under no obligation to enslave themselves. So Rousseau's thesis about the absolute sovereignty of the general will is not equivalent to the declaration of the absolute sovereignty of any and every democratic deliberation, since democratic majorities can and do err. The judgment of whether or not a democratic majority has erred in a way that dissolves the bond of obligation—whether factions have prevailed in the voting process, or whether the laws have ceased to be general and have begun to burden some citizens at the expense of others—must be left to each individual citizen.

[21] See Kant, *MM*, 6:231: "Now whatever is wrong is a hindrance to freedom in accordance with universal laws. But coercion is a hindrance or resistance to freedom. Therefore, if a certain use of freedom is itself a hindrance to freedom in accordance with universal laws (i.e., wrong), coercion that is opposed to this (as a hindering of a hindrance to freedom) is consistent with freedom in accordance with universal laws, that is, it is right."

[22] John Hope Mason offers a similar interpretation in "Forced to Be Free," 124.

[23] I thank Daniel Viehoff for pressing me to clarify this.

[24] This interpretation of Rousseau's political philosophy will be controversial, but I believe it makes good sense of what he says. For a similar reading, see Green, *Lectures on Political Obligation*, 400–415.

Conclusion

In this chapter, I pursued two main goals: the first was to suggest that Rousseau's account may have resources to construct a theory of legitimate political authority where Kant's does not. Rousseau makes the case that there is only one kind of political authority we can obey without forfeiting our freedom entirely. This is the authority of a general, rather than a particular, will: a will that protects a set of common interests equally for all members of the state, that they formulate themselves, through democratic voting, and that is imposed in the form of an impersonal law. These protected interests guarantee each citizen's freedom from personal dependence and domination. For this reason, unlike Kant, Rousseau thinks that freedom cannot possibly require us to undertake an unconditional obligation to any private person or group of persons. Rousseau also suggests that a general will imposes certain conditions on the way authority should be organized: a legitimate authority must always be democratic, everyone who is subject to the laws must have the opportunity to vote on them, and the laws must apply equally to all. Where these conditions are not met, no legitimate authority is in place. In the next chapter, I argue that when properly updated, the general will can serve as a criterion for the legitimacy of contemporary states.

My second goal was to show that Rousseau's defense of democratic authority further involves a controversial assertion, one that we will be exploring in more detail in part 2 of the book. He indicates that in order to legislate generally and impartially on one another's behalf, the citizens of a democratic state must share a certain solidarity and trust. This solidarity gives them a special concern for the freedom and welfare of their compatriots. Indeed, Rousseau's argument shows why a regard for one's own freedom can give one good reason to develop a patriotic commitment to citizenship. In order to formulate a general will, we must have some motive for taking the needs and concerns of our compatriots into account in our political deliberations. Our own interest in freedom, for Rousseau, therefore gives us a rational reason to regard common citizenship as placing us in a special relation to our fellow members. By subjectively identifying as a citizen, one engaged in the common project of defining the bounds of civil freedom in the state, we ought to feel solidarity with our fellow participants. In part 2 of this book, we will be further discussing what this "solidarity requirement" might actually entail in practice.

4

Political Obligation and Justice

Freedom and Political Obligation

I began this book by noting that many political philosophers have had an increasingly difficult time reconciling their view that the liberal state is based on the moral principle of equal freedom of persons with two widely shared convictions, both of which are summed up in the particularity assumption. The first is that citizens may have political obligations—not directly reducible to their moral obligations to other persons qua human beings—to the institutions of their own state above others, even when those other states are equally just. Vindicating this belief would require us to offer an account of how the state can have a right to rule, how it might possess legitimate political authority over its subjects. But as we saw in chapter 2, philosophical anarchists have argued, on broadly liberal grounds, that no political authority can be reconciled with individual freedom unless its subordinates have directly consented to it. If political authority is inconsistent with freedom, then it seems it must also be prima facie inconsistent with the basic principle of liberal morality, namely, the equal freedom of persons. This view ultimately leads a philosophical anarchist like Simmons to claim that all existing states are illegitimate and that their members have no political obligations.

In addition, liberal theorists have found it equally difficult to justify a second common conviction: the belief that fellow compatriots enjoy a special claim to our concern, a claim that justifies granting priority to them over others in matters of distributive justice and public good provision. Exploiting this difficulty, contemporary cosmopolitans have argued—again, on what they take to be liberal grounds—that confining egalitarian justice to the state merely draws a morally irrelevant distinction between persons, based on the purely contingent fact of borders. Priority for compatriots, they claim, is nothing but a form of discrimination. Instead, we ought to implement principles of distributive justice among all members of humanity, since we owe an equal share of moral respect and concern to them all.

Contemporary philosophers have found these two convictions difficult to justify in part, I think, because they tend to hold that the "liberal grounds" for justifying our obligations are more limited than they in fact are. Indeed, they tend to hold that to be justified on liberal grounds, an obligation must spring from one of only two possible sources: either it must be a "natural duty" of personal morality that is owed to human beings as such; or it must be a duty that antecedently autonomous individuals have contracted to undertake, by acts of promising or explicit consent. But political obligations and special duties of justice to compatriots are not readily assimilable to either of these two models. Political obligations apply within one bounded political community, and not to the entirety of humanity, in the manner of duties of personal morality. And most citizens of modern democracies cannot be meaningfully said to have consented to stand in any "special" relationship to their compatriots.

Through our consideration of Kant and Rousseau, however, we have shown that there may be a third type of value that can impose justified obligations on us: this is the value of external freedom, or independence from subjection to other private persons' wills. As I claimed in chapter 2, what justice most fundamentally requires, for these thinkers, is that persons enjoy equal freedom-as-independence. And if Kant and Rousseau are correct, the structure of the obligations that justice imposes on us is importantly different from natural moral duties to other persons or from obligations created by our own consent.

The key thing both thinkers emphasize is that we must construct a political *authority* in order to realize justice, because preserving our freedom from private persons' domination and interference requires us to be subject to the rule of law. Because external freedom is jeopardized whenever other private persons have the power to unilaterally and arbitrarily determine the extent of our rights, political authority provides us with the only possible solution to an important problem. It allows us to bring into being an institution that can define and enforce the boundaries of our sphere of freedom in a public and nonarbitrary manner, one that frees us from subjection to other persons' private interpretations of our rights. For this reason, justice is a necessarily institutional value, and the only institution in which it can be realized is the legitimate state.

This means the obligations imposed by justice have a distinctive structure. They are not obligations based on consent, as Simmons believes, because equal freedom is not something we need to consent to in order to be bound by it. Instead, if we follow Rousseau, the enjoyment of freedom as independence is a necessary precondition for the realization of all our other goals: we do not have to consent to it, because we cannot rationally choose to give it up. This makes freedom a characteristic on the basis of which our various individual wills can always be united, even if the particular ends for which we wish to use our freedom are disparate.

Kant, for one, draws an important political conclusion from this: if the state establishes conditions of equal freedom-as-independence, then it is acting on the basis of something each one of us has already necessarily willed. It is acting on a general will, which is a will we do not have to explicitly consent to in order for it to be legitimate and obligating. For this reason, if the state's laws really do establish a background condition of equal freedom, I don't have to agree to these laws or to the establishment of this particular state in order to be obligated by them. Since we are already morally required to establish the conditions for justice, and Kant has shown that such conditions depend on state institutions, we are bound to support and uphold just state institutions. Our consent is beside the point.

Of course, this approach makes our duties of justice sound somewhat like natural duties, since like natural duties, we do not have to do anything to be bound by them. In one sense that is right: the obligating power or binding force of equal freedom-as-independence is a natural one. But the particular duties that equal freedom requires of us are natural duties of justice, not duties of personal morality, and they have a structure that is unique for two reasons. First, their precise content requires specification in terms of positive law, since the value of external freedom is indeterminate with respect to our acquired rights: the terms of property, contract, and status require institutional "filling out." Second, these additional specifications cannot be defined and imposed by private persons, but must be imposed by public institutions if they are to be compatible with our independence from others' domination and control. In that sense the duties of freedom are not like natural duties, which are supposed to be fully clear and determinate without reference to any institutions. If Kant and Rousseau are right, then, equal freedom must be understood as a value that (despite its basis in a natural human capacity for self-government) can only be defined and applied within institutional structures. Justice is therefore not a value that pertains—or at least does not pertain in the same way—to private acts of morality. Since it is a value that can only be applied by institutions, it pertains first and foremost to the evaluation of public institutional acts, not to the individual acts of private persons.

As we saw in the last chapter, Rousseau adds an important additional requirement to Kant's account. He claims that, in order to be just, the will that defines our acquired rights must not only guarantee each citizen's freedom-as-independence, it must also be formulated and imposed in a certain way: through a democratic process, in which all those who are bound by the decision have an equal input, and take one another's interests into account in their voting. An essential part of freedom is to be able to understand oneself as the author of the restrictions under which one is asked to live, and Rousseau claims that we cannot attain this kind of freedom if the duties to respect others' rights are simply imposed upon us by an external force, by the private will of some particular person or group. Instead, to be fully free, we must formulate them and impose them upon ourselves. Only in this way can the laws be truly nondominating, subjecting us to our own will, and not the will of a master.

The claim that equal freedom must be mediated by institutions, which Rousseau and Kant share, must not be taken to imply that freedom cannot be thought of extra-institutionally, or that its moral content is exhausted by certain institutional relationships, which are just there as a matter of brute fact. This is certainly not true. Principles of justice can be morally constructed at any time, simply by reasoning through the consequences of what it takes to establish conditions of equal freedom-as-independence: by performing a kind of thought experiment, like the ones to which both Kant and Rousseau give a significant place. In that sense, these principles have a basis that is rationally independent of the structures that instantiate them. But Kant and Rousseau argue that we cannot realize equal freedom in a social environment unless we create democratic institutions through which we can all be subject to general, impersonal, and reciprocal laws for the definition and enforcement of our acquired rights.

Can a theory of equal freedom as an institutional value go some way toward providing the liberal justification of the particularity assumption that we are seeking? Recall the conditions that we set out in the introduction for such a justification: a successful liberal justification would have to show why a member's relationship to the state is of some moral importance, and it would have to show this by appealing only to the "universal" principles of freedom and equality and not to any purported moral force to be found in "brute facts" about the existence of an institution or an ascriptive relationship. Can a commitment to the value of equal freedom by itself explain the moral importance of the democratic state? I think it can.

A Kantian-Rousseauian theory such as the one sketched in the last two chapters has the resources to account for the conviction that states matter morally, simply by an appeal to the constitutive role of *democratic authority* in realizing a condition of justice.

Political obligation to particular democratic states, on this model, is not in conflict with a universal regard to equal freedom. Inside a legal community, consociates come—for the first time—to be linked to one another by a network of civil rights and duties that helps to secure their respective spheres of freedom in a manner on which all can rely. Legitimate law gives citizen A a set of definite obligations to citizen B: to respect her property, not to interfere with her person, to refrain from infringing her civil rights. In the absence of these publicly accepted definitions of property and rights—that is, outside the legitimate state—A's duties to B would remain indefinite, and subject only to her private interpretation, since there is no higher court of appeal that could give them an objective specification.

But no rules about our respective duties can exist unless it is possible for someone's private interpretation to be shown to be wrong, and to be overruled. One owes political obligations to a particular just state, then, not because one is specially biased in favor of it, but because only it is capable of laying down public rules of justice. The democratic state is the institution that has the authority to define what equal freedom requires over a given portion of the earth. Indeed, if what I have been arguing is correct, it is the only possible institution that could play this role.

Although this argument has established the moral importance of democratic states in realizing justice, it has not yet shown why a citizen has a special reason for allegiance to her own state, as opposed to reason for supporting democratic states in general. In part 2 of this book, we will take up this last question, and I will claim that justice does give the citizen sufficient reason for allegiance to her particular institutions, and also for solidarity with her compatriots. But before we move on to part 2, however, I would like to conclude this first part of the book by clarifying two remaining questions about the implications of the Kantian-Rousseauian view I have been developing. As we saw in the last chapter, I reject Kant's claim that justice requires us to obey all existing states, in favor of the Rousseauian view that we are required to obey only legitimate states, those that articulate a sufficiently general will. But this may seem far too vague to serve as a standard for any practical assessments. What precisely is the criterion that a citizen should use to judge whether or not a particular state is legitimate? And how does she know if she is actually under any political obligations?

In addition, on the Kantian-Rousseauian view I have been developing, the moral importance of particular states is derived wholly from their constitutive role in guaranteeing the "universal" right to equal freedom-as-independence. But this leaves us with a pressing question: what are the citizen's duties to persons outside her state? Surely foreigners have equal rights to freedom as independence as well. So do the members of states have any duties of justice to them? And if so, then how might these duties be fulfilled? Although I will not be able to offer a complete account of political obligation and of global justice—immensely complex issues in their own right—I hope at least to sketch the bare outlines of the response that a Kantian-Rousseauian theory might make to these two important questions.

Legitimate Authority and the Judgment of Institutions

If we subscribe to the basic Kantian-Rousseauian view about the institutionally mediated character of freedom, we will want some clear criteria for judging the institutions that mediate it. Do the laws of some existing state really establish conditions of equal freedom? It is hard to believe that there aren't many states whose laws and policies are so unjust that we owe them no obligations at all.

As we have seen, Rousseau claims that there is one kind of authority under which we are certain to secure equal freedom: this is the authority of a general will. But how can we judge whether the laws of a given state actually reflect such a will, or reflect it sufficiently that we might be justified in holding ourselves to be under at least a presumptive obligation? Whether the laws conform to our substantive views about justice is not a sufficient criterion for judgment, since as we have seen, it is possible for citizens to disagree about what the general will substantively requires. For this reason, if we are to derive criteria that citizens might use in judging the legitimacy of state institutions, these criteria cannot depend on their full-blown views about justice. Whatever criteria for state legitimacy we put forward must be consistent with the possibility of ongoing and reasonable disagreement about what justice ideally means. The fact of pervasive disagreement about justice might make us pessimistic that citizens can come to any reasonably public and objective assessment of the legitimacy of their institutions. But I don't think it should. Instead, I believe the way forward is to seek a consensus—or at least a greater degree of agreement—on what justice minimally requires.

Although the Kantian-Rousseauian view of the state I have been defending proceeds on grounds rather different from Joseph Raz's theory of authority, I believe we can take an interesting remark in Raz's discussion as a model for deriving a standard of legitimacy amid continuing disagreement about justice. Raz suggests that an authority can still function as an authority—it can bind its subjects even when they disagree with the substance of its decisions—even though its subordinates do not take themselves to be under an obligation to obey it when it makes a clear mistake. Defending this position, of course, entails holding that there is a significant difference between clear mistakes about justice and other kinds of possible mistakes that an authority might make. Raz describes the difference this way:

> Consider a long addition of, say, some thirty numbers. One can make a very small mistake which is a very clear one, as when the sum is an integer whereas one and only one of the added numbers is a decimal fraction. On the other hand, the sum may be out by several thousands without the mistake being detectable except by laboriously going over the addition step by step. Even if the legitimate authority is limited by the condition that its directives are not binding if clearly wrong . . . it

> can play its mediating role. Establishing that something is clearly wrong does not require going through the underlying reasoning.[1]

The basic idea that there could be clear limits on political authority without destroying the mediating function of state institutions is not peculiar to Raz, but was also shared by Hobbes, perhaps the most thoroughgoing defender of political authority in the modern tradition. Hobbes held that although a sovereign has the authorization to interpret exactly what our right to self-preservation requires, and that his directives are binding on us even when we disagree with them, there is a range of clear cases in which the sovereign's judgments are obviously inconsistent with our right to preservation, and where we are therefore released from the obligation to obey. Whenever the sovereign's acts directly threaten our self-preservation, as in the case where we are led to the gallows, forced to incriminate ourselves, to abstain from the use of food, air, or medicine, to commit suicide or maim ourselves, and the like, Hobbes thought that we can be sure that self-preservation cannot require us to obey, and therefore that we are again entitled to use coercive force in defense of our rights.[2] Hobbes's idea was that there is some "core" content to the notion of a right to self-preservation that must be recognized in any rightfully constituted state. We can disagree about what self-preservation in the fullest sense requires while agreeing that *if it requires anything, it must require at least these minimal guarantees*. No authority that transgressed these limits could be an authority that was actually interpreting our right to self-preservation, and therefore no authority that transgressed these limits could be an authority we are required to obey.

Hobbes and Raz claim, in other words, that limited authority is still authority, even when subjects do not take themselves to be under an obligation to obey when these limits are transgressed. Within the limits, the authority's directives are binding and authoritative even amid disagreement. But beyond the limits, its directives cease to apply. Could a Kantian-Rousseauian theory hold, with Raz and Hobbes, that there are some cases where a sovereign democracy could produce laws clearly inconsistent with the "core" content of the right to equal freedom? Could such a theory hold that in cases where this minimal core is infringed, the state becomes illegitimate, and that its subjects are no longer under an obligation to obey it? I think it can.

While Kant seems to deny that any private judgment of the acts of a sovereign authority is allowed, I believe his position on that score is untenable. Instead, consistently with the spirit of a Kantian-Rousseauian proj-

[1] Raz, *The Morality of Freedom*, 62.

[2] Hobbes, *Leviathan*, 144.

ect, I believe we can construct "clear" limits to the authority of the state on the basis of premises both Kant and Rousseau endorse. A Kantian theory could hold that there are (at least) three sorts of substantive criteria, conceptually independent of our full-blown views of justice, that would allow us to judge whether or not a given law is truly the act of a legitimate authority. These substantive criteria are personal inviolability, the universal allocation of property, and the institution of a fair and reciprocal system of private rights. In addition, a Rousseauian theory adds two sorts of procedural criteria to the substantive criteria outlined above: sufficient citizen solidarity and democratic political participation by all who are coerced to obey the laws.

First, let us outline the substantive criteria. The criterion of *personal inviolability* is included in Kant's innate right, a right that accrues to each person independently of positive law. Kant holds that any system of rights must protect the minimal integrity and freedom of movement of each person's own body, since this is an uncontroversial part of any person's ability to exercise his faculty of self-government.[3] We can therefore claim that no state where torture, imprisonment without due procedure, or extrajudicial coercion is allowed will be a freedom-guaranteeing state. It would wrong my innate freedom in a state of nature for someone to coerce my body without my having previously invaded his rights, and therefore this criterion applies directly to the state as well.

Second, both Kant and Rousseau suggest that each citizen has the inalienable right to a sphere of absolute negative freedom in which to pursue her own ends, in which the state cannot interfere. They both refer to this as a sphere of property, although that term should be taken in the very widest sense, including both rights to objects and to actions. Although the precise bounds of a citizen's property are subject to limitation by the general will, if a citizen enjoys *no* sphere of property in which she can pursue her own ends without interference from her fellow citizens and from the state, then we can say that her particular state cannot be based on a general will that takes into account her rights:

> For since all civil rights are founded on that of property, as soon as that is abolished, none other can exist. Justice would no longer be anything but a chimera, and government, a tyranny; and since the public authority would not have any legitimate basis, no one would be bound to acknowledge it, except insofar as he would be constrained to do so by force.[4]

[3] Again, this should not be construed as an endorsement of Lockean self-ownership. Kant nowhere defends the thesis that I own my labor and all of its products. But he does think that some degree of bodily freedom is part of the "core" concept of freedom, since without it, our faculty of self-government can find no expression in the world.

[4] Rousseau, "Political Fragments," 22.

Recall that the individual's initial reason for entering the state is to define, protect, and secure his acquired rights. His own freedom could therefore never give him a reason to obey a state that obviously refused to grant him any property (or secure sphere of personal freedom) at all. No state that established slavery or serfdom or imposed unequal restrictions on the property rights of a minority would be legitimate on this criterion.

Third, we can invoke a set of minimal conditions that must be in place in any particular state if we are to say that its laws meet the conditions of a possible general will, which fairly allocates private rights. Kant argues that no law can serve as a possible general will if it "is so constructed, that an entire people could not possibly agree to it" (*TP*, 8:297). He specifies the conditions of a possible agreement as consistency with the criteria of freedom, equality, and independence, all of which are entailed by the innate right. The criterion of freedom holds that any legitimate state must grant a sphere of private liberty to all its citizens: while the precise bounds of this sphere will vary over time and with the circumstances of a particular society, it is reasonable to believe that we can specify some minimal conditions, based on the "core" conceptual content of freedom, for saying that such a private sphere has been granted. Freedom of conscience, freedom of thought and expression, and some freedom of movement are minimal requirements of any sphere of private right, and of any ability to choose one's life-plan. The criterion of equality specifies that laws must apply equally to all: Kant claims that if a majority passes a law that applies unequally to the citizen body, then the law cannot possibly be an act of a general will: as when the state establishes hereditary privileges, or imposes a burden on one particular class of citizens. This establishes a fundamental right to equal treatment before the law. Finally, the criterion of independence on a general will also suggests important limits to economic inequality in any legitimate state. It is reasonable to think, too, that there would be similarly clear cases of the nonfulfillment of such economic claims. At a minimum, we might think that guaranteed survival would be a clear standard for the guarantee of independence: no matter what someone intends as a goal or potential exercise of his freedom, he must of necessity at least intend his own future existence in intending to accomplish that goal. Therefore, no state that did not guarantee its citizens' most basic needs would be a lawful state.

I think it is best to see bodily inviolability; property; freedom of conscience, movement, and expression; equal treatment before the law; and subsistence as minimal "Kantian" criteria for the guarantee of our equal right to freedom as independence. No state that does not meet at least these conditions is reasonably interpretable as a freedom-guaranteeing state, simply because its laws do not guarantee even the "core" content of equal freedom. By this, I do not mean to intimate the Kant anywhere endorses these criteria, just that they are consistent with his notion that a legitimate law must be one that an entire people could possibly agree to, and that they impose certain substantive limits on what a state can enact consistently with equal freedom. If a state does enact laws consistent with these minimal limits, it is a legitimate authority. When visiting a state that guarantees at least these minimal rights, for example, we should take ourselves to be bound to respect its laws. If we reside or work in such a state, we should take ourselves to have an obligation to pay taxes to its government. Most well-ordered states will implement civil rights that extend far beyond these minimal conditions, of course, and there will be disagreement over exactly which system of rights would realize justice in the fullest sense. But if freedom means anything at all, it must mean at least these minimal things. Since equal freedom is what grounds our obligation to establish and obey states in the first place, then we cannot be under any obligation to states whose system of laws is not reasonably viewed as an interpretation of equal freedom. And since the conditions are clear and minimal, the question of whether the state meets a threshold for legitimacy is not subject to the same problems of interpretive conflict as the question of what justice requires in the most ideal sense.

Rousseau goes beyond Kant, however, in adding a set of procedural requirements on legitimacy: he says that any just state must be a democratic state, since only a democratic state can impose laws in a nondominating way, and without subjecting us to the private will of another. Clear cases of disenfranchisement would be obvious violations of this procedural requirement. For Rousseau, if the majority disenfranchises any individual or class, the general will is destroyed, because it exists only where "all votes are counted." This limit can be relatively straightforwardly deduced from Rousseau's texts. Under this criterion can also be classed a set of minimal political rights that go beyond what Rousseau explicitly endorses, but are necessary to ensure the continued existence and functioning of democracy: the right to freely express one's opinion and to criticize political institutions, and the right to compete for political office.

Rousseau also imposes a fourth criterion on legitimacy: this is the criterion of sufficient trust or solidarity. Citizens in general must be disposed to manifest a concern with the freedom and well-being of all their compatriots, and not simply with a partial subset of the citizenry, if the laws they produce are to be legitimate. If this condition can be met, suggest Rousseau, then one has reason to believe that the authority of the laws will guarantee one's own freedom as independence to choose in the absence of domination, and therefore that the laws have the (moral) right to rule. But if a majority vote represents a purely factional interest, such as the interest of a religious, ethnic, or racial group, an economic interest, or a partial society, then the will articulated by that majority is not suitably general and can make no claims on the individual's obedience. Therefore it is consistent with Rousseau's theory to hold that it must be left to the citizen to judge whether or not the democracy in which he or she lives is an adequately solidaristic one: one in which he or she can trust that her own interests will be sufficiently taken into account in basic legislation about rights and duties.

How do these additional "Rousseauian" democratic-procedural criteria interact with the "Kantian" criteria of minimal substantive justice?[5] One way to formulate this question is to ask whether I can have an obligation to obey the laws of a nondemocratic state. If the laws are minimally just, in a substantive sense, but they are not enacted democratically, ought I to obey them? The right answer, I think, is that if I am involuntarily subjected to laws—that is, I am not just a casual and voluntary visitor to the state, but someone who was born there and cannot leave—I must have a say in their formulation if I am to be obligated to obey them. On this view, disenfranchised citizens do not have an obligation to obey minimally just laws, although those who do have a vote are obligated by them. There may sometimes be good reasons to obey the law even when I have not had a say in formulating it—as a minor, a temporary resident, or a subject of a just military occupation, I will be subject to laws I had no say in formulating. Still, on the Rousseauian theory I endorse, a political authority that permanently denies me the right to participate in formulating the laws is not one I can be obliged to obey. It would follow, on this view, that women did not have any political obligations to democratic states before the introduction of female suffrage, even when the system of rights these states enforced was otherwise minimally just in a substantive sense. These women could have rightfully disobeyed the laws of such a minimally just state in pursuit of their participation rights. Other enfranchised citizens, however, would have had an obligation to obey the minimally just laws on which they had an opportunity to vote, although they also had a duty to work for the enfranchisement of women.

On the view I am putting forward, then, justice requires only that we submit ourselves to democratic legal states,[6] that is, states whose directives meant the conditions for being laws, requirements that an entire people of free and equal individuals could possibly agree to; and where these laws are formulated and imposed through democratic procedures. These criteria are of course vague, but I believe they are sufficiently robust to rule out significant categories of states as illegitimate. Moreover, I think

[5] I am grateful to Daniel Viehoff for suggesting I clarify the relationship between the "Kantian" and the "Rousseauian" grounds of obligation in my theory.

[6] I mean here to provide an English equivalent for the German term *Rechtstaat*. For the view that Kant only defends obligations to the *Rechtstaat*, see Byrd and Hruschka, "Natural Law Duty," 243.

that the view of state authority I have set out in the previous two chapters is entirely consistent with a commitment to the existence of human rights, as long as human rights are interpreted not as moral duties that individuals owe to one another in their personal conduct, but rather as threshold criteria of legitimacy by which we define those institutions that in fact attain the status of democratic legal states. Human rights are not moral standards by which we evaluate the legitimacy of each and every law, but criteria that we use to assess the legitimacy of an entire political system. In cases where minimal substantive rights are broached by an institution, it no longer qualifies as an authority capable of imposing binding obligations on any of its subjects. And in cases where a group's democratic participation rights are not granted, the state does not impose obligations on those who are disenfranchised, since they cannot see themselves as authors of the constraints they are asked to obey.

When I refer, as I shall throughout the rest of this book, to the idea that equal freedom can only be defined and guaranteed within the state, I mean the term *state* to refer to the democratic legal state as I have briefly described it here.[7] A democratic legal state is a sovereign political authority in which each citizen has a right to vote (perhaps through elected representatives) and participate in the determination of his civil rights, and in which the scheme of civil rights that is enacted and enforced qualifies as a possible substantive interpretation of the ideal of equal freedom, by meeting the minimal criteria outlined above. The idea of a democratic legal state, as I understand it, is compatible with a wide variety of institutional forms, as well as significant variation in the particular scheme of civil rights that the state actually guarantees.

Federal structures, including multicultural or multinational federations, can certainly count as democratic legal states, so I do not reserve the term only for institutions where legal authority is fully centralized. Federal structures count as democratic legal states so long as the citizenry as a whole retains the right to vote on the federal constitution (including a revision in the powers of the subunits), and as long the federation grants the same basic rights to all its citizens. It is also acceptable to have differences within the federation in how these rights are implemented (different languages of primary schooling, for example, or different institutional structures for policing or health care provision) as long as these differences do not result in the unequal treatment of citizens.

Since the idea of a democratic legal state is meant to be compatible with a variety of institutional structures as well as a range of schemes of civil

[7] I am grateful to an anonymous reviewer for pressing me to be clearer about these matters.

rights, it may be useful to mention some political organizations that, in my view, would *not* qualify as democratic legal states:

- *Autocratic regimes.* States that do not grant all citizens the right to participate in defining their civil liberties, either through referenda on constitutional matters, or through the election of delegates or representatives, are not democratic legal states, and they impose no political obligations on those who are excluded from democratic participation. In addition, they impose no political obligations *on anyone*—even members of those elites who have a political say—if their laws are not consistent with the minimal substantive criteria of justice. All monarchical and autocratic states fall into this category, as well as states where lawmaking power rests in the hands of a small group. As we saw in chapter 2, the fact that such states are illegitimate does not mean that their subjects should disobey every law, since subjects will have moral and prudential reasons for obeying many laws. But it does mean that those who are excluded from participation in an autocratic state never have a reason to obey the law simply *because the law requires it*; instead, they should do as their private judgment counsels best. Indeed, there may be good reason to disobey even some otherwise minimally just laws in a struggle to gain the recognition of their democratic rights.
- *Democracies that violate the conditions of a possible general will.* In cases where the majority of the population refuses to guarantee a minority equal rights to liberty, property, and security, none of its subjects—even those who voted—have a genuine obligation to obey it, since it violates the minimal "Kantian" criteria of substantive justice. Cases of discriminatory legislation, where equal protection is denied to an ethnic, racial, or national minority, are paradigm cases of this kind of injustice. Again, this does not mean that members ought to disobey all laws, since they have moral and prudential reasons for obeying many laws. But it does mean that attempts to resist especially unjust or discriminating laws are in order. Indeed, depending on the degree of the majority's excesses, it may be warranted to use force in resistance to the execution of unjust laws, to attempt to overthrow the government, or even—as a matter of last resort—to forcibly secede.
- *Colonial empires.* In cases where a legitimate state was unjustly overthrown by a foreign power, direct colonial rule by that power is illegitimate—it is a usurper—and its subjects are not bound to obey the colonizer's laws. More difficult are cases where the regime was overthrown by the colonizer in a just war. If the colonial power is imposing a minimally just scheme of laws in the substantive sense

> outlined above, its subjects may have obligations to obey temporarily even if they do not now participate in the lawmaking process—as long as there is a good-faith effort being made to grant democratic rights to these subjects in the future. This is a "provisional" political obligation; it imposes obligations now in view of real efforts to work toward the full establishment of democratic justice. But even if the colonizer's laws are not deeply unjust, its subjects have no political obligations to the colonizer if they are denied democratic rights of participation over the long term. The foreign power should take steps to emancipate them politically, so they can establish a just state of their own. Only if the foreign power is (*a*) not an unjust usurper, and (*b*) grants the colonized rights of democratic participation and equal opportunity along with its other subjects, do its subjects acquire genuine political obligations. In this case, however, they are no longer colonial subjects: they have been incorporated as equal citizens into the state. This case is rare; it might happen where subjects of one state agree to voluntarily incorporate themselves into another state.

If a political institution meets these threshold conditions for being considered a democratic legal state, its laws qualify as a possible interpretation of the ideal of equal freedom, and they are formulated with the participation of all its citizens. This means the laws deserve respect from citizens and foreigners alike. Citizens' obligation to obey the laws is compatible with their exercising the right to dissent, to engage in public protest, and even to perform acts of peaceful civil disobedience, all of which can be seen as attempts to persuade their fellow citizens that the laws are deficient as an interpretation of what equal freedom ideally requires. But an obligation to obey the laws is not consistent with any use of coercive force by private individuals to interfere with the state's executive power. No state that implements a scheme of rights that meets the minimal criteria for a possible general will should be exposed to violence. Otherwise one would arrogate to oneself the authority to coercively define other people's rights based on one's private views, and to do that is always to threaten them with domination.

Public Goods, Redistribution, and "Patriotic Priority"

A Kantian-Rousseauian view of the state, I believe, not only allows us to justify a citizen's political obligations, it also allows us to justify a second commonly shared conviction: that citizens ought to have a special kind of concern for equalizing distributive shares between compatriots. This is because certain kinds of inequalities may do more than simply threaten citizens' well-being. They may also threaten their enjoyment of a secure sphere of self-government and autonomous choice, by forcing them into potentially dominating relations of economic dependence upon other private individuals. Since the most important justification for forming a democratic state is to abolish such relationships of domination, we have a special reason to safeguard compatriots against those inequalities that substantially jeopardize their equal status.

On the model defended by Rousseau and Kant, property relations within the state are established by and subordinate to the general will. A collectively enacted system of private law determines the holdings and entitlements that citizens can expect to enjoy, and the democratic state lays these down as authoritative and coercively enforces them within a given territory. Once she is subject to political authority, then, the bounds of a given individual's sphere of property are linked to determinate obligations on her fellow citizens to respect her sphere—in return, of course, for her respect of theirs. Since these obligations are political obligations (corresponding to our acquired rights), they bind only those subjected in common to a legitimate political authority, and as such they are subject to the same conditions to which all acts of political authority are subject: the requirements of a possible general will. To be in conformity with a possible general will, any system of property rights must adequately guarantee the freedom, equality, and independence of those coerced to obey it.

Property relations are rightfully subject to limitation by laws that are designed to abolish relations of personal dependence that might bring citizens' political equality into jeopardy, by subjecting them to a form of class domination. Kant puts it this way:

> The general will of the people has united itself into a society that is to maintain itself perpetually; and for this end it has submitted itself to the internal authority of the state in order to maintain those members of the society who are unable to maintain themselves. For reasons of state the government is therefore authorized to constrain the wealthy to provide the means of sustenance for those who are unable to provide for even their most necessary natural needs. The wealthy have acquired an obligation to the commonwealth, since they owe their existence to an act of submitting to its protection and care, which they need in order to live; on this obligation the state now bases its right to contribute what is theirs to maintaining their fellow citizens. (*MM*, 6:236)

Rousseau similarly argues for the importance of regulating inequality between citizens: he claims that while "degrees of power and wealth" need not be absolutely the same between citizens, "no citizen should be so rich that he can buy another, and none so poor that he is compelled to sell himself," and that the state has an obligation to regulate the distribution of property to this end (*SC*, 78).

To see how this understanding of property rights might generate special obligations to compatriots, imagine for a moment the case of a citizen who is disadvantaged by comparison with a middle-class American citizen. Rachel is a young single mother who lives in inner-city Baltimore. She has a low-wage job that pays her $15,000 a year and three children. Her two older children attend failing schools that receive among the lowest per-pupil funding in the country. Her employer has made threatening sexual advances to her, but she feels unable to quit her job, since she has no special skills and jobs are scarce. Finally, her landlord has recently notified her and her fellow tenants that they have to move out within months, since he is renovating her complex to make way for new luxury condos.

By comparing Rachel's holdings with those of her fellow citizens, we can see that she is subject to a form of inequality that threatens her standing as an equal citizen, as someone who is able to enjoy a sphere of freedom as independence.[8] Rachel's poverty may not threaten her basic subsistence, but it does subject her to situations in which she is exposed to the coercive power (and therefore the potential domination) of others, since it restricts her options so drastically as to leave her no other choice but to conform to these others' demands. This exposure jeopardizes Rachel's basic right to make her own choices independent of interference from other private wills. Other private individuals—for example, her employer or her landlord—can use Rachel's poverty in order to hold her hostage, and she has nowhere else to go.

Rachel's subjection to these forms of dependence and domination is not a direct function of her absolute level of goods. This is in keeping with the tenor of our Kantian-Rousseauian theory, which, unlike a more utilitarian or welfarist theory, argues that we have little reason to be concerned with persons' absolute levels of well-being once their subsistence has been ensured: instead, we care about wealth only insofar as it affects *independence*. This is because persons do not have a right to well-being or happiness; instead they have a right to a sphere of civil freedom. Were all other American citizens to be in approximately the same condition Rachel finds herself in—imagine they were *all* earning about $15,000 a year in low-skilled jobs, with children attending the same public school, and living in the same low-income apartments—then she would not be in any way dependent upon them or subject to their coercive influence. In

[8] Michael Blake highlights similar concerns about "relative deprivation" in "Distributive Justice," 258–60.

that situation Rachel would enjoy equal standing, and despite her lower level of overall well-being, her rights would in no way be jeopardized. Her skills would be as marketable as everyone else's, depriving her boss of the power to coerce her into granting sexual favors in order to keep her position. Other children would not enjoy any advantage over hers. Finally, her apartment would not be torn down, since no one would have the money to buy luxury condos, so she would not face eviction by the landlord. These reflections show that a great deal of the subjection a Kantian-Rousseauian theorist should care about is generated by inequalities that lead to coercive imbalances of power between citizens.

What about Global Justice?

It is important to say right away that I do not believe the only coercive imbalances of power we should care about are imbalances between citizens of the same state, even if we do have special reasons to care about these. For a Kantian-Rousseauian theorist, we should care about coercive imbalances of power wherever they occur, because these imbalances threaten the innate right to equal freedom-as-independence, which accrues to all persons. As a contrast to Rachel, let us now imagine our obligations to a person who is not a fellow citizen, but with whom we still share a degree of economic and social connectedness. Ernesto, our imagined foreigner, is a coffee farmer in Costa Rica. He owns two acres of land on which he grows a small crop of coffee beans every year, which he sells to the large suppliers in the city, who sell it to gourmet coffee companies that market to US citizens. He makes about $1,500 per year, barely enough to feed and clothe his family and pay for agricultural supplies. He too has three children who attend the small elementary school in their village, which is lacking good teachers and adequate supplies. No higher education is available to them. The family has no electricity, running water, television, or health care provision. Like Rachel, Ernesto does live in a stable democracy that guarantees his basic human rights. What is our relation to Ernesto? Ought we to be at all concerned about the inequalities that exist between him and us? If so, should we be concerned about these inequalities in exactly the same way we are concerned about the inequalities that exist between us and Rachel? Or in some different fashion?

Thomas Nagel has influentially argued in a recent paper that the inequality between us and Ernesto ought not be seen as a matter of concern in terms of distributive justice.[9] He advocates a "two-tiered" account ac-

[9] Nagel, "Problem of Global Justice"; for a weaker statist view, see also Blake, "Distributive Justice"; Sangiovanni, "Global Justice."

cording to which norms of distributive justice apply only to people who are members of the same state and subject to the same set of coercively imposed laws, and no standards of justice whatever apply outside the state. Between states, Nagel claims, norms of justice are simply irrelevant: instead, treaties and contracts establishing trade regimes should be conceived as a form of "voluntary association" by states that imposes no requirements of distributive justice. Trade agreements are entered into by states for the common pursuit of their mutual self-interest, and they require no further justification: the background conditions under which they are made are assumed to be fair. For Nagel, then, there is no justice outside the state. As a shorthand, we can call this position about distributive justice *statism.*

Charles Beitz and Thomas Pogge, on the other hand, have argued that the level of international trade, investment, and migration that exists in the world today is sufficient to ground the claim that there is a world basic structure that ought to be subject to distributive justice requirements.[10] On their view, too, distributive justice is an obligation we have to those with whom we stand in certain schemes and relationships of regularized interaction, and not simply a natural moral duty (à la Caney or Simmons) that we owe to other human beings as such. But, for them, since our context of economic interaction at present extends beyond the state, we should therefore accept that at present we do owe duties of distributive justice to all other persons. Pogge in particular argues that the effects of this global basic structure are so pervasive, and so harmful to the life prospects of the globally worse-off, that all of those who participate in the global economy have a negative duty not to impose such institutions on these others. To make good on this negative duty, he argues that we must reform world economic institutions in accordance with a global difference principle, maximizing the share of goods of the globally worst-off individual.[11] Let us call this position *cosmopolitan institutionalism.*

What would a consistent Kantian-Rousseauian position, of the sort we have been defending, have to say about our relation to Ernesto? Would it adopt the statist position, that Ernesto has no claims of justice on us

[10] See Beitz, *Political Theory*; Pogge, *World Poverty.*

[11] Pogge's work is somewhat difficult to characterize. In his early work, *Realizing Rawls*, he clearly argued for a global difference principle. His later book *World Poverty and Human Rights* continues to press the claim that there is no morally justified distinction between the national and the global economic order in terms of what principles of distributive justice should apply. But his actual proposals for global economic reform in the later work—a global resource dividend, a change in the international borrowing privilege, a democracy fund—seem to be aimed at establishing a fair economic order among *states*, not among *individuals.* In addition, his position relies on controversial empirical claims about the degree to which the global economic order causes poverty in poor countries.

whatsoever? Or would it take an institutional cosmopolitan view, that given the present context of global economic interaction, his claims are equal to Rachel's? Here, I wish to briefly indicate that on a Kantian-Rousseauian view, we should reject both of these positions on global justice. Since this book's primary goal is not to articulate an account of global justice, I do not have space to fully develop any such view here. But I do wish to comment on the issue, mostly to dispel the impression that the Kantian-Rousseauian position must lead directly to strong statism of the kind associated with Nagel.

It is easy to see why one might think statism would be the theory of global justice a Kantian-Rousseauian ought to endorse. After all, the main thesis of this book so far has been that states are morally valuable institutions, and that justice could not be realized without them. Being a citizen of a particular state, I have argued, is an indispensable and constitutive element of freedom, since it is only through state institutions that we can define the terms of our rights in a nondominating way. If I am right, then justice requires states; there is no way equal freedom could be attained without them.

But to move from the claim that justice requires states in order to be realized to the claim that only members of the same state are bound by obligations of justice is to commit a logical fallacy.[12] Justice does not stop at the bounds of the state, on a Kantian view; instead, all institutions are evaluable in terms of equal freedom, and if institutions impose externalities that jeopardize the freedom as independence of outsiders, then they should be reformed. Recall that for Kant, I can only justly acquire rights to property that are consistent with other individuals' innate right to equal freedom: my property must be justifiable to others. At the most fundamental level, then, each person is owed a justification of acquired rights that shows each other person's rights to be consistent with her independence. Therefore, persons outside my state are owed such a justification of my holdings just as much as insiders to it. Citizens or residents of a particular state, in other words, possess only those rights to property that (*a*) are compatible with the continued independence of their fellow citizens, and (*b*) are compatible with the continued independence of other individuals outside their state, that is, citizens of other states.

As we have seen, a Kantian-Rousseauian would certainly claim that the definition and enforcement of acquired rights, especially rights to property, requires a structure of authoritative legal institutions, and that this regime of acquired rights must be made compatible with the innate independence of all those who are subjected to it. To this extent, the Kantian-

[12] This has been well argued in a recent paper by Abizadeh, "Cooperation, Pervasive Impact," 320–21.

Rousseauian would endorse Nagel's view that principles of egalitarian justice (in particular, the concern to eliminate those relative inequalities in wealth that give some a coercive power advantage over others) should hold within the state. But Nagel's conclusion that there are absolutely no distributive principles that extend beyond the state does not necessarily follow from the idea that justice requires political authority. Instead, a Kantian-Rousseauian must also stipulate that the principles of justice imposed inside the state must be compatible with the equal freedom-as-independence of persons outside it as well. Let us call this important condition on justice the *externality condition.* Although I do not have space to fully make out the claim here, I do not believe that compatibility with the externality condition requires global equality of distributive shares. Instead, it requires a system in which private individuals are not able to coercively dominate others across borders. This is compatible with distributive inequalities, as long as those inequalities do not enable this kind of private coercion.

Given that freedom as independence does not require distributive equality, there are many ways to imagine this externality condition being satisfied. Imagine a world, otherwise like our own, in which the United States and Costa Rica were wholly autarkic states. As Allen Buchanan puts, let us imagine that these two states were "more or less economically self-sufficient units that are also distributionally autonomous."[13] In such a situation, if each of these states were internally just democracies whose absolute levels of wealth were nonetheless unequal, on a Kantian-Rousseauian view of justice, we should have no cause for concern about the inequality between Ernesto and ourselves. In such a world, we might still require a global regime to regulate certain problems of international right, including matters of border definition and immigration control, just war, and sovereign recognition. But there would be no duties of distributive justice between internally just autarkic states, because nothing about the economic arrangements of the one state could possible impair the freedom as independence of the citizens of the other. Since individuals simply do not interact across state lines, none of their actions impinge upon the external freedom of foreigners in any dominating way. In certain ways, Kant's and Rousseau's writings indicate that what they may have had in mind was something close to the world of economically self-sufficient and distributionally autonomous states envisioned here.[14]

[13] Buchanan, "Rawls's Law of Peoples," 701.

[14] This may be more true of Rousseau than of Kant. For an interesting discussion of the importance of closed states, see Rousseau's *Constitutional Project for Corsica* in his *Oeuvres Completes*, vol. 3. Kant does envision a regime of international right that would regulate trade between sovereign states. But he envisions trade as voluntary: individuals have a right (part of cosmopolitan right) to *try to establish trading ties* with other countries. See Kant, *MM*, 6:352. Fichte, a follower of Kant, explicitly advocated a regime of self-sufficient

It is clear, though, that we do not live in this autarkic world. In our world, Ernesto may sell his crop to a multinational corporation that has sufficient control over the local market to set the price he can receive. Perhaps it can deny him insurance or labor protections, because he is readily replaceable and there are no global labor standards that apply to his situation. The fact that he cannot receive an immigration visa to the United States or Europe determines the labor market in which he participates. And the global intellectual property regime may affect the price he pays for the seeds he plants or the medicine he can or cannot afford. In this sense, there are a number of ways that global interaction allows those who are not subject to a common scheme of domestic law with Ernesto to take actions that may affect his independence and ability to control his own life.

So is there anything that a Kantian-Rousseauian view can say about our relation to those like Ernesto whose independence may be affected by agents outside his own scheme of domestic law? A consistent Kantian-Rousseauian position would agree that we have responsibilities of justice to Ernesto, I believe, but its account of these responsibilities would take a form different from either the statist or institutional cosmopolitan view. The material provided by these two thinkers for constructing such a position on global distributive justice is somewhat sparse, but to begin, let us consider two features of Kant's views on property rights. First, it is clear that Kant thinks that the property rights of states (and therefore of their citizens) remain provisional (and therefore impose no binding correlative duties) vis-à-vis outsiders until there is a global juridical entity through which the property claims of each state can be recognized by each other state on the planet.

> Since a state of nature among nations, like a state of nature among individual human beings, is a condition that one ought to leave in order to enter a lawful condition, before this happens any rights of nations, and anything external that is mine or yours which states can acquire or retain by war, are merely *provisional*. Only in a *universal association of states* (analogous to that by which a people becomes a state) can rights come to hold *conclusively* and a true *condition of peace* come about. (*MM*, 6:350)

Until a universal association of states exists, a given state's property entitlements may have some basis in subjective right, but they are subject to the problems of unilateral interpretation and coercive enforcement in the same way individuals' rights would be in the state of nature. All of these

---

autarky in "The Closed Commercial State," and he did so largely out of a concern for justice. He thought that interdependence in matters of trade jeopardized the stability of justice—conceived as secure rights to a sphere of external freedom—within the state.

problems, recall, render property entitlements merely provisionally binding, so long as they are subject to a state's subjective—rather than a global authority's objective—definition, interpretation, and enforcement.

Therefore a stable global regime of mutual recognition by states of one another's property rights—in the form of a legal congress or association of states—is what it would take to convert an individual citizen's merely provisional property rights into fully conclusive ones. Until such a regime exists, an individual's rights may be conclusive vis-à-vis his compatriots, but they remain provisional for foreigners. Rousseau takes much the same sort of view. In the *Social Contract*, he declares that

> with regard to its members, the State is master of all their goods by the social contract which serves as the basis of rights within the State; but with regard to other Powers it is master of all its members' goods only by right of the first occupant which it derives from private individuals. (*SC*, 54)

And he too refers, obliquely, to an unpublished theory of "confederations" that might explain how states could themselves coexist in a condition of right, by establishing a global regime of justice. Once a global property regime comes into being, like the state, it too would have the authority to regulate property entitlements in accordance with objective positive laws. As this outline indicates, though, neither Rousseau nor Kant believes that a global juridical regime should take the form of a world state, which would enact laws of property directly binding on individuals. Instead, they thought justice on a global level was best ensured by an association or federation of internally just states that agreed to reciprocally recognize and uphold each other's property arrangements, in such a way as to guarantee the independence of the members.

For this reason, while I agree with the critics of statism that it is implausible that we owe no duties of distributive justice to those outside our state, I do not accept the cosmopolitan institutionalist view that these duties should be determined on a basis of egalitarian reciprocity between individuals. Rather, on a Kantian-Rousseauian view, I think they are best determined on a basis of egalitarian reciprocity between states, which (in the ideal case) will already have an internally just regime of acquired rights to regulate the claims of their citizens. Because justice requires state structures in order to be realized, whatever system of global justice we defend will have to be compatible with the continued existence of these states, and with their ongoing special relationship to their citizens.

Both Kant and Rousseau held that the state is a moral person, capable of possessing entitlements and claims to property vis-à-vis other entities.[15]

[15] For this language, see, e.g., Kant, *MM*, 6:343.

As institutions that credibly interpret the requirements of equal freedom in the name of their citizens, legitimate states are authorized by their citizens to perform a morally valuable task, and therefore they deserve respect. It would not be warranted, for example, to impose one more powerful state's scheme of property laws on the citizens of another state who had adopted an alternative, but still just, scheme. Such an action would show disrespect for their morally valuable effort to define the terms of equal freedom for themselves. There is an independent wrong done by the coercive dismantling of a just institution that a group of individuals have created and continue to sustain. So, on a Kantian-Rousseauian view, once a plurality of just democratic states has been established for contingent historical reasons, these states have a moral claim on us by virtue of the fact that each represents a valuable collective endeavor to interpret and realize the terms of justice for their members.

Thus, the best Kantian-Rousseauian position on international distributive justice, I submit, is *liberal internationalism.* This position stipulates that a global juridical institution (1) must be brought into being to regulate property rights; but that (2) while this institution will impose duties of distributive justice that go beyond a minimum of humanitarian obligation, these duties are distinctly different from the requirements that apply within a domestic regime; and (3) that these duties bind states, and not individuals. The primary goal of a just global property structure—to secure the reciprocal independence of well-ordered states as moral persons—is analogous to the goal of a domestic property structure, but its participants are different. There is therefore no requirement, on a liberal-internationalist view, to apply exactly the same standards of distributive equality to the international realm as to the domestic context, since a global property structure, in the main, determines the entitlements of the states that are subject to it, and regulates the interactions of citizens across state borders in a way that preserves the integrity of that state's domestic legal framework. In this sense, my view accepts the general Rawlsian position (which also has a Kantian basis) that there may be a plurality of principles of justice, each suited to the kind of context it is meant to regulate: as Rawls puts it, "The correct regulative principle for a thing depends on the nature of that thing."[16] One should expect that there will be one set of distributive principles for the international context, and another for the domestic, since they regulate interactions among different kinds of entity.[17] For these reasons, while there may be principles of distributive justice for the international realm, they will not take the form of a global

[16] Rawls, *A Theory of Justice*, 25.

[17] My position here is closest to the one defended in Cohen and Sabel, "Extra Rem Publican Nulla Justitia?"; and Buchanan, "Rawls's Law of Peoples."

difference principle or egalitarian regime between individuals. We do owe something in terms of justice to Ernesto, but what we owe to Ernesto will not be the same thing we owe to Rachel.

In a theory like the one I have been defending, then, where the essential point is that the state makes a moral difference to our obligations, we do not have to claim that the state's existence exhausts our obligations of justice. In cases where interdependence allows states and private actors to exercise control across borders in ways that could potentially compromise the independence of other states and their citizens, we have good Kantian-Rousseauian reasons to argue for duties to institute a parallel structure of juridical authority at the international level. We can think of this authority, if it were fully realized, as instituting a just global property structure that would regulate those forms of global interdependence that affect property rights across borders, including

1. state territorial claims and claims to control natural resources;
2. immigration and border control;
3. fair terms of trade between states, including tariffs, exchange rates, antidumping regulations, and subsidies;
4. certain forms of internationally recognized property, including patent rights, intellectual property, rules about the exploitation of unowned or common resources, and international antitrust law;
5. fair labor standards and environmental regulations.

Spelling out what a just global property structure—once instituted—would require is unfortunately beyond the scope of this book. Nevertheless, this brief excursus into questions of global justice is useful, I hope, in underscoring the point that a view like my own that defends the moral importance of states is not equivalent to a statist view of distributive justice. This is because, on a Kantian-Rousseauian view, states themselves are justified institutions only because, and insofar as, they are necessary to realize the equal freedom of individuals, and that means all individuals, not just their own members. Whatever externalities the states-system imposes that are at odds with equal freedom are themselves evaluable in terms of justice: while removing these externalities does not require equalizing global distributive shares, it does require a framework of rules that preclude the citizens of one state from unfairly coercing those outside their borders. Where a person's independence is pervasively affected by foreign actors, global legal regulation is necessary.

Any global justice proposal made in the spirit of the Kantian-Rousseauian view would be a liberal-internationalist account of global justice that is constructed with states as its institutional building blocks: unlike the cosmopolitan institutionalist view, it does not advocate the establishment of some alternative institutional structure that would supersede the state, and produce laws with direct and unmediated application to individuals. For that reason, a liberal-internationalist theory will concede that a special concern for equalizing distributive shares between citizens will continue to play an ongoing role in a theory of global justice, since compatriots are most likely to be implicated in relations of dependence that jeopardize their equal freedom. But it will advocate supplementing these domestic principles of justice with an additional set of principles that regulate international interdependence in a way that reestablishes everyone's freedom.

To conclude, we should emphasize that the redistributive obligations we owe to fellow citizens, like the obligations we would owe to other states under a global juridical entity, are not obligations of charity or humanitarian aid. Instead, they are obligations of respect for equal freedom-as-independence. By equalizing distributive shares among citizens who are subject to the same legal institutions, we help "to mitigate the impact of force, violence, and conflict" in relations among equal consociates under law.[18]

This argument, I believe, explains why priority for compatriots in matters of distributive justice is not a form of arbitrary discrimination based on the mere fact of state borders, in the way some cosmopolitans have claimed. Instead, such priority is based on the view that securing each person's freedom requires her to occupy the status of independent and equal citizen in a legitimate democratic state. In a parallel fashion, I have argued, a global regime of right would secure just states (and their citizens) from those forms of interference or coercive interaction that compromise their independence, and thereby help to ensure the stability of the domestic legal framework that protects their members' independence. But even in an entirely just global scheme, I have claimed, special obligations of membership would still exist and would remain morally important. As long as separate just states exist, bounded political obligations will continue to have moral force.

If my view is correct, then contemporary cosmopolitans and philosophical anarchists are wrong to argue that a commitment to freedom and equality is necessarily at odds with an acceptance of legitimate political authority. The central point overlooked by these theorists is that the equal right to freedom, however innate in our natural capacities, can neither be

[18] Waldron, "Social Citizenship and Welfare," 275.

defined nor protected without the construction of a democratic legal state. For this reason, an individual's relationship to her state and to her fellow citizens is not purely a matter of moral contingency and irrelevance. If, following Kant and Rousseau, we take the view that securing equal freedom requires we establish and uphold just states, then we will hold that it is only as members of states that we can be constituted as free and equal persons in the first place.

PART TWO

Solidarity and Allegiance

5

Freedom and Culture in Rousseau

The argument in part 1 established that our general duties of justice give us good reasons to construct and uphold democratic states, since they are necessary in order to define and enforce our acquired rights while maintaining our independence from domination by other private persons. But in the second part of the book I seek to address an important criticism that is frequently leveled against justice-based accounts of political allegiance like the one I so far have defended. The criticism is that a justice-based account cannot establish a sufficiently tight connection between the citizen's general obligation to establish and uphold just states and a special obligation to support her *particular* state or to show solidarity with her compatriots.[1] If a Canadian citizen like Sally, discussed in the introduction, has a general duty to support just political institutions, then doesn't the Swedish state have the same claim on her that the institutions of Canada do? After all, they are both just states that put in place a framework that defines and enforces people's acquired rights. What is it that distinguishes Canada from other just countries in Sally's estimation?

Those who make this criticism often emphasize that if what Sally truly values is justice—securing equal freedom for persons generally—then this value would seem to give her equal reason to support just institutions everywhere. Justice would be an end that Sally is bound to promote globally. So the argument in part 1 remains incomplete unless we can show that the justice-based reasons for establishing states also provide sufficient reasons for each citizen to uphold and support her particular state, by obeying its laws, paying taxes to it, voting and participating in its democratic process, and discharging state obligations (like contributing to war reparations). We must also show that justice gives a citizen sufficient reason for solidarity with her compatriots, by supporting welfare-state redistribution and taking their interests into special account in her political deliberations.

As we saw in chapter 1, the idea that a justice-based view cannot account for this sort of particularity was a main feature of Simmons's attack on "natural duty" theories of political obligation:

[1] This is Simmons's main criticism of natural duty theories of political obligation, recently repeated in Wellman and Simmons, *Duty to Obey Law*, 166–70.

> The problem for Natural Duty accounts . . .to which I point here is (part of) what I have elsewhere called the "particularity problem": A general moral duty to promote justice—or any other impartial value—cannot bind one specially to support or comply with one particular state or society (such as "my own"). . . . Natural moral duties will bind me as strongly with respect to persons or institutions that are not close to me as they will with respect to those that are. . . . Just Swedish political institutions merit support as much as, and for the same reason as do, just political institutions in the United Kingdom.[2]

It is noteworthy that liberal-nationalist theorists have recently seized on Simmons's arguments and put them to new uses.[3] Like Simmons, Yael Tamir and David Miller have also claimed that a purely justice-based account of political obligation cannot give an explanation of why a citizen might have greater reason to support her own just state over other states. Unlike Simmons, however, they think that a reason for the citizen's greater allegiance to her particular state does exist; but, for them, it is rooted in values other than justice. For liberal nationalists, the citizen's "special" reason for allegiance lies in her attachment to her national culture, which the state's separate institutions protect and promote. National identity, it is argued, is the additional element that, when combined with duties of justice, gives us a sufficient reason to form and uphold a state together with a particular group of others, namely, our conationals.[4]

Liberal nationalists therefore claim that national solidarity forms an essential part of a full-scale liberal theory of justice, since it helps to resolve particularity problems that purely justice-based accounts seem unable to overcome on their own. Tamir argues that "liberals have no choice but to presuppose the existence of such [national] ties and treat community as prior to justice and fairness in the sense that questions of justice and fairness are regarded as questions of what would be just or fair within a particular political community."[5]

In this second half of the book, I will examine and criticize what I take to be the liberal nationalists' most challenging claim: that an "extra" appeal to national identity is an essential precondition of a fully worked-out liberal theory of justice. Here, we will raise and answer two important

[2] Simmons, in Simmons and Wellman, *Duty to Obey Law*, 166.

[3] It should be reemphasized that Simmons himself is *not* a nationalist; instead, he is a libertarian-anarchist who believes we have no political obligations at all.

[4] As David Miller puts it, civic nationalism cannot "explain why the boundaries of the political community should fall here rather than there; nor does it give you any sense of the historical identity of the community, the links that bind present-day politics to decisions made and actions performed in the past." Miller, *On Nationality*, 163.

[5] Tamir, *Liberal Nationalism*, 118.

questions: Is some special bond of solidarity and obligation actually necessary for citizens to have reason to show allegiance to their particular institutions? And if so, what kind of bond should this be?

In this chapter, I first examine the historical roots of many of the nationalists' claims: as we shall see, the notion that citizen solidarity is an important precondition for democratic justice is already present in Rousseau's theory. Recall that Rousseau's defense of popular sovereignty as the only legitimate model of political authority, examined in some detail in chapter 3, involved a controversial assertion: he claims that in order to legislate generally and impartially on one another's behalf, the citizens of a democratic state must share solidarity with one another. On Rousseau's view, in order to articulate a will that takes the form of impersonal laws—laws that will truly protect each citizen's freedom equally—each citizen must be capable of taking up the viewpoint of the common interest, a perspective that requires him to show concern for the freedom and well-being of his fellow citizens. But if some form of solidarity is necessary for free democratic institutions to function effectively, as Rousseau argues, then we may ask: how do citizens develop it?

Rousseau is actually very ambivalent—even deeply torn—about this question. Because he emphasizes the role of cultural practices in fostering democratic solidarity, Rousseau has often been read as a cultural nationalist, and indeed, as we shall see, there is good evidence for this reading. But there are strains in Rousseau's account that contradict the cultural-nationalist interpretation. I will argue that, if we take these strains seriously, we can put together a more liberal and rationalist theory of civic solidarity from Rousseau's texts than is often recognized. And over the final chapters of the book, I will construct an argument that seeks to vindicate this liberal-rationalist understanding as superior to its cultural counterpart. The liberal-rationalist view that finds roots in Rousseau holds that while some from of democratic solidarity may be necessary for just institutions to function well, that solidarity can be generated simply by understanding the good reasons for allegiance to those institutions, and need not take the form of a shared culture or national identity.

Ultimately, Rousseau presents us with two incompatible stories of how the moral psychology appropriate to citizenship might be developed. One model of political upbringing, which I will here call the *freedom model*, is laid out in *Emile*, Rousseau's plan for the education of a wholly autonomous and independent individual. Emile's education is largely designed to prevent the development of the desires for domination and superiority that, for Rousseau, render social dependence potentially destructive. Rousseau suggests that dependence on other private persons is threatening because life in society gives rise to a new passion in us—a passion he calls *amour-propre*, or self-regard.[6] This passion impels us to obtain others' acknowledgment of our own moral importance or standing. Rousseau claims in part that the disorder and strife he attributes to our social dependence on others is due to an "inflamed" form of amour propre,[7] which leads us to try to dominate others in order to secure their recognition of our moral importance. The birth, in society, of this form of inflamed amour propre replaces our benign natural desires with competitive passions that lead us into dominating social relationships.

In order to forestall the genesis of these competitive and dominating passions in him, Emile—Rousseau's ideal citizen—is raised in the country, outside the social relations of dependence characteristic of large commercial centers. He is taught to think his own thoughts, to develop a sense of independence, and to question the wisdom of others and of received authority. In *Emile*, Rousseau aims to create a new type of citizen: one who can live together with others without desiring to dominate them, one who remains independent and free even in a social context. One of the interesting results of this new education, as we shall see below, is that when Emile's amour propre develops, it takes on a form different from that of other men. Amour propre manifests itself in Emile as a capacity to identify with others of equal standing and to form a reflective allegiance to a well-ordered state. In what follows, I trace the (perhaps surprising) process by which Emile's education-to-freedom creates a capacity for identification with others. The theory of moral-psychological development presented in *Emile* therefore offers us a possible solution—one based solely on an education to rational autonomy—to the problem of solidarity in the democratic state.

Despite the seeming promise of the education-to-freedom story, though, Rousseau departs significantly from it in some of his other writings on political education, particularly those that discuss Poland and Geneva, where he abandons it for what we might call a *culture model*.[8]

[6] I choose "self-regard" as a translation of *amour-propre* because it suggests a kind of "selfishness" and the idea of a "reflected self," both of which are inherent in *amour-propre*. We have regard for ourselves by imagining how others might regard us—hence, our self is "reflected" to us only by the knowledge of others and our internalized notions of their reactions to us. Through knowing others, we become conscious of ourselves as *selves*, rather than merely conscious of the first-order physical sensations and desires we experience. This reflective consciousness of ourselves gives us a broad range of new second-order desires attaching to this notion of self—desires to be regarded by others in certain ways. This can also lead to a particular sort of "selfishness," the other notion at stake in *amour-propre*. I will hereafter treat the term as an English word, that is, without the italics, but Rousseau's sense should be kept in mind.

[7] I take the term "inflamed" from Dent, *Rousseau*, 56–86.

[8] John Charvet's analysis of *Emile* also indicates that Rousseau is torn as to whether an education in reflective autonomy can really serve as a model for society: "The tentativeness

In these writings, he emphasizes the signs, games, festivals, and cultural practices that tie citizens to one another and that motivate them to take their compatriots' interests into account and to be loyal to their state. These ascriptive characteristics create ties that bind the citizens together without their being reflectively conscious of them: they operate, in some sense, behind the backs of the participants they unite. Allegiance to these practices and symbols aids citizens in identifying with one another, and it gives concrete cultural content to the common interest they take themselves to share.

Like Rousseau, modern theorists of the nation as an "imagined community" have emphasized the role of a common language, cultural practices, symbols, and myths in enabling citizens to more readily imagine others with whom they are politically connected.[9] In particular, cultural commonalities allow citizens who may not know one another to formulate a concrete view about one another's needs and interests. Citizens who inhabit large communities can relate to one another in the absence of direct personal acquaintance by conceiving of themselves as sharing certain traits and features. But this type of "mediated" identification has its drawbacks. When compatriots relate to one another purely as bearers of cultural traits, they are incapable of acquaintance with, and knowledge of, each other's actual needs and interests in their full specificity. Although the introduction of ascriptive characteristics does allow us to concretely imagine our compatriots, then, it also leads us to *misimagine* them at the same time. And this misimagination has negative implications for a politics of freedom and autonomy.

The Freedom Model

The main argument of Rousseau's freedom model is that once a citizen is educated to understand the role played by democratic institutions in securing his civil freedom, he will reflectively identify with his political institutions and his compatriots, and show concern for their interests as a matter of course. Rousseau asserts that we possess this capacity for reflective identification because amour propre, or self-regard, gives us the ability to form new attitudes and desires based on our beliefs. If we regard

with which Rousseau undertakes to reveal this reconciliation [of man and citizen] reflects an uncertainty in his own mind, that recurs in *Emile* and in the *Social Contract*, as to whether he is able to and has in fact brought about the desired harmony between nature and society, and whether it is not still the case that, to create the good social man or the true citizen, nature has to be suppressed." Charvet, *Social Problem in Rousseau*, 41.

9 Anderson, *Imagined Communities*, 6–10; Hobsbawm, *Nations and Nationalism*, 83–91.

our compatriots as equals and understand that taking account of their interests is necessary to formulate a general will, rightly educated amour propre can lead us to form a new cognitively based identification with them. According to the freedom model, then, an attitude of civic allegiance to our state and to our fellow citizens can be based solely on a public and transparent understanding of their role in defining and securing our rights.

Defending this freedom model, however, requires us to claim that evidence from *Emile* is relevant for understanding Rousseau's views on the psychology of citizenship. Are the views put forward in *Emile* relevant for understanding Rousseau's ideas about political education? Many commentators have held that they are not.[10] What gives their view an initial plausibility is that in Book I of *Emile*, Rousseau draws an important distinction between the political education advocated by the ancients and the "natural" education that is to be given to Emile. There he says:

> Natural man is entirely for himself. He is a numerical unity, the absolute whole which is relative only to itself or its kind. Civil man is only a fractional unity dependent on the denominator; his value is determined by his relation to the whole, which is the social body. Good social institutions are those that best know how to denature man, to take his absolute existence from him in order to give him a relative one and to transport the *I* into the common unity, with the result that each individual believes himself no longer one but a part of the unity and no longer feels except within the whole. (*E*, 39)

Rousseau indicates that the best example of such a purely civic education is found in Plato's *Republic*. Interestingly, though, Emile is not given a civic education of this kind. Emile is raised for himself, to become independent and autonomous, whereas Plato's ideal citizen is raised solely to perform a role that contributes to the common good of his society.

But Rousseau ends his discussion of ancient and modern education with an important question. He suggests that these seemingly opposed objects—producing a free and independent man and producing a citizen—may in the end be reconcilable.[11] He asks:

> What will a man raised uniquely for himself become for others? If perchance, the double object proposed [man and citizen] could be reunited

[10] See, e.g., Parry, "Autonomy and the Citizen."

[11] See Charvet, *Social Problem in Rousseau*, 39, for a similar view. Kant took the view that that Rousseau thought the autonomous man and the citizen could be reconciled. He argues that Rousseau should be read as a theorist of *education* to rational freedom, and not an advocate of regression to a more primitive condition ("Conjectures on the Beginnings of Human History," 227).

> in a single object, one would, in removing the contradictions in man, have removed a large impediment to his happiness. (*E*, 41)

He suggests that "in order to judge of this, [Emile] would have to be seen wholly formed: his inclinations would have to have been observed, his progress seen, his development followed" (*E*, 41). The answer, which comes only at the end of the book, is that Emile learns the doctrines of the *Social Contract* and himself becomes a citizen.

Because Rousseau suggests that an education to reflective independence will in the end produce a good citizen, I think the objection that *Emile* is irrelevant for understanding Rousseau's views about citizenship is misplaced. But I do think the stated objection points out something very important about the kind of citizenship Rousseau is (at least initially) drawn to. Rousseau sees ancient civic education, along the lines depicted by Plato, as flawed because it is not an education to *reflectively free* citizenship. Emile's education differs from the Platonic model because he reflects upon and affirms the political institutions under which he lives, since he understands the good reasons for constructing and upholding these institutions. Emile thinks of himself as an independent individual, then, and not simply as an entity submerged in the civic whole. He reflectively evaluates his own institutions, and he sees his commitment to them as a voluntary and rationally justified act. Ancient education—witness Plato's use of a "noble lie" to assign members of the city their various functions—did not form the citizen to think for himself, or to understand why the state was necessary to guarantee his own and others' freedom, but only to play a role within it with no necessary cognizance of how this role conduced to his own rational interests.

The upshot, I take it, is that to live up to its own promise, a Rousseauian model of civic solidarity must be one that the citizen herself is able to understand and to freely endorse from her own perspective. It should not be merely an attitude or disposition inculcated in her without her knowledge, in order to serve the interests of others (this includes the interests of society as a whole, to the extent those are not interests she can affirm from some standpoint). To be fully free, she must be able to understand the reasons for her allegiance and to endorse the democratic institutions of her own state from the perspective of their contribution to securing equal freedom.

To see how such a "freedom model" might actually give rise to the kind of civic solidarity Rousseau seeks, however, we first need to understand something more about the three basic principles of his moral psychology: the sentiments of *amour de soi*, *pitié*, and amour propre. For he argues that under the right conditions, our natural moral sentiments will *be guided by* our reason: that is, we will develop an attachment to those persons and institutions that we rationally believe to promote our freedom.

A Positive Theory of Amour Propre?

Before entering society, Rousseau claims, man is under the sway of "two principles prior to reason," self-love and pity, the first of which—*amour de soi-même*—interests him "intensely in [his] well-being and [his] preservation" (*D2*, 127).[12] This love of self, indicates Rousseau, is a "natural sentiment" (*D2*, 218) and is "always good and in conformity with order" (*E*, 213). *Amour de soi* is also "the source of all our passions, the origin and principle of all the others" (*E*, 212). This sort of self-love is a purely noncognitive instinct: it impels us to seek our own preservation by giving rise to certain brute desires in us. These desires are of the type that simply "come over" us: they arise, like hunger or lust, without any need for reflection, and they are always unshakably directed toward the external objects that naturally satisfy these appetites.

But although *amour de soi* endows with us a basic set of innate needs and desires, Rousseau thinks that humans attain the capacity for moral reflection and autonomy, complete with the ability to form new desires based on their beliefs, only with the development of the social sentiment of amour propre. The passions and desires dependent on amour propre, unlike those generated from *amour de soi*, all have an important cognitive dimension. They are not simple natural appetites, which "well up" in us in a manner beyond our control, like hunger or lust. Instead, they are artificial desires that depend upon our making certain reflective judgments, and particularly comparative reflections about our own moral standing with respect to others. Unlike *amour de soi*, amour propre "originates in comparisons" (*D2*, 218), and "grows with reason, memory, and imagination" (*D2*, 170).

When Rousseau argues that amour propre is a cognitive sentiment born of reflectiveness, he has in mind the reflection that other human beings are free and intentional beings: that they choose, and are not impelled, to act as they do. Before amour propre arises, Rousseau argues that a person will regard the actions of other humans in the same way he would any other force of necessity: "Every man viewing his kind scarcely differently

[12] I am not the first to argue that Rousseau has a positive theory of amour propre, but this is clearly a minority position in the literature. For other arguments to this effect, see Dent, *Rousseau*, 113–67; and Neuhouser, "Rousseau on the Relation." For the opposing view, see, e.g., Masters, *Political Philosophy of Rousseau*, 53–62; Charvet, *Social Problem in Rousseau*, 79–84.

from the way he would view animals of another species, can rob the weaker of his prey or yield his own to the stronger without considering these acts of pillage as anything but natural occurrences" (*D2*, 218). Amour propre, however, develops out of a recognition that other human beings are not like animals, but are rather free creatures who can be held morally responsible.

Once we recognize others as "moral" beings like us,[13] Rousseau claims that we move beyond the realm of the natural passions and into the new sphere of cognitively based emotions, because this reflection necessarily gives rise to (at least two) new sentiments in us: the twin feelings of gratitude and offense. Offense springs from the notion, not just of harm to us, but from a belief that the harm has been willed by a free being; gratitude likewise from an idea, not just of usefulness to us, but of willed usefulness. These passions are both responses not to events that occur of necessity, but to actions that are inflicted on us by others who we believe are free to do otherwise:

> Since it is contempt or the intent to harm, and not the harm itself, that constitutes the offense, men who are unable to appreciate one another or compare themselves with one another can do each other much violence when there is some advantage in it for them, without ever offending one another. (*D2*, 218)

The feeling of amour propre is incapable of arising in the absence of the belief that other human beings are beings, like ourselves, who are in some sense in voluntary control of their impulses. This leads us to react to them with a set of responsibility-attributing emotions: emotions like offense, resentment, and indignation. It is the imputation of useful or harmful occurrences to a person that makes us love or resent these as actions that are intentionally inflicted, instead of experiencing them as pleasant or painful events that merely happen.

Because amour propre is based on the knowledge that other beings are free persons, it is particularly concerned with other people's thoughts and intentions about us: with their esteem and opinions of our conduct. After all, others' actions toward us are determined by their thoughts and intentions. Our own amour propre tends to generate a demand that other persons treat us—and think of us—with respect and esteem. As free agents, others are in control of whether or not they respect us and how they regard us, and we expect to be respected and regarded as we deserve. Once we recognize others as persons, we expect them to mentally recognize us

[13] Several theorists have described amour propre in a proto-Hegelian way as a desire for recognition. See Scott, "Rousseau and Melodious Language," 808; Neuhouser, "Rousseau on the Relation," 221–22; Ripstein, "Universal and General Wills," 448.

as possessing a similar standing. And when they do not, we are not simply displeased—we feel wronged and desire redress.

Amour propre is a form of self-love, then, that does not simply relate the self to external objects, but also to other persons, and particularly to one's imagined standing in their estimation. Because amour propre depends in this way on comparisons of relative status, Rousseau suggests that it can easily give rise to competitive and destructive passions in us, including (most nefariously) the desire for domination over others. Since we desire to be recognized and treated as a being of moral importance, one way to try to gain this recognition is to force it from others, through demonstrations of our superiority or even through direct coercion of them. Indeed, in his Second Discourse, Rousseau claims that this desire for standing is the original source of all the evils that characterize man's social condition, that is, corruption, slavery, and war. It can lead man to abandon a state of peaceful independence for the pursuit of insatiable ambitions. In so doing, amour propre leads us into relations of dependence that give rise to all the psychological and social ills that man experiences in modern commercial societies.

Interpreters of Rousseau have often considered his view of amour propre to be a purely negative one, following the logic that since all the ills he diagnoses in social life arise with amour propre's development, he must therefore advocate its suppression. But together with a few other recent commentators, I wish to argue that such a conclusion is overhasty.[14] It is certainly true that Rousseau depicts in dark terms the amour propre that takes the form of a drive for domination. But there is evidence that Rousseau did not think amour propre necessarily had to manifest itself as a tyrannical impulse to superiority, and therefore that he did not find it a harmful emotion as such.

Rousseau takes the view that amour propre is the single trait that distinguishes human beings from animals; it gives rise to all our complex, cognitively based attitudes and desires; to root it out would therefore mean condemning human beings to a purely animal existence. Amour propre is the only emotion in us that has reference to the *moral* sphere: it is a sentiment that allows us to recognize other humans as beings who act voluntarily, and therefore can be held responsible: it thus provides a basis for establishing moral rules. Thus, Rousseau argues in the *Discourse on Inequality* that "mutual duties" and "rules of justice" are instituted only after reason and amour propre become developed (*D2*, 166–69).

Rousseau's project, in my view, is not to return us to a condition in which amour propre does not exist. It is to stave off the corruption to

[14] For other arguments to this effect, see Dent, *Rousseau*, 113–67; Neuhouser, "Freedom" and "Rousseau on the Relation," 221–25.

which amour propre is prone, by redirecting it away from a divisive struggle for domination and toward new objects that are consonant with a free social life. Since amour propre is a cognitively based emotion, Rousseau suggests that, when properly managed and educated, it can serve as the basis for socially desirable and rationally justified attachments. And if we look at Rousseau's writings systematically, I argue, we find just this sort of alternative account of amour propre: an account that shows how it might serve as the bond of civic solidarity in a rational state.

The Evidence for the Freedom Model

Much of the evidence that Rousseau holds a more benign view of amour propre than is usually attributed to him comes from *Emile*. There he calls amour propre "the first and most natural of all the passions" (*E*, 208), and a "useful but dangerous instrument" (*E*, 244), saying:

> The sole passion natural to man is *amour de soi* or *amour-propre* taken in an extended sense. This *amour-propre* in itself or relative to us is good and useful: and since it has no necessary relation to others, it is in this respect naturally neutral. It becomes good or bad only by the application made of it and the relations given to it. (*E*, 92)

In this passage, Rousseau does two things. First, he postulates that there is a connection between the passions of *amour de soi* and amour propre; that is, they are not fundamentally distinct impulses. While it is always our impulse to self-preservation that determines the shape of our passions, Rousseau suggests that impulse can take two forms. It can concern itself merely with our well-being of our physical body, in which case it is called *amour de soi*. Or it can concern itself with the well-being of the self in a more extended sense, with the respect and regard that others show us. To be concerned with the self in this second sense is to be concerned, not solely with one's physical well-being, but more importantly with one's dignity. Once this concern with our moral standing arises, the expressions of our desire for self-preservation are no longer merely influenced by the relations (perceived by the physical senses) in which we stand to objects; they are much more powerfully determined by our moral relationships to others.

In addition to postulating the development of amour propre out of the broader concern for well-being of the self that is characteristic of *amour de soi*, Rousseau declares that amour propre is not a necessarily bad or harmful passion in itself: it is naturally neutral. Instead, it becomes harmful only through the applications and the relations human beings give to it. By altering our beliefs about our dignity in others' eyes—the beliefs that inspire amour propre in the first place—Rousseau suggests that we can make this concern with recognition into a force for virtue rather than vice. Since amour propre springs from our beliefs about our own standing, Rousseau claims that the form taken by the passion will depend on the outcome of these cognitive comparisons.

> Since my Emile has until now looked only at himself, the first glance he casts on his fellows leads him to compare himself with them. And the first sentiment aroused in him by this comparison is the desire to be in the first position. This is the point at which love of self turns into *amour-propre* and where begin to arise all the passions which depend on this one. But to decide whether among these passions the dominant ones in his character will be humane and gentle or cruel and malignant, whether they will be passions of beneficence and commiseration or envy and covetousness, we must know what position he will feel he has among men, and what kinds of obstacles he may believe he has overcome to reach the position he wants to occupy. (*E*, 235)

As soon as Emile compares himself to others, then, his *amour de soi* is transmuted into amour propre. But this does not mean that the concern with the mental "I" must always express itself as a desire for harm to others. Beneficence and commiseration are likewise—in Rousseau's schema—passions that depend on amour propre.[15]

Rousseau's general thesis is that because the expressions of amour propre depend on our perceptions of relations of standing, by manipulating those relations of moral standing we can transform the emotions themselves. And indeed, he indicates that there is one kind of relationship in which amour propre is certain to be expressed not as a drive to domination but instead as a benevolent sentiment that can create bonds of attachment among human beings. The relation of social equality, he claims, turns amour propre to good account. Equality does this by focusing our attentions, not on our superiority to others, but rather on "our common miseries," which "turn[s] our hearts to humanity" (*E*, 221).

In order to turn amour propre toward benevolence, then, it is necessary that persons are educated to see themselves as moral equals. When someone commiserates with another human being, she feels herself secure insofar as she is not at the moment subject to his ills. But insofar as she is capable of entering the position of the suffering person—or in other words, as long as there is a fundamental equality between herself and the sufferer such that she is not exempted from assuming his status—she will

[15] Roger Masters discusses the similarities between Rousseau's account of pity in *Emile* and his account of amour propre in *Political Philosophy of Rousseau*, 42–48. He does not make the further claim, as I do, that social pity is reducible to a form of amour propre.

attribute her feeling of superior security not to a fundamental difference between them, but rather to chance. In this condition, Rousseau predicts that an individual will sense the sufferings of the other person as potentially her own, and feel compassion for him and a desire to redress his situation. Suffering creatures are "objects on which the expansive force of [Emile's] heart can act—objects which swell the heart, which extend it to other beings, which make it find itself everywhere outside of itself—and carefully . . . keep away those which contract and concentrate the heart and tighten the spring of the human *I*" (*E*, 223).

When Rousseau offers "maxims" to potential tutors, then, on how to turn their pupils' hearts to humanity and benevolence rather than to insolence and vanity, following his new educational method, he concentrates on shaping our perceptions of our own and others' moral standing: we cannot put ourselves in place of those who are superior to us, but only of those whom we know to be of equal dignity with ourselves. Teaching students to recognize their fundamental equality with others, Rousseau argues, is already to teach them to show concern for the freedom and well-being of those other people.

Reflective Identification

His analysis of the effect of equality on our desire for recognition allows Rousseau to formulate a theory of *reflective identification* as a reasoned sentiment. This reflective identification is importantly distinct from the natural pity that Rousseau had depicted earlier in his *Second Discourse*.[16] There, Rousseau had described pity as a purely animal instinct, "a repugnance to seeing any sentient Being, and especially any being like ourselves, perish or suffer" (*D2*, 127). Natural pity is prereflective, involves no cognitive component, and is seen in all creatures. But Rousseau indicates that this kind of pity is much more active in animals, and in the animal-like natural man, than it can ever be in our fully developed human state.

[16] The apparent differences between Rousseau's account of pity in the Second Discourse and in his other works are discussed by Jacques Derrida in *Of Grammatology*, 171–95; Jean Starobinski, in his notes to the Second Discourse, *OC*, 1330–31; and Scott, "Rousseau and Melodious Language." Derrida and Scott, for example, argue that Rousseau's accounts of pity are consistent and that the social pity described in *Emile* and *EOL* is simply the developed form of natural pity, which is "not fully active" in the state of nature (Scott, 809; Derrida, 182–84). But the textual evidence seems to me to contradict this view. Some form of pity seems to be fully active in the state of nature and indeed *more* active than Rousseau expects it to be in society. Natural pity, which "carries us without reflection to the assistance of those we see suffer," is stifled by reflection, which awakens amour propre. But in *Emile* and *EOL*, Rousseau claims that pity *depends* on reflection. On the basis of these textual

In *Emile* and other later works, however, he suggests that the physical commonality we once felt instinctually (and which is destroyed by the birth of reflection) can be replaced by a new reflectively mediated form of commonality. Rousseau argues that we have the capacity for cognitively based identification with one another through rightly directed amour propre:

> The social affections develop in us only with our knowledge. Pity, although natural to man's heart, would remain eternally inactive without imagination to set it in motion. How do we let ourselves be moved to pity? By transporting ourselves outside ourselves; by identifying with the suffering being. We suffer only to the extent that we judge it to suffer; we suffer not in ourselves but in it. Think how much acquired knowledge this transport presupposes! How could I imagine evils of which I have no idea? How could I suffer when I see another suffer if I do not even know that he suffers, if I do not even know what he and I have in common? Someone who has never reflected cannot be clement, or just, or pitying; nor can he be wicked and vindictive. He who imagines nothing feels only himself; in the midst of mankind he is alone. (*EOL*, 267)

This account of identification depicts it as a reflective and social, rather than a natural, passion. It requires the capacity for *mental*, and not *physical* identification with others. Such a capacity for identification does not presuppose that we feel others' physical sufferings as a sensation in our own bodies; Rousseau even argues that "to pity another's misfortune one doubtless needs to know it, but one does not need to feel it" (*E*, 229). For reflective identification to work, then, I have to "judge" or "know" that another person is suffering in order to feel anything myself. And this capacity presupposes the (mentally dependent) ability to impute sentiments to others that are similar to one's own.

Reflective identification, according to Rousseau, requires three capacities: first, I must conceive of the suffering being as a moral equal; second, I must have the capacity to impute subjective mental states to her merely by judging her situation, that is, from thinking of what I myself would feel in the circumstances; and finally, I must extend myself to her, ceding to her "that sensibility that [I] do not currently need for [myself]" (*E*, 229). This mental extension of our own being is a form of *identification*, and identification requires "transporting oneself out of oneself" (*EOL*, 267), "leaving our own being to take on [another's] being" (*E*, 223), "putting oneself in the place of the being who suffers" (*E*, 221), or "feeling

---

differences, I find it more plausible to side with Starobinski's claim that the accounts of pity are importantly different.

[oneself] in one's fellows" (*E*, 222). All these locutions seem to express the same idea: that one must extend one's own sensibility by experiencing in oneself those sensations one cognizes the other to feel. Because amour propre is aware of and sensitive to the mental contents of others, when rightly directed, it can express itself as an ability to take on the other's point of view, and thereby to feel from within his situation, as it were.

Rousseau argues, then, that one important result of his new theory of education to reflective freedom is that it demonstrates that under conditions of equal dignity and moral standing, amour propre can actually become a social virtue, one that leads individuals to identify with their fellows, and to take others' needs and interests as seriously as their own. In this way, Rousseau suggests that there is a form of commonality that is accessible to reflective human beings and that, given the right circumstances, can perform the functions required of civic solidarity. Through reflective identification, he says, "finally we enter the moral order" (*E*, 235).

Identification in the Freedom Model

After Emile's capacity for reflective identification has developed at his adolescence, his tutor turns to instructing him about politics. In *Emile*, Rousseau develops a model of citizenship in which the individual assumes political obligations consciously and on the basis of a rational understanding of the importance of the state in securing equal freedom. As he reaches adulthood, Emile learns the doctrines of the *Social Contract*, which serve him as the moral standard of justice by which to judge existing institutions. Then he and his tutor undertake a tour of Europe, comparing the positive laws of the various countries he visits to the principles he has learned. The purpose of this tour, Rousseau says, is make sure that Emile's commitment to his own country is a truly reflective and deliberate one. For "by a right which nothing can abrogate, every man, when he comes of age, becomes his own master, free to renounce the contract by which he forms part of the community, by leaving the country in which that contract holds good" (*E*, 455). So Emile leaves his own country—at least temporarily—and spends a full two years traveling to other countries in order to examine their laws and institutions.

He finds, though, that none of the countries he visits have institutions that fully correspond to the principles of the *Social Contract*, and that most states are actually much worse than his own. Even his own state (though we are to understand it is not wholly unjust) does not instantiate the doctrines of the *Social Contract* entirely. After the tour, Emile laments the injustice he has seen in all these countries, and briefly considers the idea of giving up all his property and living as a stateless person, independent and free. But his tutor persuades him that this would be the wrong choice, stating: "Do not say therefore, 'What matter where I am?' It does matter that you should be where you can best do your duty; and one of these duties is to love your native land. Your fellow-countrymen protected you in childhood; you should love them in your manhood" (*E*, 473). At the end of the story, then, Emile decides to assume the inheritance of his father's property, and in doing so, he undertakes a political obligation to his own democratic state, in full cognizance of what he is doing. Having learned the principles of legitimate authority laid out in the *Social Contract*, he understands that a well-ordered state is necessary to define and secure his property rights without subjecting him to private domination by others. And although he laments the fact that he is unable to find an existing state that is fully just, he sees that his own state is a legitimate one, and that he should work as a citizen to improve it.

Rousseau's transformation of Emile from an independent child to a loyal citizen, then, takes a two-pronged approach. First, he offers him a reasoned argument, based on his own interest in freedom, for why he should commit to obeying the laws of a legitimate state; and then, once Emile has undertaken citizenship, Rousseau seeks to show why, having been educated to equality, he will reflectively identify with his fellow citizens and his political institutions. Emile consciously elects to become a citizen: he understands the good *reasons* for allegiance to a legitimate state. And once he is inside the state, if political institutions can successfully neutralize the struggle for domination and substitute relations of equal standing in its place, his amour propre will be transformed into a new kind of sentiment, the moral sentiment of reflective identification. This transformation does not require the construction of a new national identity or shared culture, however. All it requires is that Emile understand the good reasons for his allegiance to his institutions and the importance of concern for his fellow citizens in formulating just and nondominating laws.

Although the "alternative" psychology of amour propre expressed as reflective identification is always a latent possibility for reflective human beings, Rousseau suggests that this relation cannot manifest itself in a state of nature, because the insecurity and uncertainty of power relations among men forces them into an anxious concern with their own security and standing that engenders a struggle for mastery and domination between them. But if the state can establish stable relations of equal dignity among its citizens, Rousseau holds, independent citizens will extend their amour propre to one another, transmuting it into a new form of social virtue:[17] "Extend *amour-propre* to other beings, and we will transform it into a virtue, and there is no human heart in which this virtue does not have its root" (*E*, 252).

Rousseau's account of reflective identification as the expression of amour propre under conditions of equality provides, I believe, precisely the kind of moral psychology necessary to the proper formulation of a general will, on the freedom model.[18] The freedom model of democratic solidarity suggests that citizens who are educated to be reflective, to think of themselves as beings of equal dignity, and to understand the role of democratic institutions in guaranteeing their own freedom will spontaneously be capable of formulating common interests because their amour propre allows them to engage in a kind of reciprocal perspective-taking. The account of moral development that Rousseau offers in *Emile* even goes so far as to suggest that this capacity for identification is a natural result of an autonomous and reflective education. We identify with our moral equals by imputing to them the sentiments we would feel in their situation. Only where this kind of reciprocal perspective-taking occurs can an opinion about the common good be offered from a truly general standpoint. Because each citizen assesses the interests of others from the point of view of her own (imputed) reactions and experiences in their situation, each one's view of the common interest will reflect the idiosyncrasies of her own experience to some degree: that is why assessing the common interest is an interpretive exercise. But what can be drawn from "the sum of the differences" of these interpretations, argues Rousseau, is a general will.

Rousseau further claims that the transformation involved in becoming a citizen of the rational state produces a "most remarkable change in man" by making him into a moral being, whose actions are guided by justice rather than by instinct:

> Only then, when the voice of duty succeeds physical impulsion and right succeeds appetite, does man, who until then had looked only to himself, see himself forced to act on other principles, and to consult his reason before listening to his inclinations. (*SC*, 53)

[17] See also the discussion by Scott in "Rousseau and Melodious Language," 822–29, where he argues that for Rousseau, "the full assimilation of the members into their community rests upon an extension of self-love—love of one's own—to the whole community" (823).

[18] See Arthur Ripstein's brief but intriguing analysis, where he claims that equality solves the problem of recognition created by Rousseau's theory of amour propre, because "equality emerges as the only form of mutual recognition that will allow for stable agents." This passage is in "Universal and General Wills," 448.

For Rousseau, humans become truly moral creatures by entering the state, where they are able to adopt a common standard of right as the guide by which to regulate their actions. But their ability to construct such a standard—to take on "the moral point of view"—in Rousseau's account has certain moral-psychological preconditions. Only when educated to equality and autonomy is the individual able to develop the kind of amour propre that would lead her to see others as something other than competitors to be dominated.

Amour Propre and the Culture Model

The freedom model of civic education holds out the promise that citizens who are brought up to see themselves as moral equals and to understand the role of political institutions in securing their freedom will rationally identify with these institutions and with their compatriots. But in many other political writings, as we noted, Rousseau seems to abandon the view that the education to autonomy and independence envisaged in *Emile* is sufficient to produce the sort of civic solidarity that democratic institutions require. Emile voluntarily elects to become a citizen, since he has been brought to understand the doctrines of the social contract and sees how accepting citizenship will help him to guarantee his own freedom. And he is able to show concern for the needs and interests of his compatriots, not because he believes they share cultural traits, but simply because he reflectively identifies with them. But in other works, Rousseau proposes a variety of motivational supplements to perform these functions: these supplements attach citizens to one another through a nonrational appeal to myths, traditions, and national practices.

In these writings, Rousseau indicates that patriotism, and not reflective identification, is the bond of solidarity that should unify a well-ordered democratic state. In his *Considerations on the Government of Poland*, his *Encyclopédie* article "Économie Politique," and his *Letter to d'Alembert on the Theater* he goes beyond the moral-psychological theory articulated in *Emile* to encourage legislators to use rhetorical techniques to foster love of the *patrie* in citizens. There he claims that the government of a legitimate state must undertake a broad program of public education and indoctrination to promote the identification of citizens with one another and with the state, by creating a separate and distinct national character in them.

In his constitutional proposals for Poland—a country that is subject to the "radical vice" of large size—for example, he recommends the institution of children's games, a national mode of dress, distinctive national religious rites and ceremonies, public festivals, public athletic competitions, and a system of grades and honors bestowed to reward service to the state (*Poland*, 179–86). The aim of these institutions is, at the same time, to introduce "bonds of fraternity" among the "members of the republic" (180), and as importantly, it seems, "to keep [the] people from being absorbed by foreign peoples" (180), "to keep it constantly alert and to make it forever a stranger among other men," and to institute barriers that keep it "separate from its neighbors and [prevent] it from mingling with them" (180). While Rousseau is clear that national characters do not exist naturally, in Poland's case he insists they must be actively *created* after the state has been established, and he claims that a central task of the legislator is to do just this, by prescribing cultural practices down to a manner of national dress. The aim of Rousseau's proposals is to artificially foster a "national physiognomy which will set [the Poles] apart from all other peoples"; this can be done, he postulates, simply by giving "a different bent to [their] passions" (184).

In his *Letter to d'Alembert*, Rousseau likewise emphasizes the importance of the cultural practices in the republic of Geneva, which he claims provide essential support for free government. He asserts that "there is no well-constituted state in which practices are not to be found which are linked to the form of government and help to preserve it" (*Letter*, 98). The practices Rousseau finds essential in Geneva's case are the *cercles*, small, all-male drinking and discussion clubs "that give them occasion to form among themselves dining societies, country outings, and finally, bonds of friendship" (*Letter*, 98), marriage balls, and most importantly large public festivals, which bring substantial portions of the people together face-to-face. He is particularly eloquent about the need for festivals on all possible occasions: to commemorate military prizes, to mark athletic and sailing competitions, even to celebrate around a pole crowned with flowers in the town square. These festivals, he says, are "an important component of the training in law and order and good morals" (130), and they enable citizens "to form among themselves sweet bonds of pleasure and joy," which give citizens reason "to like one another and remain forever united" (125). The festivals ensure that "each sees and loves himself in the others" and therefore that "all societies constitute but one, all become common to all" (126).

It is important to see that, despite his rhetoric, Rousseau is not really a theorist of the importance of cultural identity in the sense we often speak of it today. He is not arguing that linguistic, ethnic, or religious practices have a fundamental role in forming the identity of the individual and deserve our respect. Rousseau does not claim that culture is of any intrinsic value. Instead, he instrumentalizes culture in the service of the state. He therefore articulates a statist, as opposed to a cultural, nationalism. Unlike cultural nationalism, statist nationalism does not focus on the protection that states can provide for national cultures and for members who are interested in adhering to those cultures. Rather, it focuses on the interests states have in the cultural homogeneity of their citizenries, and the contribution that such homogeneity can make toward the realization of political values that are not derived from nor directed at the protection of particular national cultures.[19] Rousseau is interested in the contribution that a common national culture can make to democratic justice. Sharing a culture, he thinks, makes it easier for people to formulate and obey a general will that guarantees their freedom and independence.

Rousseau's instrumental attitude toward national culture can be seen in the fact that insofar as particular cultural practices—such as those of ethnic minorities—could provide focal points for factions or partial associations that might jeopardize the general will, he thinks that they ought to be suppressed, or even coercively destroyed, to make way for a more uniform and undifferentiated national identity. The real point of patriotic education, as he says in the *Letter to d'Alembert*, is to make sure "all societies constitute but one": that there are no factions or partial associations that might divide the citizenry (*Letter*, 126). For this reason, Rousseau recommends the use of what we might think of as "cultural" resources to create a concrete identity *for the state itself*, in order to promote the psychological identification that allows citizens to formulate a view of the common interest that takes everyone's freedom and well-being into account. These cultural resources foster citizens' acceptance of the state over competing smaller associations, by suppressing and destroying partial and factional ties, which might otherwise become the focus of citizens' loyalty and identification.

In this sense, Rousseau is a theorist of "nation building" *avant la lettre*. "Nation building" policies, on the classic definition, attempt to create a unitary citizen identity by instituting (by force if necessary) a uniform system of public education, a common language, universal conscription, and by promoting the assimilative acceptance of state symbols, practices, and traditions by all citizens. In the nineteenth century, the enforced creation of such national identities was often identified as crucial to the success of democratization, since they helped to further the consolidation of the state. Such policies privilege one common national identity over other cultural, regional, or ethnic cleavages that might potentially be politically mobilized. They often involve the use of a combination of coercion, strong economic incentives, and social pressure in order to suppress competing factional or regional identities and to encourage cultural assimilation.

[19] I take this wording, as well as the distinction between "statist" and "cultural" nationalism, from Gans, *The Limits of Nationalism*, 7.

Why does Rousseau think it necessary to institute policies that artificially create a uniform national identity in this way? As we saw in chapter 3, Rousseau argues that all that is formally required to create a relation of "peoplehood" between a set of individuals is their own recognition of a relationship of mutual political obligation: they must severally agree to take the general will of the group as authoritative for their actions. This recognition by each creates a collective actor, a "we"; and nothing more than that is formally necessary. *Ex hypothesi*, then, allegiance to the Rousseauian state is simply loyalty to the general will.[20] On this view, any set of individuals can become a people, if they all agree to recognize the general will of the body they form. At the limit, this could even be a group that is merely fortuitously assembled, individuals who simply happen to find themselves on a given territory together.

But what our overlapping private interests in freedom actually prescribe for us to do collectively, on Rousseau's account, remains indeterminate as long as we have made no attempt to formulate a view about the common interest, to come up with a set of interests that can be reciprocally protected for all. In order to figure out what the collective should will, each individual must be capable of taking on the perspective of all the others, to come up with a view about the interests they can share. In small societies where citizens are sufficiently equal, suggests Rousseau, this mutual reversal of perspectives happens almost as a matter of course; the general will then is almost common knowledge, since citizens' points of view and life situations are very nearly the same. In the *Social Contract*, for instance, Rousseau describes "troops of peasants attending to affairs of State under an oak tree," saying that in such a case, "The first one to propose [a law] only states what all have already sensed" (*SC*, 121). Moreover, because strict equality promotes role-reversal, the institutional inculcation of patriotism through education, festivals, cultural practices, and games is much less emphasized in Rousseau's constitutional plan for Corsica than it is in his writings for Geneva and Poland. In a country like Corsica, where all citizens devote themselves to agriculture, and luxury and personal distinctions do not exist, citizens already share the same condition. Here, perfect equality itself is sufficient for identification; imputing one's own sentiments to others is an easy task because everyone shares exactly (or almost exactly) the same experiences—therefore in Corsica, says Rousseau, "Love of country . . . is cultivated with the fields" (*OC*, 940). No special program of patriotic education is needed.

But in wealthier countries like Poland or Geneva, where luxury and class divisions are already established, and where citizens differ substantially in their experiences and ways of life, factions and partial associa-

[20] Ripstein emphasizes this point. See "Universal and General Wills," 450.

tions present a much greater risk. Here, Rousseau argues that citizen identification needs to be fostered or supplemented; it does not simply occur as a matter of course. The necessary supplement is provided for Poland by the legislator's institutions of a system of public education and the creation of national symbols, festivities, and common cultural practices.[21] Allegiance to these institutions and symbols comes to function as a stand-in for the mutual recognition required to formulate a general will.

The goal of all this artificial inculcation of patriotism is to redirect citizens' amour propre toward the "great and beautiful" object of the public good, and to make citizens feel palpably that their own private interest is the same thing as the good of the state, although they may not understand the reasons why. Rousseau therefore argues that political legislators and constitution-makers—as he sought to be for Poland—should seek to inspire a people with patriotic loyalty. To do this, he says, a legislator must "use neither force not reasoning, he must of necessity have recourse to an authority of a different order, which might be able to rally without violence and persuade without convincing" (*SC*, 71). The persuasion to loyalty and patriotism a legislator should seek to effect, he claims, is best produced through the use of a language of *signs*. Signs and images bring out persuasion without rational argument, and thus without any need to convince. To be motivated to obey the state by an image or sign does not require an understanding of the good reasons for that obedience, only a felt emotion of loyalty. And precisely this use of signs to replace discourse, suggests Rousseau, was an important feature of ancient politics, but it is one that modern peoples have forgotten:

> What the ancients accomplished with eloquence was prodigious. But that eloquence did not consist solely in fine, well-ordered speeches, and never did it have more effect than when the orator spoke least. What was said most vividly was expressed not in words but by signs. One did not say it, one showed it. The object that is exhibited to the eyes shakes the imagination, arouses curiosity, keeps the mind attentive to what is going to be said. (*E*, 322)

By using the language of signs, one can more powerfully arouse the passions than by using the words that stand in for them; this is because signs and images lessen or even erase the moment of representation that is involved in the use of language, and substitute a kind of immediate presence or concreteness. Rousseau even claims that words can approximate the power of signs to some extent, through the use of imagery, tropes, and figural language.

[21] On the notion of supplementarity as a theme in Rousseau, see Derrida, *Of Grammatology*, 141–64.

Rousseau ruminates on the judicious use of signs that was responsible for the Romans' political success: "Different clothing according to ages and according to stations—togas, sagums, praetexts, bullas, laticlaves; thrones, lictors, fasces, axes; crowns of gold or of herbs or of leaves; ovations, triumphs. Everything with them was display, show, ceremony, and everything made an impression on the hearts of the citizens" (*E*, 322). His "nation building" proposals for Poland are little more than a renewal of attention, in the manner of ancient republics, to these sorts of signs. Cultural practices, rites, and festivals are "nonverbal arguments" that can attach citizens' emotions to their fellow citizen and their state. Thus, Rousseau claims that despite subjecting the Spartans to an "iron yoke," Lycurgus was successful because he at the same time "attached [the people] to this yoke, he identified it with it, by always keeping it occupied with it" (*Poland*, 181). Rousseau hopes, then, that the institution of special cultural symbols and rituals will redirect citizens' amour propre toward patriotic identification without the use of reason or argument. The *patrie* simply has to be represented, using all the tropes of concreteness in the form of signs, ceremonies, and rites, to inspire its citizens' loyalty.

By redirecting amour propre toward a culturally and symbolically represented *patrie*, Rousseau thinks a legislator can lead the people to recognize, although perhaps not to understand, a reason for their allegiance. By the use of these motivational supplements, he creates in them a felt rather than an understood sense of solidarity, on the basis of which they will agree to override their various particular wills, without having to be convinced, through a complex chain of reasoning, that their allegiance is actually a necessary condition for securing equal freedom-as-independence:

> It is not enough to tell the citizens, be good; they have to be taught to be so; and example itself, which in this respect is the first lesson, is not the only means that should be used: love of the fatherland is most effective; for as I have already said, every man is virtuous when his particular will conforms in all things to the general will, and we readily want [or will] what the people we love want [or will].[22]

Conclusion

Why does Rousseau ultimately conclude that citizens need to be persuaded into patriotism in order to become self-ruling? In *Emile*, as we saw, he holds out the promise of a purely autonomous form of citizenship,

[22] Rousseau, *Discourse on Political Economy*, 15.

one that is modeled on convincing, and therefore on rational understanding, and not on irrational persuasion. On the "freedom model," a citizen must be able to reflect on and affirm his own political motives from the standpoint of their contribution to ensuring his freedom. Such a citizen can agree to formulate and obey a general will not because he blindly submits to authority, or because he is persuaded into an enthusiasm for symbols and signs, but simply because he is aware of the good reasons for undertaking obligations to the state. The aim of *Emile*, then, is to show how a completely autonomous man will be good for others: why he will understand the necessity of entering the state, be motivated to take the needs and interests of his compatriots into account in legislating on their behalf, and willingly obey their collective judgment about the limits to his civil rights.

But what Rousseau gives with one hand, it seems he takes back with another. In particular, he seems uncertain about whether a pure education for autonomy can truly unify the citizens of a legitimate state, by sufficiently motivating them to a concern for the freedom and well-being of their compatriots and loyalty to democratic laws. Therefore, he is always tempted to supplement an appeal to autonomy with the artificial bonds of a national culture. But these "extra" motivational resources, while compelling, at the same time threaten to subvert the politics of pure self-determination that he values. In the end, Rousseau leaves us unsure: can modern political education really be different from ancient civic education? Can citizens really learn to understand and endorse their political institutions from the perspective of their own freedom? Or must we lapse into a condition where the citizen is not raised to be reflective and free, but instead only to be unconsciously good for the whole?

6

Nationalism or Patriotism?

From the point of view of Kant and Rousseau (properly understood) democratic self-determination does not have the collectivistic and at the same time exclusionary meaning of the assertion of national independence and of the realization of the national character. Rather, it has the inclusive meaning of a legislation which involves all citizens equally.

—Habermas, "On the Relation between the Nation, the Rule of Law, and Democracy"

Like Rousseau himself, contemporary political thinking is torn over the question of whether reflective understanding is enough to provide citizens with a reason for allegiance to their compatriots and institutions or whether additional cultural reasons are also required. The *liberal-nationalist* camp—notably David Miller, Yael Tamir, and Will Kymlicka—claims that citizens' solidarity with their compatriots and allegiance to their particular state can only be justified by an appeal to the ethical importance of national cultures. Indeed, they argue that it is reasonable to maintain separate states in the first place only because these states protect our membership in distinct national cultures. National cultures, on their view, are defined by shared objective features, such as a language, a myth of origin or descent, or a common history, customs, and traditions, together with the subjective awareness that their possession of these features renders a group a distinct "people," whose members have special obligations to one another. To the extent that these objective cultural features are not present, these theorists predict, citizens will have no special reason for allegiance to their particular political institutions or concern for their compatriots. Moreover, liberal nationalists fear that, as an empirical matter, a polity without a shared national culture will be unable to "define itself to itself or to others, and [unable to] inspire or guide collective action."[1] Without a national culture, a democratic state will be ineffective at motivating its citizens to solidarity and political engagement.

Against this, members of the opposing camp—whom we can call *constitutional patriots*—defend the possibility of a political identity built solely

[1] Smith, *Ethnic Origins of Nations*, 25.

on shared citizenship.[2] On their view, citizens ought to show allegiance to their political institutions whenever those institutions embody principles of justice that are justifiable to all citizens as free and equal persons. For constitutional patriots, the citizen's understanding of the important role of the democratic state in defining his civil rights and securing his freedom provides him perfectly sufficient reason for allegiance to it and for solidarity with his compatriots. No additional invocation of a national culture is required. On their view, the "nation" is just an artificial collective created by the subjection of a group of rights-bearing individuals to a set of democratic institutions. The state's civic unity, then, is wholly given by its members' political and legal relation to one another—the relation of being both author of, and subject to, a body of sufficiently just laws.

Jürgen Habermas is perhaps the best-known contemporary advocate of constitutional patriotism in this sense: he argues that a citizen can be loyal to a particular democratic state on grounds of principle, without reference to any shared culture or national identity.[3] He claims, for example, that new immigrants to a liberal society should not be required to assimilate to majority cultural practices, but instead must simply "assent to the principles of the constitution within the scope of interpretation determined at a particular time."[4] John Rawls advances a similar notion of political community: for him, individuals are members of a political community if they endorse the conception of justice on which their institutions are based, and identify with their institutions and their fellow citizens for this reason.[5] So long as a citizen judges that her own state is well constituted—that it institutes a legal framework that accords with background principles of justice—then she is justified in her allegiance to that particular state. *Anyone*, no matter what his or her cultural or ethnic identity, is eligible to be a participant in a civic state.

The Liberal-Nationalist Challenge

Liberal nationalists have criticized purely justice-based accounts of civic unity like those put forward by Habermas and Rawls, however, on the basis that shared values and institutions are in the end insufficient to provide citizens with any good reason for their commitment to their particu-

[2] Advocates of this view include Ignatieff, *Blood and Belonging*, 5–9; Barry, *Culture and Equality*, 79–109; Mason, *Community, Solidarity, and Belonging*, 115–47.

[3] Habermas, "On the Relation." See also Cronin, "Democracy and Collective Identity."

[4] Habermas, "Struggles for Recognition," 228.

[5] For this view of Rawls's account of political community, see Mason, *Community, Solidarity, and Belonging*, 68.

lar state over other, equally just states. Why don't persons who value justice have equally good reasons to support *all* just states? What gives them a special reason to support their particular state? In light of this critique, nationalists argue that in addition to shared liberal values and institutions, a reference to a shared *national culture* is indispensable in providing citizens with a special reason to support one state over another.

Most nationalists identify national culture with certain objective characteristics that they believe members must share if the group of which they are members is to qualify as a nation. Yael Tamir declares:

> In the present work, a group is defined as a nation if it exhibits both a sufficient number of shared, objective characteristics—such as *language, history, or territory*—and self-awareness of its distinctiveness. An occasional group of individuals lacking any shared characteristics cannot, merely by the power of its will, turn into a nation.[6]

Will Kymlicka likewise argues that nationhood consists in certain objectively shared features. He defines the nation as "an intergenerational community, more or less institutionally complete, occupying a given *territory* or homeland, sharing a distinct *language* and *history*."[7] Although a bit more abstract about the nature of the characteristics in question, David Miller too defines the nation as a "community (1) constituted by shared belief and mutual commitment, (2) extended in *history*, (3) active in character, (4) connected to a particular *territory*, and (5) marked off from other communities by its distinct public *culture*."[8] What unifies these theorists is that they believe the defining feature of a nation is a shared set of objective characteristics of a certain kind—centrally a common language, history, myths, customs, or territory—which mark one group off from another, and mark the group as "national." What gives their thesis bite is not the simple claim that a group will share some features we can label a "culture." It is the claim that these cultural features have to be *national* features: language, history, myths, territory, and so on. While virtually all theorists of nationalism note that no one definitive set of these commonalities can be singled out as necessary for the existence of a nation, most of them do agree that any group that could be called national will display a "sufficient number" of them.[9]

Nationalist thinkers generally go on to offer two sorts of arguments for why cultural nationhood ought to be recognized as an important background element in liberal theories of justice. Their first argument claims

[6] Tamir, *Liberal Nationalism*, 69.
[7] Kymlicka, *Multicultural Citizenship*, 18.
[8] Miller, *On Nationality*, 27.
[9] Tamir, *Liberal Nationalism*, 65.

that access to a national culture is a necessary condition for individual freedom and autonomy. Their second, more persuasive, argument maintains that a theory of cultural nationhood is an important supplement to liberal theories of justice. Essentially, liberal nationalists have claimed that key particularity assumptions in liberal-democratic theory—like the legitimacy of borders and immigration restrictions, allegiance to our own particular states, and redistribution to needy compatriots—can only be justified if we assume that citizens share a national identity and that this identity is of ethical significance. Since I find their first set of arguments to be unconvincing, I will only briefly outline them, and turn then to focus on the second aspect of the nationalists' case. It is this aspect that most directly challenges a justice-based view.

Freedom, Autonomy, and the Nation

Most liberal nationalists argue that a national culture is an important prerequisite for the exercise of individual autonomy. In order to be autonomous, we must be capable of making choices among a sufficient range of options about how to live and which kinds of roles to inhabit. But we make these choices based on our preexisting beliefs about the value of these options, and nationalists argue that we derive our evaluative criteria largely from the culture in which we grow up. On the nationalist argument, then, cultures play an indispensable role in preparing us to be free persons, because they create the standards of value and meaning by which we choose our goals and projects. As Kymlicka puts this point, "It is only through having access to a societal culture that people have access to a range of meaningful options."[10] Nationalists go on to draw the conclusion that since it is only within such cultures that we can make effective autonomous choices, national cultures must be an indispensable precondition for liberal freedom.

Of course, this argument only establishes the need for some culture, not a particular culture and definitely not a national one, but nationalists also point out that in the modern world, people tend to live in national cultures, that they are likely to be identified or "pigeonholed" based on their national affiliations, and that adopting a new national culture can be a long and arduous process. Slighting or belittling a person's culture, or forcing him to assimilate into a new one, on their view, is coercive and disrespectful. These reasons are strong enough to justify holding other people to be under a duty to respect the individual's "right to culture": she should have a right to express her membership of her national

[10] Kymlicka, *Multicultural Citizenship*, 83.

culture publicly, and to live in a context where this culture is politically recognized in some way.[11]

The basic problem with the nationalist argument for the intrinsic value of national culture is, I believe, well recognized: it equivocates between rightly acknowledging the need for some kind of society and culture in which autonomous individuals can develop to maturity and exercise their capacity for choice, and the claim that the only kind of society that can fit the bill is a national culture, one marked by the "objective commonalities" of language, shared history, myths, and territory. This last claim seems distinctly odd. Most of us know individuals (we may even be one) who grew up in the context of more than one national culture—perhaps they had parents from two different countries, perhaps they moved from one country to another—without noticeable scarring effects on their identity or their capacity to make autonomous choices for themselves. Beginning from the example of these individuals, we might ask the question: what harm is actually done to individuals (especially to children, with whose education these arguments are primarily concerned) by exposing them to more than one national culture? If the answer is "There is no harm done," then it is very difficult to see what case can be made to support the thesis that educating children into a national culture different from their ancestral one is somehow wronging them. And if children are not wronged by being exposed to different national cultures, then respecting their autonomy does not require that the state preserve their adherence to the national culture of their parents.

While it is true that individuals do require a cultural context in order to flourish and to choose their life pursuits from among meaningful options, every historically existing society has provided its inhabitants with some such cultural context, whether it was a national, multinational, or nonnational one. As long as human life, with its inherently interpretive aspect, exists, so will human culture, and the corresponding range of roles, aspirations, and life projects that cultures create and make meaningful to us. Yet nationalists often argue as if their opponents proposed the abolition of culture altogether. To say that individuals must have access to some sociocultural context in order to flourish does not establish that this culture must be a national one, or that national cultures are intrinsically more valuable than other kinds. Indeed, that view seems to be defeated by the fact that those individuals who do not grow up in an environment permeated by one single and unitary national culture don't seemed to have suffered for it.[12] If we are deliberating about whether to

[11] For versions of this argument, see Tamir, *Liberal Nationalism*, 35–45; Kymlicka, *Politics in the Vernacular*, 227–28; Margalit and Raz, "National Self-Determination," 450.

[12] For a similar argument, see Waldron, "Minority Cultures."

preserve national cultures or to facilitate the creation of some new, more hybrid cultural form, the argument from individual autonomy and choice seems to give us no guidance in choosing between these options, since autonomy can be secured in both.

Nationalism as a Necessary Supplement to Liberal Theory

Nationalists are much more successful, however, with their second argument, which claims that a premise about the ethical importance of nationality must be added to liberal theory if liberals are to justify the assumption that citizens have a good reason for allegiance to their particular state over other, equally just states, and that citizens have special reasons to show solidarity with their compatriots. On this front, liberal nationalists argue that shared cultural identity gives us a key argument for why citizens belong together—a reason that goes beyond the mere fact that they happen to share a just state—and that such a reason is in fact necessary to justify citizens' particular allegiances.[13] This, they argue, is because cultural identity helps to resolve questions about membership, distributive justice, and political obligations, about which liberal principles of justice alone have little or nothing to say.

The general form of the nationalist argument goes something like this: consider for a moment the case of Norway and Sweden. These are both reasonably just and legitimate states, according to the criteria we laid out in part 1, and the two countries and their citizens share a high degree of convergence in their social and political values, including principles of justice. But this fact, by itself, provides no reason why Norway and Sweden should or should not (re)unite to form one political society.[14] To answer *that* question one way or another—whether Norway and Sweden should be one state or two—we have to ask the question, "With whom do the inhabitants of these countries have special reason to associate?" Nationalists claim that giving an answer requires us to look beyond liberal values to national identity. National identity, it is claimed, gives each member a special, prepolitical relationship to her conationals—a bond derived from a group's shared characteristics and history—in addition to their shared values.[15] It is the additional "factor X" that, when combined

[13] For discussion of this premise in liberal-nationalist thought, see Mason, *Community, Solidarity, and Belonging*, 117.

[14] The Norway/Sweden example comes from Norman, "Ideology of Shared Values." Similar arguments are made by Yack, "Myth of Civic Nation," 108–9; and Kymlicka, *Politics in the Vernacular*, 262.

[15] Most scholarship on the historical roots of nationalism would lead one to question the idea that nationality is really prepolitical, since many nations were created by the modern-

with liberal principles, gives us a sufficient reason to establish and support a political community together with a *particular* group of others, our conationals. As Yael Tamir puts it, "States can only justify their separate existence on national grounds."[16] Without an appeal to national identity, there seems to be no good reason—on liberal principles alone—why we should support one just state over another, or even have more than one state at all.

Beginning from this argument, liberal nationalists have argued that a national-cultural identity is also necessary to underpin a good number of other liberal-democratic assumptions:

1. *Bounded distributive justice.* Most liberal-democratic states enact redistributive schemes that benefit only their members, not the members of other states. But a simple adherence to liberal principles of justice—paradigmatically, a commitment to the value of equal respect and concern for all human beings—might seem, on the cosmopolitan arguments we canvassed in the introduction, to commit liberals to a global scheme of redistribution. Yael Tamir has argued that national identity is necessary to explain why duties of distributive justice extend only to compatriots, as we tend to take for granted, and not to all human beings everywhere. Only if liberal states have some special reason to care more about their members than about outsiders can bounded schemes of distributive justice be justified. According to Tamir, this reason is provided once we recognize nationality's moral force. For her, "The 'others' whose welfare we ought to consider most highly are those whose associative [national] identity we share.[17]

2. *Immigration restrictions.* Tamir also suggests that although liberal political theory adopts the fiction that the state arises from a voluntary contract among individuals, which they can enter or leave at will, the practices of liberal-democratic states do not accord with their "voluntarist" theory. No existing liberal democracy is currently willing to accord membership to anyone who simply shows up wishing to "join."[18] A more consistent liberal practice, she argues, would advocate the removal of immigration restrictions to better approximate a voluntarist theory. When the importance of national culture is factored in, however, the situation

---

ization activities of the modern state. But most sophisticated nationalists would acknowledge this. They divide on the question of whether this fact justifies some level of nation-building activities in the present to legitimize the boundaries of the state (David Miller); or supports political devolution to substate nationalities because nation-building is likely to be unsuccessful (Will Kymlicka; Yael Tamir).

[16] Tamir, *Liberal Nationalism*, 123.

[17] Tamir, *Liberal Nationalism*, 121.

[18] Tamir, *Liberal Nationalism*, 127.

looks different. If preserving national cultures is morally important, then liberal states should not open their borders to any newcomer who is willing to join, but instead should restrict membership to ensure the survival of their common way of life.

3. *Political obligations.* As a matter of common sense, we often suppose ourselves to have political obligations to support and uphold the institutions of our own country. Liberal theorists have sometimes attempted to account for this intuition, in a manner analogous to the Kantian-Rousseauian theory we presented in part 1, by arguing that we have obligations to those institutions to which free and equal individuals could hypothetically consent.[19] John Rawls, for example, argues that all persons have a "natural duty of justice" to support political institutions that conform to principles of justice chosen, by hypothetical consent, in an imagined original position.[20] But Tamir and other nationalists question how a natural duty of justice could ever account for our having political obligations to our own states. The natural-duty argument seems to entail that we ought to support all states that are sufficiently just and fair, or perhaps the one that is most just or fair, not necessarily our own.[21] But Tamir claims that citizens do have reason to assume special obligations to their *own* state (at least as long as it is a nation-state) because they identify with the national community it represents, and this gives them important obligations to their conationals.[22]

Miller and Tamir believe that invoking nationhood can solve the various problems outlined above—explaining why borders fall where they do, why some immigration restrictions are justified, why we have reason to redistribute preferentially to compatriots, and why we ought to support political institutions in our own country, not in just states everywhere—because nations are "ethical communities." Membership in a culturally defined nation, on their view, entails special ethical obligations to our conationals.[23] Miller stipulates that nationhood, like many other sorts of memberships and attachments, gives us an obligation to attribute

[19] There are other liberal theories of political obligation, including theories of actual consent, fair play, and gratitude, but they are extraneous to the argument here. For a discussion of these various arguments, see again Simmons, *Moral Principles and Political Obligations*.

[20] Rawls, *A Theory of Justice*, 333–42.

[21] This argument originally derives from Simmons's work on political obligation. He criticizes the natural duty argument similarly: "A natural duty of justice binds me to support all just institutions, wherever they may be. It can bind me no more to one set of just political institutions than to any other" (*Moral Principles and Political Obligations*, 155–66).

[22] Tamir, *Liberal Nationalism*, 135. The idea that national identification could provide a reason for obedience to law originally comes from Joseph Raz. See Raz, *The Morality of Freedom*, 94–99.

[23] Tamir, *Liberal Nationalism*, 88.

more weight to the interests of our conationals than to those of other people.[24] National obligations, for them, spring from the sense of identity and relatedness that leads conationals to see themselves as one group: "Seeing myself as a member, I feel a loyalty to the group, and this expresses itself, among other things, in my giving special weight to the interests of fellow-members."[25]

Miller and Tamir claim that when more formal schemes of justice are superimposed on a national community—as when the boundaries of the nation coincide with the state—the obligations that conationals already have to one another will provide members a special reason to support their particular institutions, and the members of their particular national community, and not other just institutions or their members.[26] In this case, the special obligations that conationals already owe to one another provide a firm basis for their allegiance to common political institutions and for compliance with the state's demands for redistribution to compatriots.[27]

Assessing the Nationalist Challenge

The crucial part of the liberal-nationalist case turns on the assertion that the constitutional patriot cannot explain why citizens have sufficient reason for allegiance to their particular institutions on the basis of an appeal to the value of democratic justice alone. This charge, in turn, assumes that a commitment to a universal value cannot justify allegiance to particular groups or schemes, or special obligations to fellow participants within those schemes. Since we do tend to believe that we have special reason to show allegiance to our particular institutions, some element of ethical partiality seems necessary to account for these convictions, and the idea of irreducible ethical obligations that flow from our identification with a national group is brought in by liberal nationalists to shore up these political beliefs.

In the next chapter, I will dispute the assumption that a commitment to universal principles of justice cannot justify allegiance to particular institutions, or special obligations to those with whom we share them. Before I present my own account, however, it is worth getting a clear view of the difficulties with the argument for special ethical obligations

[24] In this sense, Miller and Tamir opt for an account of ethics in which duties are derived, not from universal principles, but from facts about individual's identities, relations, and roles. For discussion of this, see Wellman, "Magic in Pronoun 'My,"' 540.

[25] Miller, *On Nationality*, 65.

[26] Miller, *On Nationality*, 83.

[27] Miller, *On Nationality*, 85.

to conationals. The main problem with the Miller-Tamir thesis is that it does not explain how a sense of identity and cultural relatedness could actually ground any political obligations. There are at least four kinds of problems with the view that simply identifying with a group is sufficient to create special obligations to it.

First, on Tamir's view, I have special obligations to any group with which I identify, including evil groups, like the Mafia.[28] But we would surely want to say that my identification with the Mafia does not give me any obligation to do what it expects of its members (like carrying out hits on rival factions). Instead, we think my identification is wrong, and should be revised. Surely only morally acceptable associations can impose obligations on their members to do what the association expects; otherwise, we would be faced with the difficult problem of justifying an entire set of supposed obligations to do wrong. And how would we then balance these against our moral duties to do right?

Second, on Miller's view, the content of our special obligations to conationals is fixed wholly by the self-understanding of the group. Different national groups may have very different understandings of what their ethical obligations to one another are, and for Miller, these beliefs are dispositive in settling the question of what obligations members are actually under:

> Some national cultures may attach value to individual self-sufficiency, for example, and will therefore construe their members' obligations to one another mainly in terms of providing the conditions under which individuals can fashion their own lives; others will lay greater stress on collective goods, and regard compatriots as having duties to involve themselves in various forms of national service.[29]

For him, then, since the American nation by and large does not acknowledge an obligation to provide health care to fellow citizens, its members have no such obligation. But that seems wrong: we don't think the existence of obligations is grounded in the fact of a group's beliefs about their obligations, but rather in the (objective) good reasons for those obligations' existence. A particular group's beliefs about their obligations could just be incorrect. To construe the truth about what national obligations exist as established by people's beliefs about these obligations is not only unduly relativist; it also invites questions about whether or not we can individuate cultural wholes with one unitary set of understandings about their members' obligations. Moreover, Miller's account is unfaithful to the way in which citizens actually debate their obligations to one another.

[28] Tamir, *Liberal Nationalism*, 101.

[29] Miller, *On Nationality*, 69.

They do not take themselves to be arguing about the social fact of what the nation already thinks, but rather about what the best account of their mutual obligations actually is, even if that account differs from what most people currently believe. It is logically consistent to argue that Americans do have an obligation to provide national health care, for example, even though they don't currently recognize such an obligation. No one would be confused or misunderstand the speaker's meaning in this case, in which the term *obligation* indicates that he is not referring to the social fact of his fellow citizens' beliefs.

Third, we should ask ourselves whether it is plausible to think I violate a special obligation to my conationals when I emigrate, or when I assimilate into another national community, as Miller's thesis entails.[30] He goes so far as to say that

> because our forebears have toiled and spilt their blood to build and defend the nation, we who are born into it inherit an obligation to continue their work. . . . This then means that, if we are going to speak of the nation as an ethical community, we are talking not merely about a community of the kind that exists between a group of contemporaries who practise mutual aid among themselves, and that would dissolve at the point at which such practise ceased; but about a community that, because it stretches back and forward across the generations, is not one that the present generations can renounce.[31]

Indeed a strict reading of Miller's view would saddle individuals with unrenounceable obligations to their ancestors, a position that seems wholly irreconcilable with liberal ideals of individual freedom. It does not seem that as a general matter, I owe my conationals any account of the cultural choices I make, or that they have standing to rebuke me for these choices. To argue that I am under an unrenounceable obligation to continue the way of life of my ancestors is, as we saw in chapter 1, to negate the liberal commitment to each person's freedom to choose the shape of his own life.

Finally, on Tamir's more voluntarist conception of national obligations, these obligations bind a person only if he identifies with the group. But one might ask what happens when an "objective" member—one who shares the relevant cultural characteristics—does not identify with the group. We generally take parents, for example, to have special obligations to their children, of the sort to which Miller and Tamir appeal. But con-

[30] In a footnote, Miller suggests that I do violate national obligations by emigrating, but that this prima facie wrong is overridden by the need to protect individual freedom. Miller, *On Nationality*, 42.

[31] Miller, *On Nationality*, 23.

sider the case of Deadbeat Dad, who no longer identifies with or loves his children. Is he no longer under any obligation to support and care for them? Most of us would say he must still do so, no matter how subjectively identified with them he feels. If we are right, then special obligations to family members, and perhaps other special obligations as well, do not rest wholly on subjective identification. At the very least, some more nuanced account of how we can divest ourselves of these obligations—surely not just by altering our mental state?—must be given.

Liberal Nationalism: Functional and Normative Claims

Liberal-nationalist arguments all pursue (and often equivocate between) two basic strategies: a normative strategy—which we have just examined—and a more motivational one. Claims that nationhood is necessary to explain boundaries, redistributive duties, and political obligations invoke the nation in order to solve certain difficulties in the normative theory of liberal democracy. Liberals, it is argued, lack a compelling moral explanation for boundaries and differential obligations, and appealing to the cultural nation can help us to fill this gap. Moreover, the claim that nationhood is necessary for individual freedom and choice aims to shows us that the cultural nation is an object of intrinsic moral value. But liberal nationalists often go beyond this to argue that nationhood is also an important motivator of democratic sacrifice and trust, and therefore is *empirically necessary* for the pursuit of liberal-democratic goals. Here, instead of invoking moral considerations, nationalists offer a empirical argument about motivation, by pointing to certain problems of commitment and sacrifice in a democracy that they hold can best be overcome by fostering a national identity. The argument is that democracy requires some solidaristic motivation in its citizens order to function effectively and that only a common national identity can generate it.

David Miller, Will Kymlicka, and Margaret Canovan have emphasized that our voluntary compliance with certain demands that the democratic state places upon us—especially demands for our tax money to support redistributive programs, and for our obedience to correctly enacted, but perhaps unpopular, laws—requires a willingness to sacrifice our own private and strategic interests in favor of the interests of our state or our compatriots. As citizens of a social-democratic welfare state, for example, we are required to make significant monetary sacrifices on behalf of those whom we do not know and will perhaps never meet. Similarly, a willingness to obey a legitimate democratic law with which one disagrees presupposes a trust that the law reflects a considered view about the common good of the polity, rather than the narrow and exploitative interest of a majority. Charles Taylor puts the point this way:

> Let's first of all take the case where the attempt is made to live out the principle of popular sovereignty through a representative democracy. The nature of this kind of society, as in any other free society, is that it requires a certain degree of commitment on the part of its citizens. Traditional despotisms could ask of people only that they remain passive and obey the laws. A democracy, ancient or modern, has to ask more. It requires that its members be motivated to make the necessary contributions: of treasure (in taxes), sometimes blood (in war); and it expects always some degree of participation in the process of governance. . . . So democracies require a relatively strong commitment on the part of their citizens. In terms of identity, citizenship has to rate as an important component of who they are.[32]

According to liberal nationalists, the only consideration that is capable of reliably motivating citizens to act beyond their self-interest in the way Taylor describes—the only reliable source of democratic solidarity and trust—is a shared national culture. This is so, liberal nationalists claim, because the nation is the largest community of common belonging available in the contemporary world. No other social identity in modern times, according to Will Kymlicka and Christine Straehle, "has been able to motivate ongoing sacrifices beyond the level of kin groups and confessional groups."[33] As Canovan puts it, the cultural nation is the "battery" on which liberal democracies run.[34]

This distinction between liberal nationalists' normative and motivational arguments is important, because if we reject the nationalists' normative claims, as I will argue we should, then we are left with the view that the nation is not particularly valuable in itself; rather it merely serves as a useful vehicle for solving certain motivational problems in democratic states. But should some equally useful equivalent be offered—one that was capable of motivating citizens to act beyond their strategic interests and leading them to sacrifice for their fellow citizens—then, on the basis of this motivational argument, we really ought to be indifferent between the nation and this proffered alternative. If there actually does exist some motivational alternative to cultural nationhood, then, liberal nationalism's power to convince must stand or fall with the intrinsic moral value of national cultures and their normative status as important sources of obligation.

[32] Taylor, "Nationalism and Modernity," 39.
[33] Kymlicka and Straehle, "Cosmopolitanism," 69.
[34] Canovan, *Nationhood and Political Theory*, 80.

In my view, it is their motivational thesis that grants nationalist arguments much of its persuasive power, and indeed, persuades many readers to attend carefully to their more controversial normative claims. But evaluating their motivational thesis is actually more difficult than it might seem. One problem is that while nationalists abundantly assert that a shared national culture is a necessary condition to motivate citizens to act together politically, they provide little hard evidence to prove that this is in fact so. And when faced with the empirical evidence of functioning democracies—as for instance, Canada, India, Switzerland, or Belgium—that seem to work reasonably well without a shared national culture, David Miller, for example, retreats to the claim that these polities function because they share a national identity, although not a national culture:

> Belgium, Canada, and Switzerland work as they do partly because they are *not* simply multinational, but have cultivated common national identities alongside communal ones, and partly because they have developed institutions (federalism, decentralization) to ensure that each community has its interests protected against incursions by the rest.[35]

Thus Miller argues that the Swiss think of themselves as *Swiss*, an identity that is superimposed upon their linguistic, religious, and cantonal allegiances, and that this identity ensures political unity among them.

The problem, of course, is that if the liberal nationalist concedes the viability of multinational democratic polities like Switzerland, then this concession seems to fatally compromise his main thesis, which is that no legitimate democracy can successfully motivate people to care about citizenship unless it is based on objective commonalities of the proper national type. If Miller allows that nations like Canada, Switzerland, or Belgium work because they share a political identity, then he is conceding that a functional political identity that is not a cultural one does in fact exist. If multinational democracies can be based on a political identity, then Miller's thesis about the indispensability of a national culture must be incorrect.[36]

But despite the existence of empirical examples that on the surface seem to contradict their thesis, liberal nationalists have remained skeptical of the possibility of functional alternatives to the nation. They argue that any form of identification that did not depend on a shared culture would be "bloodless," "overly abstract," "could not act as a substitute for national attachments," and would "lack cohesion."[37] Nationalists, more-

[35] Miller, *On Nationality*, 96.

[36] Arash Abizadeh makes this point. See Abizadeh, "Does Liberal Democracy Presuppose," 498.

[37] For these claims, see Canovan, *Nationhood and Political Theory*, 87–97.

over, persistently characterize any possible "liberal" account of political unity as one that is based solely on "universal principles," and that commits us to supporting just states everywhere.[38] But principles, complains Miller, do nothing to "give us a historical location, particularly in socially and geographically fluid societies where older source of identity such as those of family and neighborhood are weakened."[39] Indeed, without nationality, Miller claims, we must succumb to

> a view of the world as a kind of giant supermarket in which different goods and services are on offer in different places, and in which it is perfectly reasonable for individuals to gravitate to whatever place offers them the best package. On this view, national ties should count for nothing except perhaps in so far as they affect the range of cultural goods on offer in a particular place. For reasons that will be apparent, I regard such an outlook as pathological.[40]

Yet arguing that citizenship can provide the only source of unity in the democratic state is not necessarily equivalent to arguing that citizens identify solely with universal principles of justice. Instead, the fundamental locus of identification may be with a particular democratic process through which citizens act together to define their civil rights. If it is possible for citizens to identify with a particular polity even in the absence of a cultural nation, then the argument that a shared national culture is a necessary motivational condition for a successful democracy will have failed.

Constitutional Patriotism: The Redirective Interpretation

Since the nationalists' motivational thesis is at best unproven, this leaves open the possibility that we might accept Rousseau's theory as the correct account of legitimate authority in the democratic state, while denying that his thickly "patriotic" solution to the problems of democratic solidarity and allegiance is one we are constrained to accept. This very strategy is the one pursued in the account of *constitutional patriotism* recently put forward by Jürgen Habermas. Rousseau's main idea—that legitimate law can only be based on generalizable interests, which citizens must define for themselves in an exercise of democratic sovereignty—remains alive and well today in theories of deliberative democracy, like Habermas's or

[38] Tamir, *Liberal Nationalism*, 118.
[39] Miller, *On Nationality*, 165.
[40] Miller, *On Nationality*, 165.

Rawls's, which appeal to public reason.[41] Likewise alive and well, or so I will argue in what follows, is the problem of democratic solidarity, which Habermas's theory confronts anew. Beginning in the late 1980s, in his writings on politics and law, Habermas began to introduce the idea of a political motivation called constitutional patriotism, which he sees as essential to democratic politics.[42] Like Rousseau, he links the presence of this motivation in democratic citizens with the project of justifying the state as legitimate, that is, with providing a warrant that each citizen can accept for the state's application of coercive force and a reason for her cooperation in obeying and enforcing the laws.[43]

But Habermas's theory of constitutional patriotism has been widely misunderstood and has often been identified with a cosmopolitanism of human rights of the sort we examined in chapter 1 through the work of Martha Nussbaum or Simon Caney. Readings in this vein usually interpret Habermas's account as taking the form of a "strategy of redirection."[44] Patchen Markell indicates that such a strategy "claims to render affect safe for liberal democracies by redirecting our attachment and sentiment" from a prepolitical community described in ethnic or cultural terms and toward a civic community defined solely by its citizens' attachment to constitutional principles of human rights. On the "redirective" interpretation, Habermas's project is to weld universal moral norms, as these are contextualized in existing constitutions, to an affectively motivating citizen identity built around them. Constitutional patriotism, on this view, would be a sort of "constitutional faith": it would connect citizens' loyalty with abstract norms through an act of identification with their constitution.[45] But there are problems with this reading: if the bounds of our political identity are be determined by citizens' affective attachment to certain principles, then it remains unclear how Habermas could respond to criticisms along the lines of the nationalists' Norway/Sweden example. For the citizens of Norway and Sweden are surely attached to much the same set of principles, in the way the redirective view suggests. So why do they not share the same political identity?

[41] The debt to Rousseau is not only apparent in Habermas's work. Joshua Cohen, for example, has taken Rousseau as a model for his attempt to interpret Rawls's theory of public reason as an account of deliberative democracy. See "Deliberation and Democratic Legitimacy," 67–91.

[42] Habermas, *Between Facts and Norms*, appendix 2, "Citizenship and National Identity"; "The European Nation-State"; "On the Relation"; "Struggles for Recognition"; and "Postnational Constellation."

[43] See Michelman, "Morality, Identity," for an argument about how the problems of political justification and constitutional patriotism are connected in Habermas's work.

[44] Markell, "Making Affect Safe," 39.

[45] On this idea, see Levinson, *Constitutional Faith*.

This line of argument has become a very widespread objection to Habermas's idea. David Miller, for example, has characterized constitutional patriotism in this light:

> A constitution usually contains a statement of principles and a delineation of the institutions that will enact them. The principles themselves are likely to be general in form, more or less the common currency of liberal democracies. Subscribing to them marks you out as a liberal rather than a fascist or an anarchist, but it does not provide the kind of political identity that nationality provides. In particular, it does not explain why the boundaries of the political community should fall here rather than there; nor does it give you any sense of the historical identity of the community, the links that bind present-day politics to decisions made and actions performed in the past.[46]

Bernard Yack likewise subscribes to the "redirective" view of Habermas's political project, but Yack goes so far as to suggest that Habermas actually contradicts himself when he claims that constitutional principles must be situated within "the horizon of the history of a nation," since according to Yack, "this statement clearly implies that the audience for arguments about the focus of political loyalty is not some random association of individuals united only by allegiance to shared principles, but a prepolitical community."[47] Those who interpret Habermas as pursuing a redirective strategy take this to be a fatally damning criticism: if political unity is simply a matter of identifying with liberal principles, then how can constitutional patriotism ever account for our loyalty to any particular liberal democracy over any other? Indeed, Yack claims that Habermas's account is incapable of explaining events in his own country: if the German *Wiedervereinigung* were explicable solely in civic-universalist terms, then why did East Germany choose to join West Germany rather than Poland or the former Czechoslovakia?[48]

Despite its widespread acceptance, I will argue—in broad agreement with recent articles by Patchen Markell and Ciaran Cronin—that the redirective interpretation of constitutional patriotism is at best simplistic, and at worst incorrect.[49] The redirective interpretation overlooks the impor-

[46] Miller, *On Nationality*, 163.

[47] Yack, "Myth of Civic Nation," 108.

[48] Yack, "Myth of Civic Nation," 108.

[49] See Markell, "Making Affect Safe"; and Cronin, "Democracy and Collective Identity." Both authors argue that Habermas's theory should be interpreted in the light of his procedural account of law, and that constitutional patriotism describes an allegiance to the democratic *process* rather than to abstract universal principles. As will be clear, I agree with much of what they have to say. My account differs from theirs, however, in placing a much greater stress on Habermas's view of rights and on his debt to a Rousseauian understanding of legitimate democracy.

tance of particular democratic processes in defining our rights and in providing a focus for our allegiance as citizens. In so doing, it presupposes a "moral" account of rights that Habermas has explicitly rejected in his theory of law. And by discarding the redirective interpretation in favor of an account that emphasizes the importance of citizenship as collective democratic participation, as I will show in the next chapter, we can reject the criticism that constitutional patriotism cannot account for particular political loyalties.

Morality and Law

The intuitive picture of constitutional patriotism presented by the redirective interpretation relies on there being a determinate set of prepolitical human rights that exist prior to being embedded in a constitution and that are knowable to us wholly through moral reflection. These moral principles can be fleshed out in a familiar way as including protection of freedom of religion, bodily integrity, the right to speak freely, and so forth. On this view, it is the inclusion of these determinately specified human rights in any constitution that grants it its legitimacy. Insofar as citizens identify with their constitution, then, they are meant to identify with these moral principles in a form mediated by their sentiments and political history, and they become loyal to them. Of course, universal moral rights are meant to be applied in a given political context, and according to the redirective interpretation, that will lend them a particular shape that will differ somewhat from one legal system to another. As we mentioned in chapter 1, the constitutional right to freedom of speech in the United States protects the right to acts of racist speech, for example, while in Canada it does not.[50] But the redirective view sees both countries' constitutions as engaged in the very same project: welding their citizens' identities with an invariant moral principle—the right to free speech—which is interpreted slightly differently depending on context.

In choosing principles as the locus of citizens' identification, however, the redirective view overlooks Habermas's emphasis on the moral importance of democratic institutions and on the legal status of citizenship. Like Rousseau, Habermas views citizenship as a morally significant category because he thinks that democracy establishes a regulative ideal of political legitimacy, which holds "that only those statutes may claim legitimacy that can meet with the assent of all citizens in a discursive process of legislation that has in turn been legally constituted."[51] Well-constituted

[50] Michelman, "Morality, Identity," 269.
[51] Habermas, *Between Facts and Norms*, 110.

democracies aim to satisfy what Habermas calls the "idealizing presuppositions" of moral discourse so that the outcomes of democratic politics can carry a presumption to legitimate authority. These presuppositions specify that everyone affected by the law must be able to take part in its enactment, that everyone be able to participate and introduce any assertion into democratic debate, and that no one be prevented, through coercion, from exercising these rights. If these guarantees are sufficiently institutionalized, then democratic laws carry a (fallible) epistemic warrant to moral validity, because they are the product of a process of rational will-formation.

Moreover, Habermas has claimed that conceiving of democracy in this way necessitates drawing a firm distinction between law and morality. Democratic law, he suggests, should accord with morality, or have a moral basis—indeed, it must do so if it is to be legitimate—but it is not the same thing as morality. He points to at least four important differences between law and morality:

1. Law does not address a universal communication community of human beings, but rather a determinate community of legal consociates. This means that legitimate law is made in discourses that are not universal and unlimited, but are shaped by the particular characteristics and concerns of those who participate in its formation.
2. Law regulates only our external behavior as it impinges on others, and law enforces its regulations coercively. The law, therefore, addresses itself to a legal subject without concerning itself with the nature of that subject's internal moral motives. It leaves open the question of her moral orientation toward legal rules, as long as she obeys them.
3. Law specifies principles in a determinate way: it "decides which norms count as law, and the courts settle contests of interpretation over the application of valid but interpretable norms in a manner at once judicious and definitive for all sides."[52] The law, in other words, is a system of authority: it does not leave it to the private judgment of its subjects to decide what is or is not lawful, through their personal reflection on what might be the outcome of a universalized discourse of moral justification; rather, it lays down what is henceforth to be considered lawful within a determinate jurisdiction.
4. Law does not regulate only moral matters: it also regulates pragmatic issues, by implementing fair compromises between competing interest groups; and it resolves ethical-political questions regarding how this particular community understands itself with respect to

[52] Habermas, *Between Facts and Norms*, 114.

> its own political traditions and form of life. In other words, law's regulations "are too concrete to be justifiable by moral considerations alone."[53] Instead, legal norms rest on a variety of reasons, including pragmatic reasons and ethical reasons relative to the self-understanding of that particular legal community.

This sharp distinction between morality and law is important for understanding Habermas's views on rights as well as his views on civic solidarity. While those who advocate a "redirective" interpretation of Habermas's own work conceptualize rights as decontextualized moral principles that place external constraints on positive legislation, Habermas has indicated that this view is actually a misunderstanding. Against this way of construing rights, Habermas wants to conceive of the principle of democracy as a means of testing, through a discursive political process, what positive rights legal consociates should accord one another. The rights that free and equal citizens mutually grant one another should thus be consistent with the discourse principle; but that principle does not give rise to a concrete list of rights directly and of itself.

In arguing against the view that rights are to be conceived as external moral constraints on legislation, Habermas appeals to the views of Kant and Rousseau as inspirations. As we have seen, both Kant and Rousseau claim that there is only one basic human right, the right to equal freedom, and on their view, the social contract institutionalizes this single "innate" right to equal freedom, by specifying those acquired rights that citizens reciprocally grant one another in accordance with this fundamental principle. For them, any more determinate specifications of the innate right to equal freedom—as we have seen all along—have to be grounded in the general will of a citizenry that is united by being subject to a legitimate political authority. For Rousseau and Kant, then, all concrete specifications of the innate right to freedom are acquired civil rights, and they are acquired by being subject to a scheme of positive law.

To understand Habermas's legal theory, it is fundamental that we situate him within this tradition, inaugurated by Rousseau and Kant, and not within the Lockean liberal tradition, which sees the individual as the bearer of a determinate *list* of rights against the state. Habermas claims approvingly that "Rousseau and Kant pursued the goal of conceiving of autonomy as unifying practical reason and sovereign will in such a way that the idea of human rights and the principle of popular sovereignty would *mutually* interpret one another."[54] In Habermas's theory, two fundamental moral ideas—the discourse principle and the idea of legal

[53] Habermas, *Between Facts and Norms*, "Postscript," 452.

[54] Habermas, *Between Facts and Norms*, 100

form—occupy the same ground that the innate right to freedom occupied in Kant and Rousseau: "Nothing is given prior to the citizens' practice of self-determination other than the *discourse principle*, which is built into the conditions of communicative association in general, and the *legal medium* as such."[55] For Habermas, then, rights are not discovered as pregiven moral facts; instead they are grounded in the general will of a people, as expressed in their well-constituted democratic institutions.

This should not be taken to mean that Habermas is a crude legal positivist. Just like Kant and Rousseau, he thinks moral constraints on political practice do exist, but that they are given by two abstract principles: (1) that the laws must be freely enacted by each for all—and therefore that the "idealizing presuppositions" of discourse must be institutionally guaranteed, in the form of a set of basic political rights; and (2) that all laws must be general in form, such that whatever is not explicitly prohibited by the laws shall be permitted to the legal subject, in her own sphere of private autonomy. Through the exercise of popular sovereignty, then, citizens determine what particular scheme of civil rights they must mutually accord one another if they are to regulate their common life in accordance with these principles. For Habermas, this means that we have no unmediated access to human rights as such; all rights that we know are positive rights, which inhere in the various determinate political projects that have attempted to interpret what a system of equal liberties would mean under given historical conditions:

> This system of rights . . .is not given to the framers of a constitution in advance as a natural law. Only in a particular constitutional interpretation do these rights first enter into consciousness at all. . . . If talk of "the" system of rights means anything, then, it refers to points where the various explication of the given self-understanding of such a practice converge. . . . No one can credit herself with access to a system of rights in the singular, independent of the interpretations she already has historically available.[56]

But the discourse principle and the idea of legal form do give us minimal moral constraints on positive legislation. In other words, Habermas sees the formal idea of rights as enabling conditions of a practice of democratic will-formation that can attain a presumption of rationality.[57] These moral constraints are of two types.

[55] Habermas, *Between Facts and Norms*, 127; emphasis added.

[56] Habermas, *Between Facts and Norms*, 128.

[57] "Rousseau starts with the constitution of civic autonomy and produces *a fortiori* an internal relation between sovereignty and human rights. Because the sovereign will of the people can express itself only in the language of general and abstract laws, it has directly inscribed in it the right of each person to human liberties. . . . In Rousseau, then, the exercise

First, the *discourse principle* is meant to connect the practice of a democracy with morality, by giving democratic will-formation a warrant of rationality. For the outcome of a democratic discourse to warrant even a fallible presumption of rational validity, the "idealizing presuppositions" of moral argumentation must be satisfied to a sufficient degree. Democratic participation rights give concrete specification to these ideals: at a minimum, then, no political system that does not have universal participation rights for all those affected by its laws, and that does not protect their personal security, can be a legitimate democracy, on Habermas's view. But these participation rights, even though they do possess a "core" minimum content, are indeterminate enough to require a significant act of interpretation. For example, what exactly is required to warrant the assumption that everyone with the competence to speak and act is allowed to participate in democratic will-formation? Is the mere absence of exclusionary acts sufficient to warrant the assumption that this condition is fulfilled? Or must citizens also be guaranteed certain prerogatives that enable them to take part in the discussion, as, for example, the right to associate, the right to demonstrate in a public forum, or even the right to equal use of air time in public media? Further, are citizens to be guaranteed certain competences that *aid* them in developing skills necessary to participate on an equal footing, as for example, a right to public education or a right to a certain level of economic self-sufficiency? These interpretive decisions must be left up to the legal community of citizens, who will give the fundamental ideal of participatory equality a concrete specification in light of their historical and social situation.

Second, rights also establish a *legal medium* by which a set of persons can regulate their life in common. Habermas thinks that any democracy regulating itself by law will always find it necessary to adopt some scheme of private rights. As we have seen, only rights of political participation and basic rights of noncoercion and bodily integrity can be directly deduced directly from the discourse principle itself. But the idea of private rights traditionally includes a much more extensive set of protections than this: to freedom of religion, rights of property and privacy, and so on. Habermas thinks that this category of "bourgeois" rights can be deduced from the idea of law itself.[58] The positivity of law "forces autonomy to split up in a way that has no parallel in morality."[59] Legal autonomy pre-

---

of political autonomy no longer stands under the proviso of innate rights. Rather, the normative content of human rights enters into the very mode of carrying out popular sovereignty." See Habermas, *Between Facts and Norms*, 101.

[58] Both Rousseau and Kant refer to the form of the legal medium as an important constraint on political authority. Habermas explicitly states that this should be interpreted as a guarantee of traditional bourgeois rights.

[59] Habermas, *Between Facts and Norms*, "Postscript," 450.

supposes that there are legislators, who make the laws, and thus have public autonomy rights; and subjects, who obey the laws, and thus have private autonomy rights. In a democracy, however, it so happens that each citizen is both a legislator and a subject at the same time. Habermas claims that since the legal form is addressed to subjects, it is necessary to establish a category of legal personhood, which helps to define the category of the legal subject: "The legal medium as such presupposes rights that define the status of legal persons as bearers of rights."[60] Any state that wishes to regulate itself by means of positive law must institute a category of private law, which will grant the members of the state equal rights to a private sphere of autonomous decision making.

In order to regulate their common life by means of impersonal law, citizens must therefore grant each other a sphere of private liberty of an unspecified extent, subject only to the proviso that such a protected sphere (*a*) should exist and (*b*) should be equal for all. Private rights, then, are rights that citizens grant one another in order to live side-by-side in equal freedom in a legal community; but these citizens decide for themselves precisely which aspects of their behavior are to be public and which to be private. The (administrative) state then coercively enforces the rights that establish equal spheres of individual freedom against those who would violate them: it hinders "hindrances to freedom," in Kant's vocabulary. The state—conceived as a democratic association of citizens—therefore defines what the reciprocal bounds of the citizens' liberty should be: without a concrete and authoritative legislation, this sphere of liberty would remain underspecified and indeterminate, or as Habermas puts it, "unsaturated." Habermas thinks that no system of legislation could meet the criterion of generality implicit in the ideal of legal form without establishing some scheme of private rights of this sort.

Why the Redirective Interpretation Must Be Wrong

At this point, then, we can begin to see why a redirective interpretation of constitutional patriotism must be incorrect. In moving directly from Habermas's moral universalism to a determinate list of rights to which constitutional patriots are thought to be loyal, it invokes a conception of rights that Habermas himself in fact rejects. The universal moral principles that constrain positive law, as we noted, are the discourse principle and the idea of legal form. But these moral principles, as Habermas puts it, are "fundamentally unsaturated," and must be given further content and specification by democratic self-legislation: "human rights are not

[60] Habermas, *Between Facts and Norms*, 119.

pre-given moral truths to be discovered but rather are constructions."[61] Even if we agree with the argument I presented in chapter 4—that principles of equal freedom have a "core" or "minimal" content that must be respected if the state is to be a legitimate one—this minimal core still does not provide us with a full account of what equal freedom entails in a particular political context. For that reason, democratic citizenship is a project of fundamental moral importance, since every more concrete specification of the "unsaturated" moral ideals that ought to guide legislation must come about in and through the deliberations of a well-ordered legal community. Democratic citizenship is the only institution that can mediate between abstract and formal moral conditions for political legitimacy and the positive rights that particular states enact.

When read against the background of Habermas's theory of law, then, constitutional patriotism should be understood as a citizen's loyalty to a particular project of democratic citizenship, so long as that citizen can judge that this project is both legitimate and well constituted—that it institutes a procedure that accords with the minimal moral constraints imposed by the discourse principle and the idea of legal form. A well-constituted state, then, is a state whose positive law represents an effort at developing a certain regulative ideal of fully autonomous political community between equals. The constitutional patriot is loyal to her particular version of that project, as it unfolds within the institutions of her state. Because the features of that democracy and the specific positive rights it enacts will depend on the characteristics of the citizenry that make it up, her particular democracy is unique, and its laws and features will be distinguishable from others. Norway is not Sweden, then, because its precise positive interpretation of equal freedom is its own, and that interpretation depends on the characteristics of its citizenry and its history; Sweden's will be different in important respects. Viewing constitutional patriotism in this light renders it less susceptible to some of the charges that have been brought against it, as for example that constitutional patriotism can only account for a "random assortment" of individuals, without being able to bind these individuals together, or that it cannot explain how a citizen can be loyal to one particular liberal state rather than another.

Why Constitutional Patriotism in the First Place?

Having discarded the redirective interpretation, though, we must spell out more precisely what is involved in the alternative view, which sees constitutional patriotism as loyalty to a specific democratic practice. Our

[61] Habermas, "Remarks on Legitimation," 122.

elaboration of Habermas's views on rights has not yet explained why citizen solidarity is actually necessary for a well-constituted democratic procedure to be carried out. Why can't persons in general—self-interested rational actors, citizens of the world, or lazy apathetic louts—successfully participate in a procedure of democratic lawmaking? Why do they need to be constitutional patriots?

Like Rousseau, Habermas holds that an ineliminable element of civic freedom is that the addressees of the law must at the same time be able to understand themselves as its authors.[62] This is the reason why the a priori ideal of equal freedom cannot be interpreted by an external sovereign, who is set over and against democratic citizens. As subject to the laws, suggests Habermas, it must be possible for any citizen also to understand himself as the author of the constraint that is imposed on him, as one that he himself had a hand in creating, and therefore sees good reason for him to endorse and to obey. For this reason, Habermas argues, the system of private rights characteristic of modern liberal-democratic societies is itself dependent on the solidarity of citizens who engage in a rational process of popular will-formation, and who respect the laws they impose on themselves.

Like Rousseau, Habermas claims that citizens can come to an understanding about what rights they ought to accord one another as free and equal citizens only by assuming a certain standpoint, the standpoint of the "common good." To be legitimate, democratic laws must be enacted on the basis of an understanding of the general interest that citizens construct together, by taking equal account of the perspective of each individual. From within this standpoint, citizens seek to discover generalizable interests that could be willed by each for all to protect in common:

> A legal order must not only guarantee that the rights of each person are in fact recognized by other persons; the reciprocal recognition of the rights of each by all must in addition be based on laws that are legitimate insofar as they grant equal liberties to each, so that each's freedom of choice can coexist with the freedom of choice of all. Moral laws fulfill these conditions per se, but for legal statutes, they must be satisfied by the political legislator. The process of legislation thus represents the place in the legal system where social integration first occurs. *For this reason, it must be reasonable to expect those who participate in the legislative process, whether directly or indirectly, to drop the role of private subject and assume, along with their role of citizen, the perspective of members of a freely associated legal community. . . .* This combination requires a process of lawmaking in which the partici-

[62] Habermas, *Between Facts and Norms*, 33.

> pating citizens are *not* allowed to take part simply in the role of actors oriented to success. To the extent that rights of political participation and rights of communication are constitutive for the production of legitimate statutes, they must be exercised in the attitude of communicatively engaged citizens.[63]

This particular paragraph helps to illuminate what it is that *Verfassungspatriotismus* adds to a well-constituted democratic procedure, and why the procedure cannot be carried out in its absence. Like the perspective of the citizen who wills the general will, the perspective of a member of a "freely associated Habermasian legal community" is not accessible to any and all individuals regardless of their subjective orientation. In particular, Habermas suggests that the perspective of the common good cannot be accessed by citizens who take part in a lawmaking procedure in the role of strategic "actors oriented to success." In order for citizens to derive a truly general will, they must step out of an orientation to purely private interest.

For this reason, Habermas must have recourse to an additional motivation in order to solve the problem of democratic solidarity. He claims that "the democratic procedure of legitimate lawmaking relies on citizens' making use of their communicative and participatory rights *also* with an orientation towards the common good, an attitude that can indeed be politically called for but not compelled . . . to this extent, constitutional democracy depends upon the motivations of a population *accustomed* to liberty."[64] Because rights are not moral principles that can be imposed on a population from outside, but instead must be interpreted and given content by democratic citizens for themselves, these citizens must be willing to take up a "we-perspective of active self-determination."[65] Therefore, like Rousseau, Habermas thinks that citizens must share solidarity if they are to formulate and obey nondominating laws. But Habermas claims that we can account for these solidaristic motivations without any appeal to a national identity.

How can identifying with the purely legal status of citizen motivate the individual to take up the "active we-perspective" characteristic of democratic solidarity? Habermas answers by invoking one of the essential differences between law and morality: legal discourses accommodate a wide range of justifying reasons. Law not only interprets moral rights, but also contains ethical references to the collective self-understanding of particular communities, based on their shared constitutional traditions and

[63] Habermas, *Between Facts and Norms*, 31; emphasis added.

[64] Habermas, *Between Facts and Norms*, 461; see also 513.

[65] Habermas, *Between Facts and Norms*, 499.

history, and incorporates pragmatic reasons stemming from fair compromises between interest groups:

> Whereas moral rules, aiming at what lies in the equal interest of *all*, express a universal will pure and simple, laws also give expression to the particular wills of members of a particular legal community. Moreover, whereas the morally autonomous will remains in some sense virtual because it states only what could be rationally accepted by each, a legal community's political will, which of course should accord with moral insights, also expresses an intersubjectively shared form of life, existing interest positions, and pragmatically chosen ends.[66]

In contrast to a purely moral discourse, in a lawmaking discourse, the same issue can be thematized under more than one aspect: a moral aspect, an ethical aspect, or a pragmatic one. For this reason, Habermas argues that legal justification has to be open to what he calls an "ethical-political" use of practical reason.[67]

The distinction between these three sorts of justifying reasons is important for understanding why Habermas thinks citizenship can serve as a locus for particular identities and for democratic solidarity. Moral reasons, thinks Habermas, are reasons that must be rationally acceptable to all free and equal persons everywhere. The scope of their applicability is fully universal. Ethical reasons, however, must only be acceptable within a community of people who share a certain constitutional history and the traditions derived from it. The scope of their applicability is therefore limited to those people who share these particular affiliations. Pragmatic reasons, finally, are reasons of prudence or instrumental rationality: they do not require an orientation to the claims of other persons, but merely consideration of how to efficiently carry out a certain goal.

Ethical-political reasoning, then, illuminates the self-understanding, particular values, and traditions of a given political community: it answers the question "Who are we?" Ethical-political reasons are valid only relative to a particular context: "to the historically, culturally molded identity of the legal community, and hence relative to the value orientations, goals, and interest positions of the members."[68] Law can be at least partly justified on the basis of particular ethical-political reasons in a way that morality, as a set of principles that apply to persons everywhere, cannot be. This broader scope of reasons, suggests Habermas, gives law greater power to motivate citizens' allegiance and shape their particular

[66] Habermas, *Between Facts and Norms*, 151.

[67] See McCarthy, "On Reconciling Cosmopolitan Unity," 193; Hegel, *Elements of the Philosophy of Right*.

[68] Habermas, *Between Facts and Norms*, 155.

identities. For this reason, Habermas thinks that "once the status of citizenship has taken root in the legal and political cultures of constitutional democracies, democracy itself can shape the identities of citizens while gradually sloughing off its historical dependence on the ambivalent concept of the nation."[69]

The presence of an ethical-political aspect to lawmaking facilitates citizens' identification with one particular democratic process over another, since the laws of a particular democratic state will always express elements of a particular association with which a person identifies, because they depend partly on the particular mix of interests and ideals characteristic of its citizens. What citizens do in any particular procedure of democratic lawmaking is in part to clarify who they are—to articulate an understanding and a political identity that describes themselves as citizens of a given republic that draws on their own history and constitutional tradition. In coming to any shared understanding about rights, then, they are also in part expressing and reshaping this shared political identity.

Habermas is arguing, in effect, that all debates about rights have both a moral and an ethical content. Take for example the recent constitutional debates in the United States over the courtroom display of the Ten Commandments. This is in the first instance a debate about where the line between public and private should be drawn in matters of religion, and therefore a debate about rights, which in Habermas's sense qualifies as a moral-political debate. But it is also a debate about the proper place of a Christian heritage in American public life, and about how displaying and celebrating that heritage will affect those citizens who do not share this particular tradition. Is it acceptable to display the Ten Commandments in all public contexts, in some public contexts, or in no public contexts? The outcome of this debate in turn affects the self-understanding of the nation in an ethical sense: are we a substantially Christian nation who acknowledges this fact in our public rhetoric? Are we a multicultural nation who should acknowledge our Christian heritage only as part of a larger acknowledgment of other religious traditions that contribute to our history? Or are we a nation committed to doing without any public religious heritage at all?

Although all legitimate law should be interpretable as the actualization of a scheme of equal rights, in order to decide what these rights should consist in, citizens must thematize certain aspects of their common life, which depends on the particular mix of people they are, the nature of their cultural allegiances and religious backgrounds. In thematizing this common life, rather than another one, they identify themselves as citizens of a particular republic, with its particular constitutional history and char-

[69] Cronin, "Democracy and Collective Identity," 3.

acteristics. In each instance, such a debate is understandable both as a debate about which rights citizens are to accord one another in order to conduct their political life in an autonomous manner (thus a moral-political debate), and as a debate about how their particular political community is to understand its concrete identity (thus an ethical-political one). The distinctiveness of a political community, then, is given by which particular aspects of their common lives they conceive as in need of public regulation and in what ways.

The fact that constitutional debates also shape and express a collective self-understanding, on Habermas's view, gives citizens an additional reason to take up a communicative stance when entering democratic constitutional discourse, for what is at stake is not only the attainment of new theoretical insights into normative validity, but also a new understanding of one's own identity as a citizen of *this* particular state, with its history and traditions. The results of such debates therefore not only have theoretical significance as criticizable insights; they also help to define citizens' political identities. By participating in constitutional discourses to define the rights they are to grant one another as legal consociates, these citizens at the same time define their identity as occupants of a social role that has a definite social and historical past, and therefore also a special meaning for them. It is the fact that members can identify with their roles as citizens that allows citizenship to become the "driving force" behind the project of producing an association of free and equal individuals.

Habermas therefore hopes to solve this problem of democratic solidarity by making common citizenship, rather than common national culture, the focus of individual identity in a modern, heterogeneous state. He argues that because citizenship is necessarily citizenship of a particular state, with concerns and interests that can be differentiated from others, this motivational feat can be accomplished without any reference to a prepolitical, culturally defined nation. But is he right?

Is *Verfassungspatriotismus* the Cultural Model in Disguise?

Habermas's concession that legitimate democratic processes must rely on the motivational resources that are embedded in a particular ethical-political context has led some critics, often those sympathetic to the broader aims of his project, to argue that the moral claims he makes for his political theory are untenable. These critics hold that Habermas's insistence that constitutional patriotism retains a universalist core—that it is based on "the interpretation of recognized, universalistic constitutional principles within the context of a particular national history and tradition"[70]—cannot be defended, once he concedes that citizenship always draws on a particular ethical-political background. Instead, they argue that since Habermas believes that we can only "ever have access to the abstract system of basic rights as 'refracted' through particular constitutional traditions,"[71] he ought to abandon the claim that constitutional patriotism entails adherence to distinctively universalist ideals. What does it mean, these critics ask, to insist on the priority of a potentially universal moral justification if universal principles come to us in versions whose concrete content is always mediated by the self-understanding of a particular legal community?[72]

This critique is successful in pointing out some ambiguities in the concept of constitutional patriotism. On the one hand, Habermas can (and sometimes does) describe constitutional patriotism as a theory of allegiance to universal democratic principles. But when described in this sense, *Verfassungspatriotismus* becomes "empty" and "formal," since the universal moral principles that undergird democratic practice are the discourse principle and the idea of legal form, and as we have seen, these are fundamentally indeterminate or "unsaturated" ideals, that is, they depend on further specification only democratic deliberations can provide. On the other hand, Habermas can (and sometimes does) emphasize that in practice constitutional patriotism takes its content from the historical and social context in which it is situated, and that implementing an abstract system of basic rights is therefore inseparable from coming to a collective self-understanding within a particular legal community. But then it may seem the supposedly universal core of constitutional patriotism is doing none of the work. All of the content is provided by the cultural context in which these moral principles happen to be situated. It may seem, then, that—as its critics often argue—constitutional patriotism tacitly presupposes an already existing national-cultural identity.

Critiques along these lines have been offered by Frank Michelman,[73] Thomas McCarthy,[74] and Maurizio Viroli, who claims that in Habermas's theory

> the object of the citizens' love is their own particular republic; not just democratic institutions, but institutions that have been built in a particular historical context and are linked to a way of life—that is, a *culture*—of citizens of that particular republic.[75]

[70] Habermas, "A Reply," 398.
[71] McCarthy, "Legitimacy and Diversity," 131.
[72] Bernstein, "Retrieval of Democratic Ethos,"289.
[73] Michelman, "Morality, Identity," 254.
[74] McCarthy, "Legitimacy and Diversity," 135.
[75] Viroli, *For Love of Country*, 172; emphasis added.

These critics challenge the idea that Habermas's theory of constitutional patriotism is anything more than an attachment to a particular culture, even if that culture happens to be a particularly "open" and "democratic" one.

Habermas, however, resists an identification of his own project with a version of nationalism that would hold that implementing justice involves *nothing more* than clarifying the traditions and self-understanding of one culture. Although as we have seen, he concedes that the application of his theory is intertwined with processes of coming to collective self-understanding among a particular people, he wants to insist that the moral perspective can be defined independently of any of these contextual supplements, even if it requires concrete situational details in order to be applied in a given context.

There are three ways that Habermas tries to defend the universalism of his own theory and to distinguish it from a more thoroughgoing cultural nationalism.

1. First, Habermas emphasizes the transformative power of democratic discourses for collective political identities. The locus of the constitutional patriot's identity must be viewed as a process open to potentially perpetual revision, not as a static national-cultural tradition to be preserved and reaffirmed in the present.
2. Second, he stresses the separation of a common political culture from the majority culture. Any political culture will of necessity remain "ethically" imbued. But since it derives from laws that realize equality between a bounded set of citizens, and not a set of objective commonalities like language, myth, and history, a political culture can become ever-thinner. The political culture is simply defined by the overlap in needs and interests that are present in whatever national or thickly "ethical" cultures happen to inhabit a given society, and it can always be further diluted if new groups join.[76]
3. Finally, Habermas claims that there is some context-independent content to the "unsaturated" moral principles of justice, and that this content can constrain and guide political practice, even if it does not fully determine outcomes.

Habermas indicates that in modern democratic societies, a collective identity is never a fixed and finished product, but is continually "under construction" in an open and revisable process. In their democratic will-formation, constitutional patriots are also articulating a political identity, but their identity is always available for revision—it is the perpetually

[76] In this sense, as in many others, Habermas's view comes close to Rawls's advocacy of an "overlapping consensus."

alterable outcome of the political process. The reverse should not be true: if political autonomy is to remain in the ascendant, the political process cannot simply rubber-stamp an already-given national identity, defined by a tradition or by objective cultural commonalities. Habermas therefore refuses the Rousseauian appeals to a form of persuasion that would proceed "behind the backs" of political actors by invoking a prepolitical unity of language or culture. Instead, he wishes to place the production of the citizens' political identity under their own conscious control.

What Habermasian constitutional patriots are loyal to, then, is not a constitution in the fixed sense, defined by appeals to Founding Fathers, a sacred document, or the ancestral heroes of the nation; instead, it is an ongoing constitutional practice that is at the same time a collective practice of self-definition.[77] The ever-revisable quality of collective identities does not mean that cultural content disappears from the process: as we have seen, any attribution of "grouphood" will also involve the ability to distinguish some group characteristics that we can call culture, if we are so inclined. But what is essential to Habermas's goal is that cultural content in a democratic society be produced by the decisions of an autonomous people, and not simply inherited. While the decisions of any democratic society will create a determinate particular character for their community, then, citizens must be aware that the character of their community is up to them and not a received inheritance that they are destined to reproduce.

In order to foster conscious identity-production, Habermas encourages the contestation of political tradition and history:

> The inevitable pluralism of readings, which is by no means unmonitored but on the contrary rendered transparent, only reflects the structure of open societies. It provides an opportunity to clarify one's own identity-forming traditions in their ambivalences. This is precisely what is needed for the critical appropriation of ambiguous traditions, that is, for the development of a historical consciousness that is equally incompatible with closed images of history and with all forms of conventional, that is, uniformly and prereflexively *shared* identity.[78]

Public history can encourage an autonomous relation to the past, by pluralizing our interpretations of it and refusing to allow us to settle comfortably into a mythologized vision of our collective identity. While the political process necessarily draws upon its cultural background, then, if it is to encourage the conscious fabrication of collective identities, it

[77] Habermas, "A Reply," 399.
[78] Habermas, "Apologetic Tendencies," 227.

must draw on the past in a way that thematizes, contests, and pluralizes this background.

Second, Habermas argues that "the ethical integration of groups and subcultures with their own collective identities must be uncoupled from the abstract political integration that includes all citizens equally."[79] As modern societies grow to encompass a more diverse set of subcultures, the legal system should strive to be neutral among these various forms of life, rather than simply reflecting the more holistic value orientations of the majority culture. All that a democratic state can expect to require of its citizens, then, is a thinly "political" socialization—one that can be justified by an appeal to neutral reasons—and not a more thoroughgoing and fully "ethical" socialization to the majority culture. Prospective immigrants, for example, should merely be required to

> assent to the principles of the constitution within the scope of interpretation determined at a particular time by the ethical-political self-understanding of the citizens and the political culture of the country; in other words, assimilation to the way in which the autonomy of the citizens is institutionalized in the recipient society and the way "the public use of reason" is practiced there.[80]

Immigrants are not to be required to assimilate in a more thoroughgoing way to the majority culture, by adopting the prevailing style of dress, observance of holidays, language, customs, or other nonpolitical practices. Some commentators, including Thomas McCarthy, have questioned whether a political culture can ever truly be "decoupled" from the majority culture in quite the way Habermas imagines.[81] Doesn't a democracy require a national political language, for example, and won't that generally reflect the language of the majority? And won't other standardized public decisions, about holidays, for example, or school curricula, reflect the culture of the majority?

Many of Habermas's other remarks suggest that what he has in mind is not the absolute decoupling of politics from its cultural background—criticisms like McCarthy's make it clear that that is unlikely to be possible anyhow—but instead a process that strives to politicize the equation of the political culture with the majority culture, again disentangling democratic politics from a received cultural background that is construed as beyond revision. Thus, while Habermas urges that immigrants accept the fixed constitutional settlement in place at the time they immigrate, he also

[79] Habermas, "Struggles for Recognition," 224.

[80] Habermas, "Struggles for Recognition," 228.

[81] See Cronin, "Democracy and Collective Identity," 5; McCarthy, "Reconciling Cosmopolitan Unity and National Diversity," 195.

indicates that once they become citizens, they form part of the state's ethical-political culture and as such have the power to shift the prevailing constitutional interpretation over time:

> This constitutional alternative has the implication that the legitimately asserted identity of the political community will by no means be preserved from alterations *indefinitely* in the wake of waves of immigration. Because immigrants cannot be compelled to surrender their own traditions, as other forms of life become established the horizon within which the citizens henceforth interpret their common constitutional principles may also expand. Then the mechanism comes into play whereby a change in the cultural composition of the active citizenry changes the context to which the ethical-political self-understanding of the nation as a whole refers.[82]

For this reason, although at any given time there may be a political language or a set of national holidays in place, these features are never entrenched beyond democratic revision because of their status as defining features of a national identity. Instead, these decisions are open to revision and reconsideration, as the cultures composing the citizenry shift.

Finally, the moral point of view inherent in Habermas's theory supposes that there is, at least theoretically, a "best answer" to questions about rights, which stands outside any nation's traditions or self-understanding. This is the answer that you, I, and the rest of our democratic community would come up with, if we had infinite time, full information and access to all the reasons, and all the "idealizing presuppositions" of discourse were fulfilled. Habermas thinks that the way in which we argue about moral claims, including rights, makes it clear that we must be presupposing a rationally justified answer of this sort. We argue, that is, as though our exchange of reasons had the power to convince, which means we must think there is a cognitive standard for evaluating these issues. This is what Habermas means, rightly interpreted, when he says constitutional patriotism is "based upon the interpretation of recognized, universalistic constitutional principles within the context of a particular national history and tradition."[83] All constitutional practices presuppose the same principles because they all argue about rights in a way that presupposes a single right answer at which free and equal citizens might potentially arrive.

To be a constitutional patriot, then, is to be loyal to a democracy that can be interpreted as trying to approximate in practice this universal regulative ideal of public reasoning, by coming up with positively enacted civil

[82] Habermas, "Struggles for Recognition," 229.
[83] Habermas, "A Reply," 398.

rights that can credibly claim to be based on an unforced agreement among equals:[84]

> The advantage of a recourse to "constitutional patriotism" lies in the universalist meaning of the core of this kind of patriotism, thus providing an implicit overlap with the patriotism of other communities. . . . The performative meaning remains the implicit but stable point of reference, though any attempt at its explication is only one among various possible versions.[85]

Because all constitutional patriots subscribe to the supposition of a "single right answer," they can always critique their current political practices from the same moral standpoint, that of a freer and more equal political community. And when they do so, Habermas indicates, they are presupposing an "idealized agreement" that would hold the "final truth" about what civil rights actually are—once and for all—required to realize freedom and equality. Yet because the "final truth" about rights stands in a moment of idealized justification that we cannot reach, we can never be sure that the rights we accept here and now do in fact approximate this ideal. Instead, we have to leave them open to challenge by better reasons or as yet unknown considerations that may arise in the future.

Habermas believes, however, that this moral ideal can serve as a meaningful moral constraint on positive self-legislation, because it can rule out certain laws as inconsistent with the core content of the discourse principle and the idea of legal form. It does so in two ways: first, the universalist content implicit in the discourse principle can declare laws that disenfranchise citizens, violate their bodily security, or grant special privileges to some groups at the expense of others as unjust, regardless of how they comport with a nation's self-understanding. These laws and practices are simply not consistent with the moral standpoint of a free and equal political community. Second, Habermas thinks that the discourse principle can serve as a directional guide to public policy by prescribing greater inclusivity in our political practices, and counseling tolerance when groups disagree. For this reason, Habermas can defend the claim that constitutional patriotism involves more than the mere elucidation of the cultural self-understanding of a given society. Any society whose self-understanding would require intolerance, the disenfranchisement or exclusion of some of its members, the privileging of one group above others, or the violation of citizens' basic rights to freedom, can be criticized from a moral perspective that is independent of that self-understanding. Although the universalist content implicit in the democratic ideal is purely

[84] Frank Michelman offers a similar interpretation in "Morality, Identity," 254.

[85] Habermas, "On Law and Disagreement," 193.

formal, and requires the motivational and situational resources of an ethical-political context in order to be determinately applied, the fact that republican citizenship is based in universal ideals of freedom and equality gives it a "thinly" transcendent moral content.

Conclusion

Habermas's theory of constitutional patriotism goes a long way toward reappropriating the promise of the "freedom model" of Rousseauian democracy, one that would emphasize a politics of reflective and critical autonomy rather than the collective reaffirmation of a political unity secured through symbols and cultural practices. But liberal nationalists have remained skeptical, criticizing his views as too abstract, and even bloodless. One reason for this is that Habermas's ideas about constitutional patriotism are often vague. In particular, it is sometimes unclear how identification with a democratic process is really different from identification with a national culture. This vagueness about how identification as a citizen might proceed and what marks it off from a cultural model leads many critics to charge that Habermasian constitutional patriotism is merely liberal nationalism in disguise.

While I think Habermas's theory can probably be rescued from these charges, I also believe that the notion of constitutional patriotism would be more credible and would command wider assent if a clearer account could be given of how exactly loyalty to a democratic practice differs from loyalty to a shared culture. Habermas's key insight—that shared citizenship can serve as effectively as the cultural nation in providing a source of political unity—needs to be underpinned by a more precise theory of citizen identification if his rehabilitation of the freedom model of Rousseauian politics is to convince. In the next chapter, I attempt to fill this gap. There, I will develop insights from the philosophy of action that I think support the conviction that a functional alternative to cultural nationalism is possible, and that it can take the form of a purely civic political allegiance.

7

Democracy as Collective Action

As we saw in the last chapter, the crucial part of the liberal-nationalist challenge turns on the assertion that constitutional patriotism cannot explain why citizens have sufficient reason for allegiance to their particular institutions, or for solidarity with their compatriots, on the basis of their commitment to justice alone. Indeed, a key worry about Habermas's position is that insofar as he has a good response to this liberal-nationalist challenge, that response may entail an appeal to just the sort of histories, traditions, and ethical identities that nationalists claim are so important. If the thesis that a commitment to justice can be the sole source of democratic solidarity and civic allegiance is to be proven, then it must be clearly shown that citizens could have good reason for allegiance to their state even when they do not share a particular national identity.[1]

In this chapter, I dispute the assumption that a commitment to universal principles of justice cannot justify our allegiance to particular institutions, or solidarity with those with whom we share them. Instead, I provide an alternative account of these differentiated obligations and attachments, one that does not appeal to any national-cultural identity. A key problem with the liberal-nationalist position, I believe, is its tendency to take ascriptive identity groups as paradigmatic sources of social unity. But we are perfectly familiar with everyday groups that are not founded on any ascriptive commonalities, that pursue values or goods that are putatively universal, and yet do not lack for unity and cohesion—think, for example, of a reading club, a university, or a charitable organization. In this chapter, I hope to reformulate and defend what I believe is the best liberal view of political allegiance and unity, partly by analogy to the unity of these everyday groups.[2] In doing so, I believe I am harkening

[1] The liberal nationalist, of course, holds that an appeal to national identity will always be necessary: for him, a commitment to a universal value cannot justify allegiance to particular groups or schemes, or special obligations to fellow participants within those schemes. Instead, like Simmons, liberal nationalists argue that a commitment to principles of justice ought to give us equal reason to support just institutions everywhere. Tamir holds that there are national values "hidden in the liberal agenda" (*Liberal Nationalism*, 69). Miller too makes this claim quite explicit: "The consistent ethical universalist ought to be a cosmopolitan" (*On Nationality*, 79).

[2] Later in this chapter, however, I will emphasize that the state is also in a crucial respect different from everyday groups, because it is not a voluntary association. Like Kant, I shall argue that we have a duty to belong to the state, independently of our own consent. Hobbes

back to a classic account of nationhood, articulated (in different ways) by Hobbes and Kant. These thinkers are clear that what makes a group into a "people" is not a relation of cultural belonging, but a purely juridical relation, which brings into being an artificial "civil person."[3] Moreover, Hobbes argues that states are not the only kinds of civil persons in existence: corporations, clubs, and associations are also civil persons, and the nature of their unity shares important features with the state's, although belonging to these groups is optional in a sense that belonging to the state is not.[4]

Unlike Hobbes, though, I will use a modern philosophical concept to elucidate the analogy between democratic states and everyday groups: I will argue that both sorts of collectives are unified by the structure of shared intentions their members possess. I will also argue that justice gives us reason to form a shared intention to participate together with our fellow citizens in a democratic process. Once we see this, I think, it will be easier to explain why our reason for supporting our particular political institutions and for solidarity with our compatriots ultimately derives from, and can be wholly justified by, a commitment to universal principles of justice, since justice requires us to contribute to a shared intentional practice. To flesh out this idea, though, we will first need to make an excursus into the philosophical literature on collective intentionality.[5] Then we will examine in detail one example of an everyday group in which participants act on shared intentions: the practice of an orchestra. Finally, I will suggest that although a democracy differs in (at least one) very crucial respect from an orchestra, there is good reason to think the social unity of the democratic state can be explained along much the same lines, that is, simply from a shared intention to act together.

---

makes a somewhat similar distinction: he emphasizes that a state is a union, while everyday groups are mere associations.

[3] Hobbes, *On the Citizen*, 73. Kant refers to the state as a moral person in *MM*, 6:43. For a useful account of the concept of the people as ultimate constituent power of the state, see Hont, "Permanent Crisis."

[4] Hobbes, *On the Citizen*, 73: "Although every *commonwealth* is a *civil person*, not every *civil person* (by converse) is a *commonwealth*. For it may happen that several persons will, with the permission of their commonwealth, unite as one person for the purpose of transacting certain business. These will now be *civil persons*, as companies of merchants are, and any number of other groups, but they are not *commonwealths*, because they have not subjected themselves to the will of the group simply and in all things, but only in certain matters defined by the commonwealth."

[5] I have learned much from Attracta Ingram's article "Constitutional Patriotism," collected in Primoratz, *Patriotism*, 217–31, in which she mentions the idea of collective intentions as one possible way of understanding the purely political unity at stake in constitutional patriotism. What follows is a more extensive development of that idea.

Shared Intentions

There are many goals that individuals have reason to value, but that they can pursue only through collective cooperation, through creating or joining groups and institutions. We cannot play football alone, we cannot dance the tango alone, and we cannot be married alone. In our everyday moral life, I believe, we are accustomed to think that our participation in these institutions and groups changes our moral relationship to the other members pursuing these goals with us, even if we have no preexisting cultural or relational ties to them. Here, I want to take up three questions: (1) What attitudes or mental states explain our commitment to shared cooperative activities of this sort? (2) Does our participation in collective cooperation actually change our moral relationships to the other participants? (3) If it does, how does it do so?

It is out of an interest in understanding the preconditions of collective cooperation that philosophers have recently grown interested in the phenomenon of shared intention: many theorists have claimed that collective cooperation is undergirded by shared intentions. A (very rough) description of a shared intention might go as follows: I have a shared intention whenever I think of myself as doing something because and insofar as we are doing something together.[6] Suppose I am a member of the ballet, and we are dancing the *Nutcracker.* In this case, one could say of me that it is my goal that we dance the *Nutcracker* together, and, as a result I intend that we do this by means of my dancing the part of the Mouse King.[7] I am not simply performing the bodily motions that make up the part of the Mouse King alone and without reference to anyone else; instead, my action only makes sense within a frame that includes the actions of others. What I intend, then, is to pursue a joint goal—our dancing the *Nutcracker*—by means of my own personal contribution. Later in the chapter, I will show that we ought to view democratic participation as a shared intentional practice of a similar kind.

Collective cooperation of this sort is a common social phenomenon, and no one would deny that it plays an important role in our lives. But there is a dispute among philosophers over whether such cooperation really requires shared intentions to be possible, and also over how these intentions are structured. We can distinguish three possible positions in the debate: one position views collective cooperation as strategic coordination by individuals, another as the sharing of intentions across individu-

[6] Searle, *Construction of Social Reality*, 23–26; Bratman, "Shared Cooperative Activity."
[7] This is Searle's way of putting it in "Collective Intentions and Actions," 412.

als, and a third as the formation of a "plural" or group subject. These positions are differentiated by their responses to two questions: first, what is it that holds the intention that gives rise to a collective action—is an individual or a collective (understood as an entity distinct from the individuals composing it)? And second, what are the nature of the intentions that explain collective action—are they "we-intentions" that refer to the actions of a group or collective entity, or are they "I-intentions" that refer only to the actions of an individual self?

1. *Collective cooperation as strategic coordination by individuals*: Some philosophers (notably David Lewis, Russell Hardin, and many rational choice theorists) have attempted to understand collective action simply as a form of strategic coordination on the part of individuals. They hold that the actions of groups can be explained by postulating *individuals* who hold I-intentions.[8] On their view, individuals are the holders of the intentions that give rise to collective action, and these intentions have as their propositional content goals that are totally "self-referential." This need not mean that the goals in question are selfish, in any objectionable sense, but that the goals of the individuals engaged in collective action are individual goals, not the goals of any group. Defenders of the strategic coordination account argue that this can be the case even when the achievement of a particular individual goal depends in part on the actions of other people.

To see what this means in practice, let's take an example. Imagine it is Friday night and I want to go to a good party. This is a totally self-referential goal: it refers only to my own ends, not to the shared ends of any group. But my self-referential goal will only be achieved if other individuals show up, because it will not be a good party if I am the only one there. Perhaps, though, I have formed a belief about what other individuals will be doing tonight, and therefore about the preconditions for achieving my goal. Say this morning I heard the following rumor: "A bunch of people are getting together at Mike's." Then my belief that the other people will go there gives me reason to go to Mike's as well. If everyone else that shows up at the party goes through the same kind of thought process that I do—that is, they deliberate about the conditions for attending a good party, recall that they heard the rumor, form the expectation that others will be at Mike's, and as a result, go there—then this party will be a party of strategically coordinating individuals.

2. *Collective cooperation as shared intentions or ends*: Defenders of this second view claim that collective action should be explained by postulating individuals who hold group-referring intentions. The crucial dis-

[8] See, e.g., Lewis, *Convention*; Hardin, *Collective Action*.

tinction between this position and position 1 is that, here, collective action occurs when individuals intend to do something together—when their own individual mental states make reference to a group act that they jointly intend to bring about. Although individuals possess the intentions that explain collective action—these intentions exist only in individual minds—the goal to which they refer is irreducibly collective. For the theorist of shared intention, groups exist as a result of the interrelated attitudes of individuals who pursue joint goals, and not as separate entities in the real world. This view has been put forward, in different versions, by Michael Bratman, Christopher Kutz, and Seumas Miller, and it is the one I will use to model democratic citizenship in this chapter.[9]

To see how this would play out in practice, imagine that Mike, Emma, John, and I plan to have a party tonight. On the shared intention view, when I set out for the party later this evening, I aim at achieving a joint goal—our shared project to have the party—and I view my own action as a means contributing to this goal. The strategic view can accommodate the fact that I wouldn't be going to the party if I didn't think Mike, Emma, and John were going too. But for the shared intention theorist, I would not be going if I didn't conceive *us* as having the goal of throwing a party together, and if I didn't believe that Mike, Emma, and John conceived *us* as having this goal too, and intended to do their parts in achieving it. My intention, then, is just an ordinary intention held by a particular individual. But the content of my intention references a collective goal: I have an awareness of the relation in which my action stands as a means to a group end, and I wouldn't be performing it otherwise.[10]

3. *Collective cooperation as plural subject*: This position holds that collective action should be explained by postulating a new group-entity that holds we-intentions about its own actions. Margaret Gilbert, for ex-

[9] Christopher Kutz, *Complicity* (Cambridge: Cambridge University Press, 2000), and Miller, *Social Action*. There is some dispute among these theorists as to whether or not the irreducibly joint component of the individuals' mental states is a we-intention or the weaker notion of a collective end. Bratman argues, as I will discuss in more detail below, that I can intend that "we X." He has been criticized for this formulation by those who think that to intend an act is always to believe that I can cause the act. Since group acts consist of contributions by individuals, to intend the group act, on this view, would be to believe that I can *cause* the contributions of other individuals, which is incoherent. Therefore Seumas Miller, for example, holds that I intend only my own contribution but also have a conception of a collective end, which it is my goal to promote. I will discuss this problem again below, in footnote 21 of this chapter. I think that we *can* intend group acts, if we are precise about what is meant by that formulation. But not much turns on my being right about this, since my view could be reformulated in terms of the weaker notion of collective ends, so long as we are clear that there is some irreducibly collective component of the mental states of individuals who perform joint acts.

[10] Kutz, *Complicity*, 71.

Table 7.1
Object of Intentional Action

		"I action"	*"We action"*
	"I"	Strategic coordination (Lewis, Hardin)	Shared intentions or goals (Bratman, Kutz, Miller)
Entity holding intention to act	"We"	Null set: (Collectives with intentions over individual actions)	Plural subject (Gilbert)

ample, argues that when individuals intend to perform a shared activity together, they form a plural subject, a corporate entity not ontologically reducible to the individuals composing it: "If 'we' refers to a plural subject of a goal," Gilbert argues, "it refers to a pool of wills dedicated *as one* to that goal."[11] For Gilbert, these plural subjects can also possess beliefs and intentions that are not in any way reducible to the beliefs and intentions of individuals. On her view, as a member of a plural subject, we also have associative obligations to the other members to continue performing our roles, until the plural subject dissolves itself and ceases to exist. It is not sufficient for an individual alone to renounce a shared belief or intention in order to cease to be bound by it. As long as a plural subject exists, for Gilbert, we are—not morally, but associatively—obligated to it. Table 7.1 summarizes the three positions.

Why the Strategic Coordination Account Is Inadequate

Defenders of the strategic coordination view claim that the we-intentions supposedly involved in collective action can be fully analyzed or reduced to self-referential I-intentions. On their view, what we are doing when we speak colloquially of a group's intending something is speaking metaphorically. What we ought to say—consistent with methodological individualism—is that all or most members of that group intend to do something (under certain conditions of belief, including their beliefs about their strategic situation and about the acts of other people). The worry that motivates this position is that intentions only exist in individual heads, and speaking of a group's intending something sounds suspiciously like

[11] Gilbert, *Living Together*, 186.

positing a group mind of some sort. Where would such a collectivity exist, over and above its members?

Defenders of the strategic coordination view suggest that what makes a situation one of collective cooperation is that individual subjects with I-intentions are aware that they find themselves in a coordination situation. In this case, they all prefer to choose the action they believe the other person(s) will choose, or to match the choices of the others. What each agent intends to do is therefore sensitive to his beliefs about what other people will do, and his own individual goals are only satisfied if they all coordinate on the same action (or rule for action).[12] As long as it is common knowledge that their situation is one of coordination, he might stress, their resulting action is necessarily an act of collective cooperation. Is the strategic coordination account sufficient?

I believe the strategic coordination view is in fact an inadequate model to account for many cases of collective cooperation, particularly the kinds of joint actions—dancing the *Nutcracker*, planning a party, and participating democratically—that we are interested in here. To see this, consider the following cases:

1. *The Queen Bees.* Imagine a town in which two wealthy ladies—Mrs. Pennypacker and Mrs. Vandelay—each wish to be the undisputed social doyenne. Neither of the women can stand the other, and each has assembled an entourage of followers among the town's leading lights. But despite her loathing for Mrs. Vandelay, Mrs. Pennypacker knows that the parties Vandelay attends will be very prominent affairs, at which she would do well to be seen. Even better, if she goes to the same parties as Vandelay, she may gain a delightful opportunity to humiliate Vandelay in public, cementing her claim to be the hostess *du jour.* So Mrs. Pennypacker is careful to deliberate about which parties Mrs. Vandelay will attend, and to attend the very same ones herself. As it turns out, Mrs. Vandelay goes through exactly the same thought process. She knows that the parties at which Pennypacker appears will be very well attended. Moreover, if she goes, she may get the coveted chance to show up Pennypacker once and for all. So she is careful to think about which parties Pennypacker is likely to attend and to go to those as well. Both ladies, then, go to the same parties, and both attend in the knowledge that

[12] The qualification about rules for action is meant to account for solutions to coordination problems in which each participant perform a different action to achieve a desired outcome—like Lewis's paradigmatic case of sharing a convention where the original caller calls back if we get disconnected on the telephone, while the original callee waits. But one could still describe them as coordinating around the same *rule* for action—"If one was the caller, call back. If one was the callee, wait."

her choice to attend depends on the choice of the other (i.e., both are aware that each is matching the other). Indeed, they show up watching one another, and knowing they are watching one another, and saying to themselves, "That Mrs. Vandelay/Pennypacker is only here because I am. She's trying to steal my thunder." Are Vandelay and Pennypacker acting together?

2. *The Counterprotesters.* Imagine two bands of protesters, one for gay marriage, one opposed. Both know that they have received a permit from the city to demonstrate on the same day. But neither group is exactly sure of the other group's marching route. What is most important to each band's organizer, though, is that they march as close as possible to where the other group is marching, so that they can drown out the other group's message by shouting, waving signs, maybe throwing a punch or two. The problem, though, is that neither organizer is yet sure where the other band will go. So both organizers attempt to replicate the other organizer's decisions as to the best protest route. And as a result, they both decide that marching down Broadway is likely to be the salient option, since it is a wide and important street with a lot of foot traffic and passersby. As a result, both organizers think it fairly likely the other group will take it. On the appointed day, then, both groups march down Broadway, screaming over the top of each other, waving their signs, and generally getting in one another's way. Are they acting together as one group?

It seems intuitively clear that neither set of people has acted together. They may have coordinated with one another, but there is an important sense of "acting together" that does not apply to them. The reason they are not acting together is that there is no joint project of partygoing or protesting between them, just two separate individual projects the realization of which, in these particular cases, happen to depend on each agent's (or group's) coordinating his choices with the choices of the other person (or group). So even if what they are doing is common knowledge between both, and they walk down the street or into the party watching one another, and believing that A knows that B is watching him, and that B knows that A is watching him, and that A knows that B knows that A is watching him, and that B knows that A knows that B is watching him, and so on, it is still not a shared project, since neither one regards the other as "a partner in a joint enterprise."[13]

Despite its initial plausibility, then, the strategic coordination analysis of group cooperation is technically compatible with many situations in

[13] Kutz, *Complicity*, 78.

which we would intuitively say that no group act is occurring. This is because the strategic account counts as a group act any situation in which two or more individuals must successfully coordinate with one another, even when they coordinate in order to achieve two purely private goals. But there is a sense of acting together as one group that this definition misses out: the sense of acting together as sharing a joint goal. If we believe that the above examples are not in fact group actions, then we must specify further criteria that could successfully exclude such examples (where the strategic coordination account does not). For a joint action to exist, then, each member of the group must not only form the same intention, and not only because the other person has formed that intention, but these intentions must also reference the fact that they are doing something together as a group. These intentions, in other words, must be formed from the perspective of the first-person plural.[14] To successfully analyze group cooperation, then, we need to move from the I-intentions postulated by the strategic coordination view to we-intentions, that is, to take up either the shared intention or plural subject view.

Although I do not want to pursue the case in detail here, I think that in moving to we-intentions there are good reasons for wishing to avoid the plural subject account.[15] Gilbert's main reason for thinking that the shared intention view is insufficient is that it cannot explain what she takes to be an essentially normative dimension of joint action, which generates a (nonmoral) associative obligation on each member to do his part and a right of other members to rebuke him if he does not. But I do not think that Gilbert has successfully demonstrated that any sui generis obligation attaches to joint action that cannot be accounted for by the instrumental normative force of an individual's intentions and decisions, when they are combined with general moral obligations toward others, as I will argue below.[16] In what follows, therefore, I will pursue the shared intention account, although I think my views could be revised to fit the plural subject view, if it is shown to be correct.

Michael Bratman, whom I follow here, recommends the following analysis of shared intention, which describes a "public and interlocking

[14] Kutz, *Complicity*, 80–81.

[15] For this view, see Gilbert, *Living Together*, 177–213. More plausible versions of the plural subject view include Rovane, *The Bounds of Agency*, and Pettit, "Groups with Minds," 167–93. In adopting an irreducibly holist position, Pettit emphasizes the role of procedures for collective rationality that allow groups to hold beliefs and commitments that are not held by their members. But I think that these beliefs could still be explained in terms of individual intentions, namely an individual intention to take the results of a group's procedures as authoritative.

[16] For an argument that she has not, see Miller, *Social Action*, 85–90.

web"[17] of individually held, but "we-referring" intentions We intend to J if and only if:

1. (a) I intend that we J and (b) you intend that we J.
2. I intend that we J because of (1a) and (1b) and meshing subplans of (1a) and (1b); you intend the same.
3. (1) and (2) are common knowledge between us.[18]

Bratman's conditions indicate that we both must possess a commitment in favor of the joint activity, and that we must both be aware of this fact—it must be "out in the open" between us. Let us call this the *basic we-intention*. On the basic view, we form a collective agent—a "we"—whenever we mutually recognize a "we-attitude" that each one of us individually possesses. If I intend that we paint the house together, and you intend that we paint the house together, and we mutually recognize each other's intentions, then we already form a collective agent. Nothing else is necessary.

Bratman adds further conditions to the basic we-intention, however, because he sees two possible problems involved in stopping here. First, we could both intend to undertake an activity and both be aware of that fact, but we might not be planning to do it by means of both of us carrying out our intentions. If the activity is truly to be a shared one, though, we must achieve the goal by means of each of us acting on our intentions, and not by some other means. For us to actually share an intention I must not physically compel you or otherwise subvert your capacity to act for yourself.

Second, to share an intention, we must also adopt joint or meshing subplans that will ensure we pursue a unified and public course of action together. Suppose we both want to paint the house together, but I want to paint it blue and you want to paint it red.[19] For us to actually act together—to form a collective agent—we must negotiate some common intentional plan in the face of this potential conflict. If I poured blue paint into your can while you were not looking—imagine you are colorblind—I might bring it about that we acted on my own preferred subplan. But if I were to do that, we would not in fact fully share an intention, since you would think that we have a shared intention to paint the house red. Although by tricking you I will have gotten you to *behave* in the way that I want, we are still really intending two different things.

Bratman's definition also stipulates that in order for us to share an intention, I must intend that our goal be realized by means of both your and my respective intentions; and you must intend the same. I reflexively

[17] Bratman, *Faces of Intention*, 9.
[18] Bratman, *Faces of Intention*, 118–19.
[19] Bratman, *Faces of Intention*, 121–22.

intend the success of your intention, we might say. Because of this condition, Bratman holds that the state of "interlock" that characterizes a condition of shared intention is not merely cognitive.[20] It is not enough for Bratman—as it is for the defenders of the strategic coordination view described above—for me to intend only my own goal and to form a belief about what your goals happen to be. I must intend a shared goal, which requires that we act together. Because I regard you and I as undertaking a project together, I should do what I can to see that our joint project is successful, since what I intend is that *we* do something, and not merely that *I* do it. As Bratman puts it, "Each agent needs to embrace as her own the efficacy of the other's relevant intention."[21]

[20] Bratman, *Faces of Intention*, 124.

[21] Bratman, *Faces of Intention*, 125. As I mentioned at footnote 9 of this chapter, there is a controversy in the literature over Bratman's view that I can reflexively intend your action in virtue of my joint intention. Theorists like Seumas Miller and Christopher Kutz argue that it is preferable to hold that I intend only my own contribution, but that I orient that contribution toward a collective end I have and to which I believe you will also contribute. They argue that we can only intend those actions we can actually bring about, and that I cannot bring about your action. Therefore I cannot intend your action, even within the frame of a we-intention. Although this matter takes us far afield, I should mention that in my view the Miller/Kutz objection rests on too narrow a view of intending. It is a commonplace of action theory that we always intend actions under a description, and that various descriptions of the same behavior are always possible. When I intend an individual act, we are comfortable with the fact that I can intend it under a description that includes elements beyond my direct control. For example, suppose I intend to pick up the telephone and press some buttons. This act could be redescribed (in a wider frame) as intending to call you in London. Or it could be redescribed (in a narrower frame) as intending to move my hands in certain ways. Now, under the wide description, certain aspects of my action are not under my control. I can't bring it about that I call you in London unless my phone works, the network is not down, I do not suffer a heart attack as I pick up the receiver, etc. Yet we don't think this means I can't intend to call you in London, but (on pain of logical contradiction) must rather intend only to move my hands, since that is what is under my control, and then see what happens. As long as I have no reason to disbelieve that these other factors are in place, I can intend my act under the wide description (calling you in London). Now let us suppose that I picked up the telephone in 1930, when switchboard operators still existed. Is there some special feature of the fact that it is a person and not a network that connects me, which entails that I cannot intend to call you in London, under the wide description, but only to move my hands, under the narrow one? I can't see why it would. As long as I have no reason to disbelieve that the operator will answer and connect me, then I can intend to call you in London. In doing so, I do no disservice to my conception of the operator as a free agent. She could decide to abandon her post at any moment. I just have no reason to think that she has done so. On Bratman's view, a we-intention can function like this. Let's say I intend to dance the part of the Mouse King in the *Nutcracker.* We could redescribe this act (within a narrower frame) as intending to move my feet and arms in certain ways. Or we could redescribe it (within a larger frame) as my intending that we dance the *Nutcracker.* As long as I have no reason to disbelieve that your part will be performed, I can intend this larger description of the action, since if your part is performed, I do have control over the collective action (whether or not we dance the *Nutcracker*), just as if the operator connects me, I do have control over whether or not to call you in London (I could hang up).

Everyday Cooperative Activity: The Orchestra Case

Now that we have an account of shared intention, let us return to our central question: can a commitment to a universal principle or value—like the value of justice—give us reason for allegiance to particular cooperative schemes (like our own democratic state), and for solidarity with fellow participants within these schemes? Recall that the liberal-nationalist argument is that a commitment to justice is not sufficient to ground allegiance to a particular just state. Instead, justice ought to commit us to contributing to just states everywhere. This view of justice, however, neglects the fact that justice—like playing symphonies, or teaching at a university—is a value that requires our cooperation together in a joint intentional practice in order to be realized. Justice, on the view I have been defending, requires us to bring into being a set of democratic institutions, and to participate together in enacting the laws imposed by these institutions. I submit that when a universal value is one that requires cooperative action to be realized, it can give us sufficient reason for allegiance to the particular schemes and institutions that act to instantiate it. To examine whether this is so, let's begin by looking at an everyday group.

Consider the following case:

> *Joining the orchestra.* I play the trombone. Beethoven is my favorite composer and I value playing his symphonies. I cannot play them alone, so I decide to join the town orchestra. Suppose that I have been a member of the orchestra for a number of months now. One day, I wonder to myself: does belonging to the orchestra give me any obligation of *membership* with regard to *this* orchestra, and to my fellow players? I joined the orchestra because I valued playing Beethoven's music, but that is a universal value, and there are other orchestras out there that play Beethoven too. Why stick to my own? Has joining given me "new" reasons to do so?

Prudential Reasons

It is clear that, just by joining the orchestra, I have brought some new prudential reasons into being for myself. Joining means making a new personal commitment. We generally take our intentional commitments to carry a presumption against easy reversibility. Relative to desires, intentions have the feature of stability over time; this allows them to organize the pursuit of our lower-order desires. So my intention to play my part in the orchestra gives me some reason to act on it, by performing my role. To the extent I do not act on it (i.e., because I cannot get up in the morning, or chronically get drunk before performances), I behave irrationally.

Second, the fact that I intend a shared goal may give me some prudential reason to aid others in performing their parts sometimes. By intending a shared goal, I am subject to a certain rational pressure to aid the other participants, if giving aid does not derogate too much from my other ends. This is because a shared goal, by definition, can only be achieved if both your and my intentions are effectively realized. Let's say, for example, that our clarinetist has lost her job and cannot afford to replace her broken instrument. I have a stronger reason to contribute five dollars to the orchestra's collection for her than I do to give my neighbor—who has also fallen on hard times—the same amount of money toward her new instrument. We might express this by saying that I have an interest in the clarinetist's purchase, since her having the instrument advances a goal that I share, whereas my neighbor's having a new clarinet does not. How strong my (prudential) reason to aid the clarinetist is, though, depends on how much I value our playing together, and whether aiding her will frustrate my other goals.

None of my prudential reasons give me a very strong case for "sticking with" my orchestra, though. The main difficulty is that while there is an instrumental reason to follow through on the intentions we have, there is no obligation not to revise them in favor of different ones. So while I may have some reason to perform my role and to support my fellow players today, if tomorrow I decided to take up basketball rather than Beethoven, that reason would disappear. Moreover, our prudential reasons to perform our roles and to support others will often be weak. Viewed in a wholly prudential light, then, the value to me of playing in this orchestra is just the value to me of playing Beethoven together plus the value to me of not having to revise my intentions once they are formed.

If prudential reasons are the only ones that orchestra membership gives us, then its obligating force is minimal. But consider:

> *The fickle player.* Suppose I value playing Beethoven together with others. But I am fickle. I do not take membership in the orchestra to give me any new reasons for action, besides the prudential ones already mentioned. Instead, I am disposed to support any group when it seems like it would be effective in playing together. Small things make a difference to my decisions. If I am on the north side of town this afternoon, I might play with orchestra A; on the south side, tomorrow, orchestra B. What I value is playing Beethoven together. It doesn't matter to me with whom I do it. Notably, I do not take the fact that I joined the town orchestra in the past to give me a special reason to show up to their practice tomorrow. Nor do I take the fact that the town orchestra has already promised to play a concert in the fall to obligate me to do anything then.

The fickle player takes the sort of view to which the cultural nationalist argues his civic counterpart must fall prey: she thinks that her reason to support a goal that is undertaken in many places gives her equal reason to support it in all these places. What is wrong with the fickle player? Someone who adopted the identity-based view of special obligations endorsed by David Miller and Yael Tamir might say that her problem is that she has not subjectively identified with the town orchestra, and therefore that she isn't a member in the full sense that would include special obligations. But that seems to put the matter the wrong way round. Our response to the fickle player's case is not that since she does not feel any obligation to the town orchestra, she is therefore released. Instead, we believe that membership in the town orchestra gives the fickle player some moral obligations whether she identifies with the group or not.

Moral Obligations of Membership

CONSENT-BASED OBLIGATIONS

The reason membership affects our player's ethical situation, whether she acknowledges it or not, is because she consented to join the orchestra. Her consent to join brought into being new moral reasons for playing her role in their joint practice, and her behavior fails to acknowledge these reasons. By consenting to join the orchestra, the player acquired new obligations to others, including the obligation to play her role; to consider the needs and claims of other players in contexts relevant to the orchestra; to warn the other participants if she will no longer play her role; and to exit the orchestra in a way that does not jeopardize the other players' goals.

Joining the orchestra affects the way in which our player's duties of respect and concern for other people should be expressed. While we have duties of respect and concern to all human beings at the most basic level, this does not license the further conclusion that we are bound to treat all human beings in exactly the same way at all times. We may treat them differently as long as we can justify this by pointing to a fact about our relations that is morally relevant. Our consent to enter a joint enterprise is such a morally relevant fact. This is because consenting to join such an enterprise leads others to expect that we will contribute to their joint project, and induces them to rely on us to perform our role. We have a duty of respect to avoid manipulating their legitimate expectations and thereby inflicting harm to their joint project through their reliance on us. Our fickle player refuses to recognize this. She voluntarily leads the other players to form an expectation that she will contribute to their orchestra, and then fails to acknowledge that their expectation is legitimate, or that it makes any claim on her.

So it would be wrong for the fickle player to induce the expectation in her fellow players that she will perform her role—by consenting to join the orchestra—when she had no intention of following through. Despite this, we do not want to imply that our player has an unconditional duty to continue to playing in the trombone section indefinitely, for as long as the orchestra remains in existence. Our consent may change the landscape of moral obligation, but it does not change it irrevocably. Still, her obligations to the other players demand that she not revoke her shared intention to play together with the orchestra in a capricious or precipitous way.

So what does she owe, morally speaking, as a matter of respect to the other players, if after some months she gets tired of playing the trombone and would rather take up basketball? If her intentions change, she has reason to act to prevent losses to the other players that could arise from her nonperformance. At the very least, she owes fellow orchestra members sufficient warning before leaving, so that their project is not destroyed. It would be wrong to just decide one day to stop showing up to practice. Moreover, she may have an obligation to help them find a replacement trombonist, if one is not forthcoming. And if the group is already booked for a show, she may have an obligation to come play even though she would rather not, so that the others do not suffer undue losses. If she *does* let the others down, she has an obligation to compensate them in some way. None of these obligations add up to a duty to stay in the orchestra forever. But they do create a duty on her not to act in a way that imposes undue harm on the orchestra, since she has induced her fellow players to form legitimate expectations of her behavior by consenting to join their practice.

COLLECTIVE OBLIGATIONS

Recall that the fickle player also did not take the fact that the town orchestra had booked a concert in the fall to obligate her to do anything then. The fall concert is an obligation of the collective as a whole: if the individual players have reasons to perform their parts, then they derive from a logically prior obligation of the orchestra. As a trombonist, our player may have had nothing to do with actually making this agreement: perhaps the booking department schedules all the orchestra's engagements. Nevertheless, because she consented to join the practice, as long as she believes that her fellow orchestra members share the intention to show up and play, she still has an obligation to go play at the fall concert as well, even if this involves some inconvenience to her (perhaps, when it comes time, she would rather go to a party). So clearly voluntary membership can create wholly new obligations: these obligations burden individuals, but they actually derive from logically prior obligations of the collective as a whole.

Through their voluntary participation in the orchestra, members may even incur obligations of which they were not aware when they signed up. Consider the following case: suppose the town orchestra rents a historic house for its fall concert. That evening, just as they reach the crescendo of Beethoven's Ninth, the valuable stained glass windows in the house shatter unexpectedly, unable to withstand the vibrations caused by the instruments. Perhaps the orchestra should have chosen someone to inspect the house beforehand, but it did not. And unfortunately, the orchestra does not have liability insurance. Who should compensate the house's owner?

It is commonly supposed that in order to be responsible for a harm, I need to have made a difference to its occurrence. If the harm would have occurred anyway, no matter what I had done, I am not responsible for it, since I made no difference to it. It is also commonly supposed that to be responsible for a harm, I have to have had some control over it, such that I could have prevented its occurrence if I had wanted to.[22] The trouble is that in many collective acts, like the situation we just imagined, neither principle appears to be satisfied.

If our player had decided to stop playing her trombone just before the crescendo, the windows would have broken anyway, because of the vibrations made by the rest of the players. For this reason, her playing her part did not make a difference to the window breakage: the window breakage was overdetermined. Or suppose that just before the crescendo, she has seen that the windows might break, and tried to yell to stop the playing. Deafened by the rest of the instruments, no one would have heard. This means the breaking of the windows was not under her control: there was nothing she might have done to stop it. Moreover, each individual member of the orchestra can say the same thing about the broken windows that she can say. On this view, no one is individually responsible for breaking the windows. No individual is responsible because no one was causally pivotal to the outcome—the windows would have broken even if she had not made her contribution to the symphony—and because the outcome was not under any particular person's individual control—there was nothing she could have personally done to stop it.

The trouble with this logic, of course, is that it leaves no one responsible for the breakage and therefore leaves the house owner uncompensated for the wrong that has been done. But clearly the breakage did not come about on its own; rather it was caused by the orchestra acting together. It is the orchestra as a whole that had full control over whether or not the windows were broken, by choosing to play Beethoven's Ninth in the house on that evening. We should therefore assign responsibility for com-

[22] This way of putting it is drawn from Kutz, *Complicity*, 3–7.

pensating the owner to the orchestra as a whole, and not to the particular members who make it up. The orchestra is responsible for replacing the windows out of its common funds, or, if these funds are insufficient, for levying contributions from its members. Either way, of course, the effective burden of compensation will devolve upon individual members, who will have to forgo free lunches at practice (if the common fund is used, say) or some outside spending that month (if special contributions are levied). The players are responsible even though they weren't aware that they were "signing up" to this obligation when they joined. This is because, simply by joining, the players have incurred a liability to the burdens required to meet the collective's obligations.

If the above account is correct, then, voluntary membership in associations like the orchestra does change our moral reasons for action, by giving us "new" reasons that go beyond the reasons we had for joining the group in the first place. It does so in two ways: first, by inducing legitimate expectations in others that we will contribute to their joint enterprise; and second, by opening us up, as individuals, to the imposition of new duties to fulfill sui generis collective obligations. We can model the moral reasons of the members of the orchestra, then, using a two-tiered structure:

Tier 1		*Tier 2*		*Outcome*
Individual's goal/value (requires collective action for realization): playing Beethoven's symphonies	consent to → join orchestra	we-intention to regard myself as member of orchestra and to contribute to collective goal ↓ Gives rise to moral reasons	mutual responsiveness → mutual support	Performance of Beethoven's Ninth

1. To treat fellow-players with respect
    a. By refraining from manipulating their expectations
    b. By showing respect and concern in contexts related to the orchestra
2. To play my part in fulfilling collective obligations

It is worth noting that membership creates these new moral reasons for us, on my argument, regardless of whether individuals identify with the group of which they are members. If they consent to join a valuable cooperative practice, they have obligations to their fellow members and to those affected by the group's activities no matter how they feel about the group right now, and whether they subjectively identify with it or not. Before concluding this section, however, I should state two essential caveats to what has been said so far. First, on my view, consent to collective enterprises give us obligations of membership only if the enterprise is morally valuable. Joining a group of bank robbers does not give me obligations of membership to play my role in robbing the bank. If the joint enterprise actually produces an (objective) bad, then a member is not under an obligation to keep contributing to the enterprise, since she does not actually have a good reason to have consented in the first place. As soon as she realizes that she has misapprehended her first-tier reasons, she should also realize that she has no second-tier obligation of membership.

Second, a member is only under an obligation to perform her part in the collective enterprise if she believes her fellow members also intend to perform theirs. So if I belong to the orchestra and we have committed to play a concert in the park today, then I have a reason to go play in the park as long as I believe my fellow players intend to do so. But if I know, for example, that the entire wind section got drunk last night and won't show up, then I do not have a reason to go down to the park by myself. In this case, our shared intention has failed, and, no matter what I do, we will fail to meet our collective obligation. But because the orchestra is liable for damages, as a member of the orchestra I may owe compensation to whomever we promised the concert.

Let's take stock of our (rather complex) argument so far. Recall that we are scrutinizing a key element in the liberal-nationalist case: the claim that a commitment to a universal principle or value cannot give us reason for allegiance to particular schemes and institutions, or for solidarity with our fellow participants in those institutions. Nationalists claim that we need some special reason—beyond the fact that citizens wish to do their part in realizing a condition of justice—to justify their allegiance to a particular state and solidarity with their compatriots. Our strategy was to approach this problem obliquely, by considering whether a similar special reason would be necessary to account for people's allegiance to everyday groups pursuing goods of (presumptively) universal value. The trombone player's reason for joining the orchestra is a universal one: she thinks that playing Beethoven is valuable (everywhere). But the fact that there are other schemes out there within which she could pursue this good is no reason to abandon her particular commitment to the town orchestra. For once she has joined, she has brought into being new reasons to support it and to show respect and consideration to the fellow members who are relying on her contributions. These additional reasons of membership are derived from her basic commitment to the value of playing Beethoven, which prompted her to join in the first place. But there is nothing about the universality of her first-tier commitment that conflicts with her second-tier commitment to this particular orchestra. So, in this section, we have seen that consenting to a particular practice is an important way of generating a special commitment to it. In the sections to follow, we will take up the question of whether consent is the only way of generating such a commitment.

Democracy as Shared Cooperative Activity?

In the next sections, I will argue that we should understand a democracy as a shared cooperative venture along similar lines, and I will claim that like the orchestra, it too generates obligations to play our role, to treat compatriots with respect and concern in relevant contexts, and to contribute to fulfilling collective obligations.[23] Once we interpret democracy in this light, I believe, there is no reason to think that we need to appeal to special cultural commonalities in order to justify our commitment to a particular democracy any more than we need to appeal to them in order to justify our commitment to a particular orchestra. There are two main reasons, however, why one might initially be skeptical of my claim that democracies can be analyzed along similar lines as orchestras. I will call these two objections the *no clear goal* objection and the *voluntary association* objection:

1. *No clear goal objection*: While the members of an orchestra are obviously acting together in the service of a well-defined goal—to play Beethoven's symphonies—it may not seem that fellow citizens are participating together in an activity with a shared goal that is similarly well defined. Of course, compatriots do sometimes act together—as in voting, or paying taxes, for example—but it may not seem that their acting together is in the service of a shared purpose of which each participant is aware. Perhaps each citizen merely has private instrumental or expressive reasons for voting; or perhaps his voting is simply irrational, and therefore not to be readily explained.[24] In order to make plausible my claim that a democracy can be analyzed along the lines of other joint intentional activities, then, I must offer an account of the shared goal guiding the participants.

[23] Other efforts to apply Bratman's theory to the state have been made. See Kutz, "Collective Work of Citizenship"; Coleman, *A Practice of Principle*, 90–97; Shapiro, "Law, Plans, and Practical Reason." My account is closest to Kutz's, but differs significantly from all three.

[24] As is charged in the famous voter's paradox.

2. *Voluntary association objection*: Orchestras, dance troupes, and football teams are all examples of voluntary associations that individuals join in order to further their aims. We consent to join these activities, and our obligations to play our role and to show special respect to our fellow members derive from that fact. But it seems difficult to model the democratic state as a voluntary joint activity in this way. This is because most of us are *born* citizens of the state in which we live and the costs of exit from our birth state can be quite high: we may be forced to leave behind friends and family, be thrust into an unwelcoming cultural environment, and have to learn a new language. Given these barriers to exit, it seems difficult to describe even the most democratic of states as a voluntary association. If this is so, can a democracy really be understood as a shared cooperative activity, participation in which generally seems to be voluntary, at least in other cases?

Against these two objections, I argue that democratic citizenship can be modeled after other shared cooperative activities. Meeting the objections, however, will entail making some important revisions to the paradigm we established in the orchestra example. If I am correct, though, the democratic state is a joint practice in which we act together to secure a common end, and its unity can be explained on lines similar to the unity of other practices in which we commonly act together. We do not need a "special reason" of the sort provided by linguistic, ethnic, or cultural commonality in order to justify our allegiance to it.

The No Clear Goal Objection

The no clear goal objection asks: if a democracy is meant to have a shared aim, by analogy to cooperative groups like an orchestra, what could that aim possibly be? I submit that there are two such aims: a "Kantian" one—to coercively impose one objective scheme of rights and duties on all who are subject to the state; and a "Rousseauian" one—to define that scheme of rights and duties through our democratic participation together, in a just and nondominating way.

As we have seen, Kant argues that states play a constitutive role in the realization of justice by defining and enforcing an objective definition of our rights and duties. Each individual has an interest in possessing guaranteed civil rights (rights to property, contractual relations, and legal status) that depend on a public system of laws, because otherwise she would be subject to domination and control by other private persons in her projects. Establishing an objective system of rights and duties requires we coordinate our behavior with one another. Laws are not just enforced through directly coercive acts on the part of the authorities; they depend much more pervasively on large-scale patterns of behavior on the part of people who orient their actions to these laws, who take law to have a moral salience that affects their practical reasoning about what to do. By obeying the law, then, residents of a particular state help to make their acquired rights an effective reality. No system of law could maintain itself were those to whom it addresses itself to refuse to let law affect their practical reasoning.

Likewise, by paying taxes, members actively contribute to sustaining the institutions that enforce these rights against those individuals who refuse to comply voluntarily. Were we to cease paying taxes, again on a large scale, our rights would mean nothing in practice, since there would be no state capable of coercing those who infringed them. What it means for something to be my property is simply to have a system of social behavior coordinated around my possession of it: to have my right over it generally recognized and respected by my fellow citizens, and to have a coercive agency capable of enforcing my right against those who refuse to recognize it. By obeying the law and paying taxes, then, members contribute to the coercion of other people in accordance with an objective scheme of rights and duties. Kant argues that we are required by justice to coordinate our behavior through a state in this way, since equal freedom cannot be guaranteed in a situation where various private interpretations of justice compete with one another. It is constitutive of justice, for Kant, that it be defined and enforced by a public institution as one unitary scheme of law.

To contribute to this shared Kantian goal, it is not necessary that each member who obeys the law and pays taxes actively intend the entire system of public coercion that the state puts into effect. The resident may simply be intending not to get himself punished, or to obey the law, and may not be in any way conscious of the acts of his compatriots and their overall connection to a system of public coercion. Still, we can say that the residents are in fact contributing to the public coercion of one another even though they don't intend the entire joint project. Our resident's actions are causally linked to an ongoing collective process—the public coercion of other people on a state's territory in the name of justice—and he can be expected to be aware of that fact, if he reflects on it. By orienting our behavior toward the law and paying taxes, then, we are aiding in that state's forcible imposition of a particular scheme of rights and duties.[25]

[25] Thomas Pogge presents a somewhat similar view of our collective responsibility for imposing institutions in *World Poverty*, 66–67.

When the state we live in is a democracy, however, each citizen not only helps to coerce other members of the state by paying taxes and obeying the law; she also has the obligation to deliberately involve herself in the political process. The Rousseauian goal of a democratic state is to formulate a just scheme of rights and duties by acting together. And in contributing her voice and vote to the political process, the democratic citizen is party to a shared intention in a more robust way than when she simply obeys the law.

Why is it fitting to conceive of the democratic process as one in which we act together, as a joint intentional practice? We began our discussion of collective action with the observation that there are many goals of value to individuals that they cannot achieve unless they join a group and regard themselves as members acting together with others. If Rousseau is correct, then the formulation of just laws is a goal of this sort. This is true in two senses: in intending that we enact law together, I must (*a*) consider your interests in formulating my own opinion, and therefore regard myself as a member of a group that also includes you; and (*b*) I must also intend that your opinion about the common interest be effectively taken into account. If your opinion is not considered, I would simply be imposing my private will on you, not contributing to the formulation of a (non-dominating) general will. In participating and voting, then, my intention is not simply that I formulate law. Rather, I intend that *we* formulate a set of just laws together, which means I must also intend that your contribution be effective. In participating democratically, I must conceive of myself as "promoting a shared endeavor to which others will also contribute."[26]

This means that the law that defines our civil rights only has legitimate authority if it is the outcome of a fair collective process, one in which each person, as an equal citizen, has a right to contribute his voice and vote; and in which the participants must reflexively intend the success of each other's contributions. The democratic formulation of just laws, on this view, is necessarily a joint action. By taking part in social movements, debating political issues, voting for representatives, and retaining a right of participation in the revision of their constitution, on this view, then, citizens *do* act in the service of a shared aim: the "good" that democratic citizens ultimately produce together is the just specification of their own civil rights.

So citizens and residents in a democratic state have two sorts of collective goals. The first is one that they need not actively intend, but to which all residents' actions do in fact contribute: this is the coercive imposition, through the state, of an objective scheme of rights and duties on

[26] See Kutz, "Collective Work of Citizenship," 486.

their compatriots (the Kantian goal). And the second goal—if it to be successful—must be the subject of an active we-intention on the part of citizens: this is the formulation of just and nondominating laws that take everyone's interests into account and to which each citizen has the chance to contribute (the Rousseauian goal).

The Voluntary Association Objection

As we saw a few pages ago, the obligations of an orchestra member—like obligations of members of other voluntary associations—are grounded in her consent: that is, they depend on the player's having joined the orchestra and undertaken a commitment to her fellow players. Of course, the player who joins the orchestra does not thereby make an implicit promise to remain with the group forever. She certainly has the right to leave, if her goals and interests change. But the fact that she joined the practice has given her new obligations to show respect for her fellow players' expectations in ways that are relevant to the orchestra. Her duties of respect for her fellow players demand that she not quit just before a performance, that she consider their needs when making decisions for the group, and that she contribute to discharging collective obligations. But still, what generated these duties to the orchestra was her consent to join: no one who hasn't joined is obligated to pay for the broken windows from the fall concert, or to show up to play in the park.

Can We Have Involuntary Obligations of Membership?

Now we should ask: is consent the only way to justify special obligations like those the orchestra member has to her orchestra? Or are there other grounds for special obligations as well, grounds that place an individual under an obligation to do her part, to show respect for other members, and to contribute to discharging collective responsibilities even if she has not "joined" a particular practice? I submit that there are cases in which an act of consent or "joining" is not necessary to give me obligations of group membership. Especially relevant are cases where I already have some pre-existing moral duty to do something that can only (or best) be accomplished by my acting together with some group. In such cases, I do not have to voluntarily undertake to "join" in order to have a good reason to cooperate with the group. Instead, special obligations to contribute to the joint activity are grounded not in my consent, but in my pre-existing moral duty. Consider the following case:

> *The involuntary fire brigade.* Suppose I awaken in the middle of the night to find that my neighbor's house is on fire and his children are

> trapped inside. I have a duty to do what I can to help save the children as long as this does not entail great risk for myself. One way for me to act on this duty to rescue would be to grab a bucket, fill it up in my bathtub, and carry it over to throw on the fire. This is not likely to be very effective at saving the children, however. Suppose, though, that a fire brigade shows up, but they are one man short. They need someone to sit in the truck and man the controls if they are to put out the fire. If I help them, there is a high probability we will together save the children. Would I be justified in refusing to join forces with them, even at a much greater risk of the children's death?

In this instance, I do not think I am at moral liberty to refuse to act together with the brigade, regardless of whether I had any history of "joining" or "consenting" to be part of their enterprise.[27] The reason it is not up to me to refuse is that I am already bound to do the best I can to save the children and now that the brigade is here, the proper way to fulfill that duty is to act together with them. Therefore my preexisting duty of rescue underwrites a more specific duty to act together with the brigade in this instance, even if I have not previously consented to membership in their enterprise.

Moreover, once I have begun to sit in the fire engine and handle the controls, it would be wrong of me to simply jump up and leave, even if I left to do something that was also directed toward my duty of rescue—say by helping another group set up a cordon around the fire—as long as that is not clearly a better strategy. This is because the other brigade members are now relying on me (legitimately, since I have a positive duty to aid in the rescue). By jumping out now, I place the success of the entire joint enterprise at risk, and jeopardize everyone's attempts to fulfill her duty. So my general duty to rescue is in this case particularized to the brigade once it shows up, if it is the best option; and it remains binding once the other members have formed the expectation that I will contribute. I owe it to them either to perform my role or to give them sufficient warning that I cannot do so and help to find a replacement, at least until either (*a*) we have together fulfilled our duty and rescued the children or (*b*) it is clear that our joint efforts will not succeed.

[27] I don't mean this to imply that I can rightfully be coerced to join the fire brigade; that conclusion would require the additional step of showing that this duty is one I can be coerced to perform. Many countries do actually enforce "Good Samaritan" duties—duties of rescue in cases of minimal risk—in one form or another. I mean to sidestep the debate over these practices here. But I think I can certainly be *criticized* and *blamed* for refusing to join the fire brigade in this situation, whether or not I had any past agreement or history of membership with them, even if it turns out I cannot be coerced.

In our involuntary fire brigade example, a (partially) organized group already existed. But there are other cases in which a collection of individuals may be responsible for forming themselves into a group in order to carry out some moral duty. Consider the following case, paraphrased from a paper by Virginia Held:

> *The passive subway riders.* Consider seven unacquainted and able-bodied people sitting in a subway car. One of the people gets up, pushes the smallest person to the floor, and starts to beat and strangle him. It is possible that no one of the other five people could subdue the strangler all by himself. But the five of them together certainly can, probably without serious injury to themselves (the strangler has no knife or gun). If the subway riders just sit there, watching while the person is strangled, can we hold them responsible for their failure to act together as a group?[28]

I think we can certainly hold the subway riders responsible for their failure to act together. Unlike the fire brigade, however, the subway riders are encumbered by an additional responsibility: in order to fulfill their duty by acting together, they must first constitute themselves into a group. No one is obliged to risk life and limb against the strangler all alone. But they are obliged to act together, since that is the only way to save the victim, and therefore they are obliged to create the conditions that make joint action possible, by communicating their intentions, and the like. Just as with the involuntary fire brigade, what grounds their duty to form a group is in the first instance their duty to rescue, a duty incumbent on them as human beings. It doesn't matter that they didn't consent to being faced with this situation in the subway car, that they may not identify with the other riders, or would prefer not to act together with them. They have a duty to constitute themselves into a group, since that is the right way to save the person being strangled. If they refuse to do so, we can hold them morally responsible.

Duties of Membership in a Democratic State

The crucial difference between the state and our orchestra example, I believe, is that the state cannot be understood along the lines of a voluntary association, but is instead analogous to the involuntary examples we outlined above in terms of what grounds our obligations of membership. This is because we have an unconditional duty, binding on us independently of our goals and choices, to participate in a just state. In taking this position, I am following Rawls, who similarly argues that we have a

[28] Held, "Random Collection," 475.

"natural duty of justice" to "comply with and to do our share in just institutions when they exist and apply to us; and . . . to assist in the establishment of just arrangements when they do not exist, at least when thus can be done with little cost to ourselves."[29] Rawls, in turn, follows Kant, who, as we have seen, argues that we have a (coercively enforceable) duty of justice to enter the state.[30]

If we accept the Kantian-Rousseauian argument I have defended so far, we will hold that the duty of justice requires us to bring into being a public institution—the democratic state—that can define and enforce rights to property and to bodily inviolability in a way that is consistent with everyone's independence from private coercion, and the threat of domination it provokes. This duty of justice can only be fulfilled through institutions; it cannot be fulfilled by private persons acting on their own. And these duties of justice are not based on consent or voluntary adoption. Instead, they are natural duties, like the duty of rescue, to which we are bound simply in virtue of being rational agents, and which can be coercively enforced.

Since the natural duty of justice is a duty that can only be fulfilled through the establishment of a public juridical institution, every other person who is subject to potential coercion by our actions has a right that we do our part to bring such an institution into being and to uphold it. In keeping with our analysis of democracy as a joint intentional practice, I believe we ought to interpret the natural duty of justice as a duty to a) cooperate in the state's coercive imposition of a unitary scheme of rights and duties, by obeying the law and paying taxes; and b) to do our part to see that the scheme we impose is a just one, by forming a shared intention to participate in the democratic process that defines these rights.

If this is correct, then the important question is this: which particular state does a given individual have a duty to uphold and to participate in? The answer, I think, is that an individual is under a duty to do his part in establishing and upholding institutions together with *that group of people whose rights are regularly affected by his acts*. That means the natural duty of justice is particularized in the following way:

a. *Duties to establish a state in the state of nature.* Where no state currently exists, each person is under a duty to do his part in a collective endeavor to create one. In this sense, those individuals who refuse to constitute themselves into a just state can be held morally responsible for not doing so. They are exactly like the Passive Subway Riders. They stand by

[29] Rawls, *A Theory of Justice*, 334.

[30] Kant calls this the "postulate of public right": "When you cannot avoid living side by side with all others, you ought to leave the state of nature and proceed into a rightful condition" (*MM*, 6:307).

while their own rights and the rights of those with whom they interact are subjected to determination through violence, although they could overcome this problem by coordinating their behavior through a public institution. Kant would say that although these individuals do one another no wrong in enforcing their own views of their rights on one another, given that they jointly intend to remain in a state of nature, they do "wrong in the highest degree" by refusing to constitute themselves as a state. They are collectively shirking their natural duty of justice.

Jeremy Waldron has referred to this idea as Kant's "Proximity Principle": where people cannot avoid living side-by-side with others, in a way that their actions necessarily affect one another, they have a duty to bring into being a juridical institution, since that is the only way they can possess property without compromising other people's freedom.[31] Therefore, in a state of nature, we would have a duty to establish a state together with whomever our control of resources affects, that is, with whomever we regularly interact. Since we at present remain in an international state of nature, and since our actions regularly impinge on the freedom of others across borders, as we saw in chapter 4, we have an unfulfilled collective duty to constitute ourselves into an international juridical institution now.

Thus, any group of individuals whose acts regularly affect one another's rights and who do not currently have a set of legal and political institutions are obliged to create one. With whom? With all those persons on whose rights their actions regularly impinge, regardless of their nationality or cultural affiliations. On this view, the "people" who form a state do not have to be bound together by any prior ties at all; they might be an occasional group that simply happens to find themselves together on a piece of territory. Still, however it is that they came to be in a situation where their acts impinge on one another, they require a state to regulate their interactions. Members of a state are bound together solely by their territorial situation, a situation that brings them into sustained contact with each other.

b. *Implication in existing states*. In the contemporary world, no one lives in a state of nature anymore, and our territorial situation is today defined not by interactive proximity but by state jurisdiction. But there are a large number of existing states in our world, many of which can make a plausible claim to legitimacy, so which one of these states in particular do we presently have an obligation to uphold, by obeying the law, paying taxes, and the like? I submit that we have an obligation to uphold that existing state in which our actions regularly affect the legitimate coer-

[31] Waldron, "Redressing Historic Injustice," 136–37; Waldron, "Kant's Legal Positivism," 1555.

cion of other people, and therefore impinge on the security of their rights. This amounts, in effect, to a "Kantian" natural duty to uphold the state on whose territory we reside.

As a member of a state, in complying with the law, paying taxes, and enjoying the security of one's own and others' rights (especially rights to property, as we saw in chapter 1), one is already implicated in coercing one's compatriots. By orienting my behavior to the laws and paying my taxes, I help to impose a set of laws on the particular group of people on this territory, not on all human beings everywhere. The acts of a resident of Sweden do not contribute in the same way to the coercive imposition of laws on residents of South Africa, for example. Whether or not she refuses to orient her behavior to South Africa's property laws does not undermine South Africans' security of possession, unless she is temporarily present in their territory as a tourist. But whether she orients her behavior to Sweden's laws does impinge on her compatriots' property rights. Similarly, if she refuses to pay taxes to South Africa's government, she is not jeopardizing the welfare or social rights of South African citizens or the integrity of their legal authorities. They never expected or relied upon her contributions to secure their rights in the first place. But if she refuses to pay taxes to the Swedish government, she is threatening the security of her compatriots' rights. Simply by being present in the territory, then, I contribute to the coercion of the other subjects of its legal system. I do this either by orienting my behavior to the laws governing that territory and paying taxes—thereby helping to impose a coercive legal order on others—or refusing to do these things—thereby coercing these others through my private will rather than through a public institution, something from which I have a duty to refrain. Just by being present in a territory, then, I acquire obligations to uphold the legal system that governs it, if that legal system is sufficiently legitimate. This is because I have a prior duty of justice to regulate all of my interactions involving external resources through a juridical authority.

It is hard to imagine how one could extricate oneself from implication in a coercive scheme of law, unless it is by colonizing another planet or becoming a hermit, and thus withdrawing from social interaction altogether. But on the Kantian view, being involuntarily implicated in a legal scheme does one no wrong, since one already has a prior duty of justice to uphold a legitimate state. In the same way, being involuntarily implicated in the fire brigade did our next-door neighbor no wrong. He already has a duty of rescue to help save the children, and although he did not ask for the brigade to show up, now that they are here, he has a duty to act together with them.

Similarly, although I did not choose the group of people on this territory, I wrong them when I refuse to regulate my actions through the political authority that governs their territory, and that is what gives me a particular obligation to them, whether I acknowledge it or not. On the Kantian view, this means one ought to obey the state's laws wherever one is, and contribute one's tax money to the state where one resides or owns property as long as that state is legitimate. If one does not voluntarily form the intention to do these things, then one can be rightly coerced to do them.

The Kantian account of state membership and political obligation, then, is primarily a territorial account, as we should expect from a theory that emphasizes the moral importance of the state in defining and securing our rights to property. It is by acting in a way that has repercussions on the freedom of other people within a given territorial space—and thus merely by being present within that space—that one acquires obligations to uphold the state that governs it, by obeying the law and paying one's taxes. Tourists and residents in another state's territory are "temporary members" of a joint law-enforcement practice, rather like "fill-in" players in an orchestra. They have an obligation to play their role, by respecting others' rights, orienting their behavior to the law, and so on, but their connection with the state is fleeting and impermanent. And they lose these obligations when they exit the territory, because then their actions no longer regularly contribute to the coercion of members of that state.

But the fact that my acts contribute to the public coercion of other people through the state also gives rise to important responsibilities to these other people. If I am helping to coerce my compatriots in accordance with a scheme of rights and duties that is unjust or dominating, then my acts are contributing to a public wrong. I have a responsibility to do what I can to redress that wrong. If the laws of my state violate the minimal threshold criteria outlined in chapter 4, I may have a duty to disobey the law, or to act together with my fellow citizens to depose the current government. But even if the laws meet these minimal threshold criteria, they may still contain significant injustices, or they may not be formulated in a way in which each citizen's interests receive an adequate hearing. How can I do my part to prevent the imposition of an unjust or dominating scheme of rights on others?

One way of doing what I can to redress this wrong is to actively involve myself in the democratic process. In addition to "Kantian" obligations to uphold the state, then, the natural duty of justice also grounds "Rousseauian" obligations of democratic participation. Following Rousseau, I argue that the way to ensure that the scheme of rights and duties that one's state imposes is just and nondominating is for it to be the outcome of a collective endeavor in which each person participates, in a way that takes every other member's interests into account. Even if the principles of equal freedom have a "core" or "minimal" content that must be respected—those threshold conditions that we outlined in chapter 4—these conditions still do not provide us with a full account of what equal freedom entails. Forming a shared intention to participate together with others in defining a scheme of positive civil rights is therefore an essential part of realizing justice on a particular territory. Democratic citizenship mediates between an abstract ideal of free and equal citizenship, and the particular rights that achieve this ideal for *this* group of citizens in their particular circumstances.

If a well-ordered democratic state already exists and one is a permanent member of it—in the sense outlined above: that one's actions pervasively affect the imposition of a coercive legal system on other members within a given territory—then one is under an additional duty to form a shared intention to participate together with others in formulating the laws the state coercively imposes. Like the territorial duties of obedience to law and payment of taxes, Rousseauian duties of participation are particularized to one democratic process and to one particular set of citizens. If the Swedish citizen does not participate or vote in South African elections, then, we need not fear that the interests of someone who is coerced to obey South African laws go unheard in formulating those laws. As long as she is not a permanent resident there, the Swedish citizen is not coerced to follow South African laws: they are not even addressed to her. But if a group of South African citizens is systematically disenfranchised from contributing to the formulation of South African law, then we do have reason to worry that the laws that result will be unjust or dominating: this group of citizens has not had the chance to voice their interests in the political process, or to contribute their view of the common good.[32] Democratic justice, on this view, requires us to act together and to think of ourselves as a group. If I refuse to vote, participate politically, or to support others' efforts to make fair use of their political rights, then I show a lack of regard for the role citizenship plays in defining a fair scheme of rights and imposing that scheme in a sufficiently nondominating way.

This Rousseauian view of the importance of democratic citizenship in realizing justice also has important implications for granting citizenship, as we can see from the case of the Swedish citizen who permanently resides in South Africa. According to this view, all permanent residents on a state's territory ought to be citizens. It is fitting to extend a higher status of membership to those whose lives are pervasively shaped by the institu-

[32] Clearly citizens are not wronged by the enforcement of the civil, criminal, and tax laws, if they are sufficiently just. But I also don't think it is wrong to make voting a legal duty, as countries like Australia do, although this is bound to be more controversial.

tions of a territory over the long term—just as it is fitting to allow permanent members of the orchestra a say that fill-in players do not have. So a territorial theory of citizenship, like the Kantian-Rousseauian one, cannot endorse an ethnic or cultural basis for the granting of civic rights. Anyone who is pervasively subject to coercive expectations to obey the law within a certain territory must have a path to acquiring citizenship rights within that territory: this group of people includes those born there as well as those who reside there over the long term. It may be proper to institute residence requirements—proof of a relatively enduring connection to the state and its territory—as a prerequisite for citizenship. But to deny a permanent resident citizenship is to refuse to recognize his innate right to freedom, since he ought to be able to understand himself as the partial author of the constraints he is forced to obey.

Last, a Kantian-Rousseauian view of the state implies that citizens, just like members of an orchestra, have important collective responsibilities to those on whom their joint practice inflicts injury or injustice. A collective responsibility to redress injustice can be owed either to insiders or to outsiders to their territory. For example, if part of the population on their territory is currently disenfranchised, citizens are under a collective obligation to redress the situation, by changing the law and by paying compensation. It may be true that no individual citizen made a difference to the group's disenfranchisement. Perhaps the policy of discrimination enjoyed such support that no matter what she had done, no particular citizen could have changed the outcome. Thus no one was pivotal in determining the policy. And perhaps the policy was also not under any particular citizen's control, since it was only the result of the entire group's discussion and voting that determined whether it was imposed, and no citizen had control over the entire process. Moreover, each other citizen can say about the policy exactly what our representative citizen can say: he had no control over it and was not pivotal in deciding it. But clearly the democracy as a whole had collective control over the policy. So it is the democracy as a whole that owes compensation and redress, perhaps in the form of affirmative action policies to benefit this excluded group. We can apply the same analysis to policies that violate the rights of outsiders to a democracy. Even though the outcome was not under the control of any individual citizen, and was not determined by his particular actions, the democracy as a whole still owes compensation to those outsiders whom it injures, and in their capacity as members, citizens can be expected to contribute to it.

On my view, then, we *do* have special moral reasons to participate politically in our own democratic process, to obey the laws of our particular state (when they are legitimate), to pay our taxes to the authorities of our country, and to contribute to discharging the state's collective responsibilities; and these reasons are grounded in our natural duty of justice, which demands that we establish, and contribute to, a shared intentional practice of democratic legislation. If the above account is correct, then I believe we can sketch the structure of an individual citizen's commitment to a *particular* democracy along lines similar to those developed in the orchestra case, using our earlier two-tiered model. In both these cases, a universal value that requires a practical commitment to cooperation with others can give one reason to acquire the attitudes characteristic of membership in a particular group.

Tier 1				*Tier 2*		*Outcome*
Natural duty of justice (requires collective action to secure justice)	→	produce common scheme of law	→	Duty to act as democratic citizen	→	Formulation/ imposition of just scheme of law
				↓		

1. Moral duty to act as member of some state. (I cannot renounce duty of justice)
2. Obligation to perform my "Kantian" duties to uphold a scheme of law—pay my taxes, orient my behavior to law
3. Obligation to perform my "Rousseauian" duties of citizenship:
   a. To vote and participate in the democratic process
   b. To do what I can to see that my fellow citizens' participation rights are guaranteed
4. Obligation to help discharge *collective responsibilities* the state as a whole may acquire by voluntary commitments or by inflicting harm through our joint acts

The essential difference between the orchestra and the democratic state, then, is not so much in the type of obligations to which they gave rise—in both cases, I have an obligation to play my role in a joint practice, to treat fellow participants appropriately, and to contribute to discharging collective responsibilities. The difference is in what *grounds* these obligations. In the case of the orchestra, our obligations are grounded in our consent to the practice. In the democratic state, our obligations are grounded in the natural duty of justice, to which we are bound independently of our will. Beyond that, however, the substance of these obligations—and the relations they establish between us and our fellow members—is much the same.

Do We Need a Shared National Culture?

With all this in place, let us briefly return to reconsider the liberal-nationalists' case. Recall their assertion that the constitutional patriot cannot explain why citizens have sufficient reason for allegiance to their particular state, or for showing solidarity with their compatriots, on the basis of justice alone. Instead, nationalists claim that citizens need some special reason—like the moral importance of national identity—to justify their obligations and attachments to particular states. In our earlier orchestra example, though, we saw that a universal value—like the beauty of Beethoven's symphonies—can be perfectly sufficient to justify participants in undertaking obligations to a particular group, and in adopting an attitude of membership in that group. No mediating invocation of cultural ties or ascriptive commonalities was required to ground solidarity in that instance.

In the democracy case, the only significant difference, as we have seen, is that a commitment to justice is not a voluntary one: instead, it is a natural duty. But as we saw, there are good reasons for thinking that the production of just legislation must be a collective undertaking; and thus that our natural duty of justice gives us obligations to form a shared intention to participate together in a democratic process. Now we must ask: why can't our sense of membership in a particular democratic state be accounted for in a completely parallel fashion? That is, if we understand that the natural duty of justice requires us to cooperate in producing democratic legislation, then why isn't the aim of securing justice by itself enough to account for our attitude of membership in our own state?

In this vein, we can easily explain why we identify with our orchestra—because in it, we act together with our fellow players, and we endorse that shared activity, since it produces a valuable good for all members. We don't need to invoke any cultural commonalities to explain that sense of membership. One can say, then, that we feel a rational sense of membership in the orchestra: we value our membership because it allows us to pursue goals we care about. But it is no more mysterious why we might feel a sense of membership as a citizen of a particular democratic state. By acting together with our fellow citizens, we produce a set of just and nondominating laws, and that is a valuable good for each person. Like the orchestra, then, the democratic state is a collective in which it is possible to feel a rational sense of membership, and we do not need to invoke a shared national culture to undergird it. If the above account is correct, then a reflective understanding of our duties of justice is perfectly sufficient to ground our identification as citizens. Just as Rousseau argued in

Emile, a commitment to equal freedom-as-independence—when rationally reflected on—is by itself enough to generate a commitment to citizenship and solidarity with our compatriots. Nothing else—and in particular, no commonalities of language, culture, or history—is required.

Two Illustrations

Now that we have seen how our natural duty of justice is particularized within a democratic state, we understand that justice can ground important obligations of membership. To underscore and illustrate this point, consider thc following cases:

1. *The Swedish taxpayer.*[33] Suppose a wealthy Swedish businessman, having read Yael Tamir, David Miller, and A. John Simmons, is totally convinced by their argument. Up to now, he had supposed that his commitment to justice gave him a good reason to support the Swedish state, by paying his taxes. But now he realizes he was wrong. Instead, his commitment to justice only gives him reason to support the just state of his choice. Convinced that he can both save money and do his moral duty, he goes straightaway and files business incorporation papers in the Cayman Islands, sparing himself millions. After all, the Cayman Islands is a reasonably just state. Has our Swedish taxpayer done anything wrong?
2. *The reparations shirker.* Suppose, in the aftermath of World War II, the UN had ordered the payment of reparations for unjust deeds on all sides. As part of the program, the United States was ordered to pay reparations to Japan and Germany for the bombings of Hiroshima, Nagasaki, and Dresden. An average U.S. citizen in 1945 made no difference to these acts. He also had no control over them. Would he have had more reason to pay additional taxes to discharge the reparations than a citizen of Iceland, say, would have had?[34]

If Tamir and Miller are correct, the constitutional patriot cannot provide any account of why civic membership could give the Swedish taxpayer or the reparations shirker any reasons to contribute, beyond those a supporter of justice anywhere would have. Indeed, the Miller-Tamir thesis suggests that a commitment to liberal principles gives these individuals no

[33] I owe this example to a conversation with Martin Sandbu.

[34] I have made this case easier for myself by assuming a reasonably just state that owes a collective obligation for committing an unjust act. A full theory of collective political responsibility would need to consider whether any obligation is imposed by membership in unjust states, a much more difficult problem. A full theory would also need to consider the limits of dissenters' obligations in an involuntary group like the state.

special reason to contribute at all, apart from their fear of being punished by the state: instead, some invocation of their cultural identity is required. But once we see that democracy is a shared intentional practice, we can explain why they have reason to contribute on grounds of justice alone.

The Swedish taxpayer should contribute to Sweden's tax receipts and not to tax receipts in the Cayman Islands because he and his fellow citizens have together enacted laws regulating property in their society, which give each citizen social rights that this tax revenue is meant to finance. In enacting these laws, the citizens legitimately relied on and expected each other's contributions in order to uphold the social rights they guaranteed. By choosing to send his check to the Cayman Islands, our taxpayer disregards his fellow citizens' reliance on his contribution to secure their rights. Different schemes of acquired rights are possible and just. But being a member of a state means that one is committed to upholding a *particular scheme* of acquired rights. Other members are relying on the Swedish taxpayer's contributions to secure their rights, and by refusing to orient himself to Sweden's tax laws, he is coercing them in a way that is unjust. The Swedish taxpayer has a duty of membership, derived from his natural duty of justice, to avoid inflicting harm on his fellow citizens by manipulating their reliance in this way.

The reparations shirker should contribute because reparation for harm to civilians in war is a collective obligation that falls on the state as a whole. If citizens generally refused to recognize any obligation to pay in such cases, the victims of their harms or negligence would go uncompensated.[35] Moreover, it was their acting together that caused the harm in question—their tax dollars paid for the bombs, their army flew the planes, their constitution authorized the decisions in these cases. Our average citizen may not have made an individual difference to the occurrence of these events, but he is part of a collective that together had full control over the infliction of these harms. Therefore the collective is responsible for compensating the victims, and the individuals in the collective have obligations to do their part to discharge this responsibility.

To conclude, I should add a few caveats to the brief account I have given. First, just as belonging to a group of bank robbers does not give us an obligation to rob the bank, my account does not entail that belonging to an unjust state gives us an obligation to do what it says. Recall that our first-tier reason for participating in the state is a natural duty of justice. No natural duty of justice can undergird a second-tier membership reason to commit injustice. There may be difficulties about how far we are obli-

[35] I do not mean to suggest that there is no question of individual criminal liability for the decision makers in these cases. That is an important additional question separate from collective liability for compensation.

gated to a state that is only partially just, but no state that *clearly* fails to treat its members as equally free, in accordance with the criteria laid out in chapter 4, has a right to their allegiance. Second, just as the orchestra player does not have an obligation to play a concert if she knows her fellow members will not show up, I also do not have an obligations to pay my taxes or comply with property laws if I know my compatriots will not do so. To do so would be to undertake a burden that does not in any way conduce to achieving the collective end, that is, the establishment of democratic justice. State coercion, however, will generally be sufficient to provide assurance in this respect, and to place me under a genuine obligation to contribute. Third, just as the orchestra member is not obligated to stay in the orchestra forever, citizens of just states are not obligated not to emigrate. They are free to emigrate to other states, provided that they either renounce their membership in the state where they are citizens, or prove a permanent connection to two states, and show that they are able to discharge both sets of political obligations. There is no reason, therefore, to think that civic allegiance could not be a "portable" attitude.

I believe, then, that a careful consideration of democracy as a collective activity shows that the liberal-nationalist critique of civic nationhood is wrong. But it should be emphasized that this reconstruction of constitutional patriotism cannot (and should not) defend all aspects of current practice in liberal states. All it shows is that a commitment to principles of justice is consistent, in theory, with an allegiance to particular democratic states, and with a sense of membership and solidarity with our compatriots. But constitutional patriotism of this kind is a normative ideal, not a description of existing practice, and as such it can serve as a tool of critique. Since it advocates thinking of just states along the lines of everyday groups like clubs, it also endorses reforming existing states to function more like clubs. This is particularly important, I think, when it comes to assessing current immigration and citizenship practices, many of which are inconsistent with liberal principles. A liberal state can only justify its preferential treatment of its citizens if there are merely contingent, but not ascriptive, reasons for outsiders' exclusion. This means no liberal state should deny citizenship to those who are forced to comply with its laws on a long-term basis. And no theory of constitutional patriotism can underwrite ethnic or nationality preferences in immigration policy, the denial of citizenship to everyone born on the territory, or preferences for skilled or wealthy immigrants like the ones contemporary liberal democracies actually show. So a full account of constitutional patriotism will require a number of prescriptions for the reformation of our practices, though I must defer more discussion of these to future work.

8

Conclusion

Recall that in chapter 1 we initially raised the problem of political obligations by considering the case of Sally from Toronto in some detail. Our commonsense moral intuitions at that stage supported the view that being a Canadian citizen makes some moral difference to what Sally ought to do, by shaping her practical responsibilities. For example, we held that, at a minimum, she ought to

1. obey Canadian laws rather than US laws, as long as these laws were sufficiently just;
2. participate in Canadian elections and political debates;
3. pay her taxes to Canadian revenue authorities, rather than to the authorities in some other just country of her choice; and
4. contribute to welfare redistribution in Canada to secure the social rights of her fellow citizens.

We remained agnostic about whether Sally might be subject to additional duties of citizenship, as for example, the duty to serve in the military during a just war, to perform civil service, or to contribute to reparations owed by her state. Instead, we focused there on a seemingly intractable problem with such political obligations: how, on a liberal view that emphasizes the importance of universal freedom and equality, might the obligations that we attributed to Sally actually be justified? Liberals do not countenance other unchosen obligations to groups that we are born into. So why should they concede that we have unchosen obligations to the state?

We saw there that vindicating our commonsense intuitions about Sally's obligations of citizenship on liberal grounds actually posed a difficult challenge, one that many contemporary theorists have thought impossible to overcome. Cosmopolitans have claimed that, on reflection, we ought to hold that special obligations of citizenship are fundamentally incompatible with liberal values, which attribute the same moral worth to all individuals everywhere. They conclude that our obligations of justice should not be limited in any way by state boundaries. And liberal nationalists agree with cosmopolitans that liberal values alone cannot show obligations of citizenship to be justified, although they argue that this lacuna actually points out the hidden importance of the nation to our political thinking. Neither of these schools, however, believes that citizenship can be shown to be of any moral significance on liberal grounds alone.

This book has presented a sustained argument to the effect that we can in fact vindicate Sally's obligations of citizenship on liberal grounds alone, and that a commitment to justice by itself may provide Sally with sufficient reason to support her democratic institutions and to show solidarity with her compatriots. In other words, I have claimed that realizing the central value that liberals care about—a condition of equal freedom-as-independence among individuals—requires us to undertake political obligations to a legitimate democratic state. My argument, developed at length over the course of the book, had two basic parts.

First, I claimed that cosmopolitans go wrong in overlooking that fact that the democratic state plays a key role in defining some of our duties of justice to others. Whereas cosmopolitans and critics of political authority like Simmons assume that our duties of justice are clear and determinate interpersonal obligations, I drew on Kant's political writings to question this assumption. Kant holds that prior to the state's establishment, our moral duties of justice are indeterminate with respect to certain key questions, particularly the rightful extent of our property and the limits of our "acquired" (or "civil") rights. As we saw, Kant claims that this indeterminacy makes it necessary to construct an institution to provide some public definition of each person's acquired rights by legislating positive laws. Otherwise, we could not be securely free, since each person would retain the ability to interfere with us at every moment according to his private view of justice. And Rousseau adds that the only way for us to impose an objective definition of each person's civil rights consistent with freedom is on the basis of a democratic general will. If Kant and Rousseau are correct, then a condition of justice requires democratic state institutions. Our natural duty of justice therefore does not counsel just acts on our part toward other individuals (including strangers), but instead urges us to act together to construct, uphold, and obey just democratic states.

As we saw, though, the general argument for state authority was only partly effective, taken by itself, in establishing that a citizen like Sally has obligations to her particular state, Canada, and to her particular compatriots, the Canadians. Liberal nationalists claim that any general argument to the effect that Sally has duties of justice to states should actually require her to support all just states equally. I argued in the last chapter that this claim rests on the false view that commitment to a universal value can never undergird a commitment to particular institutions in which we cooperate with others in order to instantiate and realize this value. What particularizes Sally's obligations to Canadian institutions and her Canadian compatriots is the fact that they are acting together to fulfill their natural duty of justice, by democratically defining a fair scheme of acquired rights. Since Sally has a general duty to do her part in establishing just institutions, she also has reason to make sure that those institutions she personally participates in imposing are not unjust, and that by imposing them, she is not wronging her fellow members. Moreover, she has reasons of respect not to manipulate the reasonable expectations of her compatriots that she will in fact contribute to realizing their joint scheme. These considerations give her sufficient reason to participate politically in her own democracy, to engage in civil disobedience against unjust policies, and to provide the tax contributions and the obedience to sufficiently just laws that are required in order for her fellow citizens' acquired rights to be effectively recognized and respected. But none of these reasons why Sally should show allegiance to her own institutions and support for her compatriots, in my view, requires any further appeal to Sally's national identity, her emotions and sentiments, or her culture. Democratic solidarity and civic allegiance can be grounded in a commitment to justice alone, as long that commitment is recognized as one that requires us to act collectively with others in a democratic process.

One thing a liberal theory of citizenship cannot do, however, is tell us why we should have separate states in the world at all, or why borders happen to fall where they do. A Kantian-Rousseauian view can only tell us that legitimate democratic authority (in one state or in many separate states) is necessary for a condition of equal freedom. It does not tell us how many of these authorities we should have. But in my view this is in no way problematic. For a Kantian-Rousseauian theory can give the citizen perfectly good reasons for allegiance to the particular democracy in which she lives. In the same way, there is no a priori answer to how many fire brigades, or football teams, or universities we should have in the world, or which particular people should be members of which ones. But that does not negate the fact that I have perfectly good reasons to do more for my university or for my football team than for other, equally good, universities and teams. These reasons are not due to the fact that I am strongly subjectively identified with my university over others, or that I am partial to its members, but simply to the fact that, in it, I act together with others to instantiate and realize the value of higher learning in *this* place rather than *that* one. My appreciation for learning is a universal value that gives me perfectly sufficient reason to support my own students and colleagues and not students and colleagues in other places.

If the two parts of my argument have met with any success, then I believe they go a long way toward showing that traditional liberal accounts of civic unity and obligation may in fact be far stronger than has been recently made out. I therefore hope that this book can contribute to the larger project of offering a defense of liberal citizenship against the assaults that have recently been made on it by both cosmopolitans and nationalists. Dissolving the apparent dilemma of liberalism's commitment to particular states is, in my view, a necessary first step to a more complete vindication. For there is much to admire in the traditional account of liberal citizenship, and it would be far premature for us to abandon it.

Bibliography

Abizadeh, Arash. "Cooperation, Pervasive Impact, and Coercion: On the Scope (Not Site) of Distributive Justice." *Philosophy and Public Affairs* 35 (2007): 318–58.

———. "Does Liberal Democracy Presuppose a Cultural Nation? Four Arguments." *American Political Science Review* 96, no. 3 (2002): 495–509.

Anderson, Benedict. *Imagined Communities*. London: Verso, 1983.

Arneson, Richard J. "Do Patriotic Ties Limit Global Justice Duties?" *Journal of Ethics* 9 (2004): 127–50.

Barry, Brian. *Culture and Equality*. Cambridge: Cambridge University Press, 1993.

———. "Humanity and Justice in Global Perspective." In *Ethics, Economics, and the Law*, ed. J. Roland Pennock and John W. Chapman, 219–52. New York: New York University Press, 1982.

Beitz, Charles. *Political Theory and International Relations*. Princeton: Princeton University Press, 1979.

Bernstein, Richard. "The Retrieval of the Democratic Ethos." In *Habermas on Law and Democracy: Critical Exchanges*, ed. Michael Rosenfeld and Andrew Arato, 287–305. Berkeley and Los Angeles: University of California Press, 1998.

Blake, Michael. "Distributive Justice, State Coercion, and Autonomy." *Philosophy and Public Affairs* 30 (2001): 257–96.

Brandt, Reinhardt. "Das Erlaubnisgesetz, oder: Vernunft und Geschichte in Kants Rechtslehre." In *Rechtsphilosophie der Aufklärung*, ed. Reinhardt Brandt, 233–85. Berlin: de Gruyter, 1982.

Bratman, Michael. *Faces of Intention: Selected Essays on Intention and Agency*. Cambridge: Cambridge University Press, 1999.

———. "Shared Cooperative Activity." *Philosophical Review* 101 (1992): 327–41.

Buchanan, Allen. *Justice, Legitimacy, and Self-Determination: Moral Foundations for International Law*. Oxford: Oxford University Press, 2004.

———. "Rawls's Law of Peoples: Rules for a Vanished Westphalian World." *Ethics* 110, no. 4 (2000): 697–721.

Byrd, B. Sharon, and Joachim Hruschka. "The Natural Law Duty to Recognize Private Property Ownership." *University of Toronto Law Journal* 56 (2006): 217–82.

Caney, Simon. *Justice beyond Borders: A Global Political Theory*. Oxford: Oxford University Press, 2005.

Canovan, Margaret. *Nationhood and Political Theory.* Cheltenham, UK: Edward Elgar, 1996.

Carens, Joseph. "Aliens and Citizens: The Case for Open Borders." *Review of Politics* 49, no. 2 (1987): 251–73.

Charvet, John. *The Social Problem in the Philosophy of Rousseau.* Cambridge: Cambridge University Press, 1974.

Cohen, Joshua. "Deliberation and Democratic Legitimacy." In *Deliberative Democracy: Essays on Reason and Politics*, ed. James Bohman and William Rehg, 67–91. Cambridge, MA: MIT Press, 1997.

———. "Reflections on Rousseau: Autonomy and Democracy." *Philosophy and Public Affairs* 15 (1986): 275–97.

Cohen, Joshua, and Charles Sabel. "Extra Rem Publican Nulla Justitia." *Philosophy and Public Affairs* 34 (2006): 147–75.

Coleman, Jules. *A Practice of Principle.* Oxford: Oxford University Press, 2001.

Criminal Code of Canada, Section 318–19, http://laws.justice.gc.ca. Accessed 4/26/2008.

Cronin, Ciaran. "Democracy and Collective Identity." *European Journal of Philosophy* 11, no. 1 (2003): 1–28.

Dent, N.J.H.. *Rousseau.* Oxford: Basil Blackwell, 1988.

———. "General Will." In *A Rousseau Dictionary.* Cambridge, MA: Blackwell Reference, 1982.

Derathé, Robert. *Jean Jacques Rousseau et la Science Politique de son Temps.* Paris: Presses Universitaires de France, 1950.

Derrida, Jacques. *Of Grammatology.* Trans. Gayatri Chakravorty Spivak. Baltimore: Johns Hopkins University Press, 1976.

Forst, Rainer. "The Basic Right to Justification: Toward a Constructivist Conception of Human Rights." *Constellations* 6, no. 1 (1999): 35–60.

Gans, Chaim. *The Limits of Nationalism.* Cambridge: Cambridge University Press, 2003.

Gilbert, Margaret. *Living Together.* London: Rowman and Littlefield, 1996.

Gildin, Hilail. *Rousseau's Social Contract: The Structure of the Argument.* Chicago: University of Chicago Press, 1983.

Gomberg, Paul. "Patriotism Is Like Racism." In *Patriotism*, ed. Igor Primoratz, 105–11. Amherst, NY: Humanity Books, 2002.

Goodin, Robert E. "What Is So Special about Our Fellow Countrymen?" In *Patriotism* ed. Igor Primoratz, 141–58. Amherst, NY: Humanity Books.

Green, Leslie. *The Authority of the State.* Oxford: Clarendon Press, 1988.

Green, T. H. *Lectures on the Principles of Political Obligation.* In *Philosophical Works.* Bristol, UK: Thoemmes Press, 1997.

Grotius, Hugo. *The Rights of War and Peace.* London: T. Warren, 1654.

Habermas, Jürgen. "Apologetic Tendencies." In *The New Conservatism: Cultural Criticism and the Historians' Debate.* Ed. and trans. Sherry Nicholsen. Cambridge, MA: MIT Press, 1989.

———. *Between Facts and Norms.* Trans. William Rehg. Cambridge, MA: MIT Press, 1996.

———. "The European Nation-State: On the Past as Future of Sovereignty and Citizenship." In *The Inclusion of the Other: Studies in Political Theory*, ed. Ciaran Cronin and Pablo De Greif. Cambridge, MA: MIT Press, 1998.

———. "On Law and Disagreement: Some Comments on Interpretative Pluralism." *Ratio Juris* 16, no. 2 (2003): 187–94.

———. "On the Relation between the Nation, the Rule of Law, and Democracy." In *The Inclusion of the Other: Studies in Political Theory*, ed. Ciaran Cronin and Pablo De Greif. Cambridge, MA: MIT Press, 1998.

———. "The Postnational Constellation and the Future of Democracy." In *The Postnational Constellation: Political Essays*, trans. Max Pensky. New York: Polity, 2001.

———. "Remarks on Legitimation through Human Rights." In *The Postnational Constellation: Political Essays*, trans. Max Pensky. New York: Polity, 2001.

———. "A Reply." In *Habermas on Law and Democracy: Critical Exchanges*, ed. Michael Rosenfeld and Andrew Arato, 381–452. Berkeley and Los Angeles: University of California Press, 1998.

———. "Struggles for Recognition in the Democratic State." In *The Inclusion of the Other: Studies in Political Theory*, ed. Ciaran Cronin and Pablo De Greif. Cambridge, MA: MIT Press, 1998.

Hardin, Russell. *Collective Action*. Baltimore: Johns Hopkins University Press, 1982.

Hart, H.L.A. "Are There Any Natural Rights?" In *Human Rights*, ed. A. I. Melden, 61–75. Belmont, CA: Wadsworth, 1970.

Hegel, G.W.F. *Elements of the Philosophy of Right*. Ed. Allen Wood. Trans. H. B. Nisbet. Cambridge: Cambridge University Press, 1991.

Held, David, ed. *Democracy and the Global Order: From the Modern State to Cosmopolitan Governance*. Stanford, CA: Stanford University Press, 1995.

Held, Virginia. "Can a Random Collection of Individuals Be Morally Responsible?" *Journal of Philosophy* 67, no. 14 (1970): 471–81.

Hobbes, Thomas. *Leviathan*. Ed. Richard Tuck. Cambridge: Cambridge University Press, 1996.

———. *On the Citizen*. Ed. Richard Tuck and Michael Silverthorne. Cambridge: Cambridge University Press, 1998.

Hobsbawm, Eric. *Nations and Nationalism after 1780*. Cambridge: Cambridge University Press, 1990.

Hont, Istvan. "The Permanent Crisis of a Divided Mankind: Contemporary Crisis of the Nation-State in Historical Perspective." *Political Studies*, special issue, ed. J. Dunn (1994): 183–91.

Hruschka, Joachim. "The Permissive Law of Practical Reason in Kant's *Metaphysics of Morals*." *Law and Philosophy* 23 (2004): 45–72.

Hume, David. *A Treatise of Human Nature*. Ed. P. H. Nidditch. Oxford: Oxford University Press, 1978.

Ignatieff, Michael. *Blood and Belonging*. New York: Farrar, Straus and Giroux, 1993.

Ingram, Attracta. "Constitutional Patriotism." In *Patriotism*, ed. Igor Primoratz, 217–31. Amherst, NY: Humanity Books, 2002.

Kant, Immanuel. "Conjectures on the Beginning of Human History." In *Kant's Political Writings*, ed. Hans Reiss, trans. H. B. Nisbet. Cambridge: Cambridge University Press, 1991.

———. *Kant's Gesammelte Schriften*. Ed. German Academy of Sciences. Berlin: Walter de Gruyter, 1900–.

———. "On the Common Saying: That May Be Correct in Theory, but It Is of No Use in Practice." In *Practical Philosophy*, ed. Mary Gregor. Cambridge: Cambridge University Press, 1996.

———. "Theory and Practice." In *Kant's Political Writings*, ed. Hans Reiss, trans. H. B. Nisbet. Cambridge: Cambridge University Press, 1991.

Kersting, Wolfgang *Wohlgeordnete Freiheit*. Berlin: de Gruyter, 1984.

Korsgaard, Christine. "Morality as Freedom." In *Creating the Kingdom of Ends*. Cambridge: Cambridge University Press, 1996.

———. "Taking the Law into Our Own Hands: Kant on the Right to Revolution." In *Reclaiming the History of Ethics: Essays for John Rawls*, ed. Andrews Reath, Barbara Herman, and Christine Korsgaard, 297–328. Cambridge: Cambridge University Press, 1997.

Kutz, Christopher. "The Collective Work of Citizenship." *Legal Theory* 8, no. 4 (2002): 471–94.

———. *Complicity*. Cambridge: Cambridge University Press, 2000.

Kymlicka, Will. *Multicultural Citizenship*. Oxford: Clarendon Press, 1995.

———. *Politics in the Vernacular*. Oxford: Oxford University Press, 2001.

Kymlicka, Will, and Christine Straehle. "Cosmopolitanism, Nation-States, and Minority Nationalism: A Critical Review of Recent Literature." *European Journal of Philosophy* 7, no. 1 (1999): 65–88.

Levinson, Sanford. *Constitutional Faith*. Princeton: Princeton University Press, 1989.

Lewis, David. *Convention: A Philosophical Study*. Cambridge, MA: Harvard University Press, 1969.

Locke, John. *Second Treatise of Government*. Indianapolis: Hackett, 1980.

Margalit, Avishai, and Joseph Raz. "National Self-Determination." *Journal of Philosophy* 87, no. 9 (1990): 439–61.

Markell, Patchen. "Making Affect Safe for Democracy? On Constitutional Patriotism." *Political Theory* 28, no. 1 (2000): 38–63.

Mason, Andrew. *Community, Solidarity, and Belonging: Levels of Community and Their Normative Significance*. Cambridge: Cambridge University Press, 2000.

Mason, John Hope. "Forced to Be Free." In *Rousseau and Liberty*, ed. Robert Wokler, 121–38. Manchester: Manchester University Press, 1995.

Masters, Roger. *The Political Philosophy of Rousseau*. Princeton: Princeton University Press, 1968.

McCabe, David. "Patriotic Gore, Again." In *Patriotism*, ed. Igor Primoratz, 121–37. Amherst, NY: Humanity Books.

McCarthy, Thomas. *Ideals and Illusions: On Reconstruction and Deconstruction in Contemporary Critical Theory*. Cambridge, MA: MIT Press, 1991.

———. "Legitimacy and Diversity." In *Habermas on Law and Democracy: Critical Exchanges*, ed. Michael Rosenfeld and Andrew Arato, 115–53. Berkeley and Los Angeles: University of California Press, 1998.

———. "On Reconciling Cosmopolitan Unity and National Diversity." *Public Culture* 11, no. 1 (1999): 175–208.

Melzer, Arthur. *The Natural Goodness of Man*. Chicago: University of Chicago Press, 1990.

Michelman, Frank. "Morality, Identity, and Constitutional Patriotism." *Ratio Juris* 14, no. 3 (2001): 253–71.

Miller, David. *On Nationality*. Oxford: Clarendon Press, 1995.

Miller, Richard W. "Cosmopolitan Respect and Patriotic Concern." In *Patriotism*, ed. Igor Primoratz, 167–85. Amherst, NY: Humanity Books, 2002.

Miller, Seamus. *Social Action: A Teleological Account*. Cambridge: Cambridge University Press, 2001.

Mulholland, Leslie. *Kant's System of Rights*. New York: Columbia University Press, 1990.

Nagel, Thomas. "The Problem of Global Justice." *Philosophy and Public Affairs* 33 (2005): 113–47.

Neuhouser, Frederick. "Freedom, Dependence, and the General Will." In *Foundations of Hegel's Social Theory: Actualizing Freedom*. Cambridge, MA: Harvard University Press, 2000.

———. "Rousseau on the Relation between Reason and Self-Love (*Amour-Propre*)." *Internationales Jahrbuch des Deutschen Idealismus* (2003): 221–39.

Norman, Wayne. "The Ideology of Shared Values." In *Is Quebec Nationalism Just?* ed. Joseph Carens, 137–59. Montreal: McGill University Press, 1995.

Nussbaum, Martha. "Patriotism and Cosmopolitanism." In *For Love of Country*, ed. Joshua Cohen, 3–17. Boston: Beacon Press, 1996.

O'Neill, Onora. *Bounds of Justice*. Cambridge: Cambridge University Press, 2000.

Parry, Geraint. "Autonomy and the Citizen." In *Rousseau and Liberty*, ed. Robert Wokler, 99–121. Manchester: Manchester University Press, 1995.

Patten, Alan. *Hegel's Idea of Freedom*. Oxford: Oxford University Press, 1999.

Pettit, Philip. *Republicanism*. Oxford, Clarendon Press, 1997.

———. *A Theory of Freedom: From the Psychology to the Politics of Agency*. Oxford: Oxford University Press, 2001.

———. "Groups with Minds of Their Own." In *Socializing Metaphysics*, ed. Frederick Schmitt, 167–93. New York: Rowman and Littlefield, 2004.

Pogge, Thomas. "The Bounds of Nationalism." In *World Poverty and Human Rights*. Cambridge: Cambridge University Press, 2000.

———. "Cosmopolitanism and Sovereignty." In *World Poverty and Human Rights*. Cambridge: Cambridge University Press, 2000.

———. *Realizing Rawls*. Ithaca, NY: Cornell University Press, 1989.

———. *World Poverty and Human Rights*. Cambridge: Polity Press, 2002.

Rawls, John. *Political Liberalism*. New York: Columbia University Press, 1993.

———. *A Theory of Justice*. Cambridge, MA: Belknap Press of Harvard University Press, 1971.

Raz, Joseph. *The Morality of Freedom*. Oxford: Clarendon Press, 1986.

Ripstein, Arthur. "Authority and Coercion." *Philosophy and Public Affairs* 32 (2004): 2–35.
———. "Universal and General Wills: Hegel and Rousseau." *Political Theory* 22, no. 3 (1994): 444–67.
Rosenfeld, Michael, and Andrew Arato, eds. *Habermas on Law and Democracy: Critical Exchanges*. Berkeley and Los Angeles: University of California Press, 1998.
Rousseau, Jean-Jacques. *The Discourses and Other Early Political Writings*. Ed. Victor Gourevitch. Cambridge: Cambridge University Press, 1997.
———. *Emile*. Trans Allan Bloom. New York: Basic Books, 1979.
———. *Letters from the Mountain*. In *The Collected Writings of Rousseau*, vol. 9, ed. Christopher Kelly and Eve Gracc. Hanover, NH: Dartmouth College Press, 2001.
———. "Letter to d'Alembert on the Theater." In *Politics and the Arts*, ed. Allan Bloom, 3–123. Ithaca, NY: Cornell University Press, 1960.
———. *Oeuvres Complètes*. Ed. Bernard Gagnebin and Marcel Raymond. Paris: Pléiade, 1959.
———. Discourse on *Political Economy*. In *The Social Contract and Other Later Political Writings*, ed. Victor Gourevitch. Cambridge: Cambridge University Press, 1997.
———. "Political Fragments." In *The Collected Writings of Rousseau*, vol. 4, ed. Roger D. Masters and Christopher Kelly. Hanover, NH: Dartmouth College Press, 1994.
———. *Projet de constitution pour la Corse*. In *Oeuvres Complètes*, ed. Bernard Gagnebin and Marcel Raymond. Paris: Pléiade, 1959.
———. *The Social Contract and Other Later Political Writings*. Ed. Victor Gourevitch. Cambridge: Cambridge University Press, 1997.
Rovane, Carol. *The Bounds of Agency*. Princeton: Princeton University Press, 1998.
Sangiovanni, Andrea. "Global Justice, Reciprocity, and the State." *Philosophy and Public Affairs* 35 (2007): 2–39.
Scheffler, Samuel. *Boundaries and Allegiances*. Oxford: Oxford University Press, 2001.
———. "Relationships and Responsibilities." *Philosophy and Public Affairs* 26 (1998): 189–209.
Scott, John T. "Rousseau and the Melodious Language of Freedom." *Journal of Politics* 59, no. 3 (1997): 803–29.
Searle, John R. "Collective Intentions and Actions." In *Intentions in Communication*, ed. Philip R. Cohen, Jerry Morgan, and Martha E. Pollack, 401–15. Cambridge, MA: MIT Press, 1990.
———. *The Construction of Social Reality*. New York: Free Press, 1995.
Shapiro, Scott. "Law, Plans, and Practical Reason." *Legal Theory* 8, no. 4 (2002): 387–441.
Simmons, A. John. *Justification and Legitimacy*. Cambridge: Cambridge University Press, 2001.
———. *The Lockean Theory of Rights*. Princeton: Princeton University Press, 1992.

———. *Moral Principles and Political Obligations*. Princeton: Princeton University Press, 1979.

Smith, Anthony D. *The Ethnic Origins of Nations*. Oxford: Basil Blackwell, 1986.

Smith, M.B.E. "Is There a Prima Facie Obligation to Obey the Law?" *Yale Law Journal* 82 (1973): 950–76.

Sreenivasan, Gopal. "What Is the General Will?" *Philosophical Review* 109, no. 4 (2000): 545–81.

Talmon, J. L. *The Origins of Totalitarian Democracy* New York: Praeger, 1961.

Tamir, Yael. *Liberal Nationalism*. Princeton: Princeton University Press, 1993.

Tan, Kok-Chor. *Justice without Borders: Cosmopolitanism, Nationalism, and Patriotism*. Cambridge: Cambridge University Press, 2004.

———. "Patriotic Obligations." *Monist* 86, no. 3 (2003): 434–53.

Taylor, Charles. "Nationalism and Modernity." In *The Morality of Nationalism*, ed. Robert McKim and Jeff McMahan, 31–55. Oxford: Oxford University Press, 1997.

Tuck, Richard. *The Rights of War and Peace: Political Thought and the International Order from Grotius to Kant*. New York: Oxford University Press, 1999.

Viroli, Maurizio. *For Love of Country*. Oxford: Clarendon Press, 1995.

Waldron, Jeremy. "Kant's Legal Positivism." *Harvard Law Review* 109, no. 7 (1996): 1535–66.

———. *Liberal Rights*. Cambridge: Cambridge University Press, 1993.

———. "Minority Cultures and the Cosmopolitan Alternative." In *The Rights of Minority Cultures*, ed. Will Kymlicka, 93–119. Oxford: Oxford University Press, 1995.

———. "Redressing Historic Injustice." *University of Toronto Law Journal* 52 (2002): 135–60.

———. "Social Citizenship and Welfare." In *Liberal Rights*. Cambridge: Cambridge University Press, 1993.

———. "Special Ties and Natural Duties." *Philosophy and Public Affairs* 22 (1993): 3–30.

Weinrib, Ernest. "Propter Honoris Respectum: Poverty and Property in Kant's System of Rights." *Notre Dame Law Review* 2003:795–828.

Wellman, Christopher Heath. "Is There Magic in the Pronoun 'My?' " *Ethics* 110 (2000): 537–62.

Wellman, Christopher Heath, and A. John Simmons, *Is There a Duty to Obey the Law?* Cambridge: Cambridge University Press, 2005.

Yack, Bernard. "The Myth of the Civic Nation." In *Theorizing Nationalism*, ed. Ronald Beiner, 103–18. Albany: State University of New York Press, 1999.

Index